Railways in the Netherlands

Railways in the Netherlands

A Brief History, 1834–1994

AUGUSTUS J. VEENENDAAL, JR.

Stanford University Press
Stanford, California

Stanford University Press
Stanford, California

© 2001 by the Board of Trustees of the Leland Stanford Junior University

Railways in the Netherlands is an expanded version of *De IJzeren Weg in een Land vol Water*,
© 1998 A. J. Veenendaal, Jr./De Bataafsche Leeuw.

Printed in the United States of America on acid-free, archival-quality paper.

Library-of-Congress Cataloging-in-Publication Data

Veenendaal, A. J.
   [IJzeren weg in een land vol water. English]
   Railways in the Netherlands : a brief history, 1834–1994 / Augustus J. Veenendaal, Jr.
     p. cm.
   Includes bibliographical references and index.
   ISBN 0-8047-3947-1 (alk. paper)
   1. Railroads—Netherlands—History.   I. Title.

  RF77.V44   2001
  385'.09492—dc21

2001020912

Original printing 2001

Last figure below indicates year of this printing:
10 09 08 07 06 05 04 03 02 01

Designed by Princeton Editorial Associates.
Typeset by Princeton Editorial Associates in Palatino and Gill Sans.

CONTENTS

LIST OF MAPS

PREFACE

A concise survey of the history of railways in the Netherlands did not really exist until the Dutch version of this book appeared in 1998. J. H. Jonckers Nieboer published a general history of Dutch railways back in 1908, but he focused almost entirely on the political and legal side of railway building and said little or nothing about the economic and social side of these railways, and nothing at all about the working of them. Jonckers Nieboer's book was all that was available for a long time, and when he updated his work in 1938, he retained the same emphasis. Since 1945, and especially since the 1970s, a flood of literature on specialized subjects such as locomotives, rolling stock, and railway stations has become available. But still missing was a concise survey of all facets of the history of Dutch railways, one that would both appeal to the general public and fill the gap for the serious rail buff. My Dutch book *De IJzeren Weg in een Land vol Water. Beknopte Geschiedenis van de Spoorwegen in Nederland, 1834–1958* was meant to fill that gap. Published by De Bataafsche Leeuw of Amsterdam in 1998, it was well received and sold out in six months, so that a second, improved edition was released later that same year.

For the non-Dutch speaker interested in general Dutch railway history, however, nothing was available. My discussions with Norris Pope, director of Stanford University Press, suggested that English-speaking readers would welcome a book along the same lines as the Dutch work. The result is not a straight translation of the earlier Dutch text. I have added material to acquaint the non-Dutch reader with some of the history of the Kingdom of the Netherlands essential to an understanding of railway development there. I have also reorganized the text, subdividing the original five chapters into seventeen smaller ones and leaving out a few details of interest only to a Dutch public. Finally, I have brought the story forward to the 1994.

I have replaced the lengthy Dutch bibliography with a comprehensive bibliographic essay, and I refer interested readers with some knowledge of Dutch to that. There I have included all available literature in languages other than Dutch, but publications in English are unfortunately very rare.

———

Norris Pope, director of Stanford University Press, with whom I had collaborated on an earlier book, showed much interest in this work right from the start. When he first saw the Dutch copy of *De IJzeren Weg in een Land vol Water*, he immediately encouraged me to write an English-language edition and offered helpful ideas and suggestions for that somewhat challenging project. The idea of continuing the story from 1958, the end of the Dutch book, to the present day was his.

A great number of illustrations in this book came from the collection of the NVBS, the Netherlands Association of those interested in Railways and Tramways, or Dutch Railfan Association, for short. As honorary keeper of this collection since the early 1970s, I knew very well the wealth of photographs available and could freely use the ones I needed for this book. They deserve to be seen by more people than just the members of the NVBS.

The handsome maps in this volume were drawn by my friend Dick van der Spek, of the Netherlands Topographic Service. Working in close cooperation with me, he has succeeded in providing a good deal of information in these maps, which are in my opinion models of clarity.

I thank my good friend G. Bonno van Dijk, M.A., history teacher at the Municipal Gymnasium of Haarlem, for his expert comments, not only on the first Dutch version, but also on this English edition. His experiences as history teacher at Hope College in Holland, Michigan, proved most useful here.

Last of all, I thank my wife, Jannie. Always a helpful and interested critic, she listened patiently to my endless and at times undoubtedly boring stories about railways and railwaymen and never tired of offering comments and ideas. I owe her a lot and I dedicate this book to her.

Augustus J. Veenendaal, Jr.
Pijnacker, the Netherlands

ABBREVIATIONS

AM	Aachen-Maastricht Railway Company
ANRM	General Netherlands Railroute Company
AR	Antwerp-Rotterdam Railway Company
ARD	General Regulations for the Railway Service
ARV	General Regulations for Railway Traffic
AS	Almelo-Salzbergen Railway Company
ATO	General Transportation Company
BE	Bentheimer Railway Company (Germany)
BME	Bergisch-Märkische Railway Company (Germany)
CME	Cologne-Minden Railway Company (Germany)
CME	Chief Mechanical Engineer
CS	Central Station
DB	German Federal Railway Company
DP	Delftsche Poort Station (Rotterdam)
DR	German National Railway Company
ESM	Electric Railway Company
EUR	Eastern Union Railway Company (England)
GCB	Grand Central Railway (Belgium)
GER	Great Eastern Railway Company (England)
GOLS	Guelders-Overijssel Regional Railway Company
GoTM	Gooische Tramway Company
GS	Gooische Steam Tramway Company
GT	Ghendt-Terneuzen Railway Company (Belgium)
GTW	Guelders Tramway Company
GWR	Great Western Railway Company (England)
HESM	Holland Electric Railway Company

HS	Holland Railway Station (The Hague)
HSL	High Speed Line
HSM	Holland Railway Company
HTM	Tramway Company of The Hague
ICE	High Speed Train (Germany)
KNLS	Royal Netherlands Railway Company "William III"
KPEV	Royal Prussian Railway Company
LCDR	London, Chatham & Dover Railway Company (England)
LM	Liège-Maastricht Railway Company (Belgium)
LNER	London & North Eastern Railway Company (England)
LTM	Limburg Tramway Company
MET	General Tramway Company
MT	Malines-Terneuzen Railway Company (Belgium)
NBDS	North Brabant-German Railway Company
NCS	Netherlands Central Railway Company
NFLS	North Frisian Regional Railway Company
NHT	North Holland Tramway Company
NMBS	Belgian National Railways Company
NOLS	North Eastern Local Railway Company
NRS	Netherlands Rhenish Railway Company
NS	Netherlands Railways Company
NTM	Netherlands Tramway Company
NV	Netherlands Association of Railway and Tramway Workers
NVBS	Netherlands Association of those interested in Railways and Tramways
NZH	North and South Holland Tramway Company
NZOS	Netherlands South Eastern Railway Company
ORE	Railway Research and Study Office
PCB	Protestant-Christian Association of Railway and Tramway Workers
RAI	Fair Buildings (Amsterdam)
REB	Rhenish Railway Company (Germany)
RTM	Rotterdam Tramway Company
SBB	Swiss Federal Railway Company
SDAP	Social-Democratic Workers Party
SNCF	French National Railways Company
SS	State Railway Company
TEE	Trans Europe Express
TNHT	Second North Holland Tramway Company
UIC	International Railway Union
ULS	Utrecht Local Railway
WD	War Department (Great Britain)
WSM	Westland Steam Tramway Company
WTC	World Trade Center (Amsterdam)
IJSM	IJssel Steam Tramway Company
ZHESM	South Holland Electric Railway Company

I want to transfer this wonder of human ingenuity to the soil of the
Netherlands so that it may act as a mighty driving force for lifting up
commerce and industry.

WILLIAM ARCHIBALD BAKE
(1834)

Not only is private industry immensely more powerful than all
state enterprises, it is also much cheaper, and moreover the supervision
of the construction and working of railways is much more easily accomplished
than when the state would charge itself with this function.

JOHAN RUDOLF THORBECKE
(1858)

Introduction

The Kingdom of the Netherlands became an independent country in 1815 after the fall of the French emperor Napoleon Bonaparte. It comprised the territory of the former Republic of the Seven United Netherlands, or Dutch Republic, which had been carved out of the Spanish territories in the Low Countries in the late sixteenth and early seventeenth centuries. Under William of Orange-Nassau the Silent, the Netherlands had revolted against the Spanish king in 1566, and after eighty years of guerrilla and full-scale warfare, the seven northern provinces were recognized as an independent power.

For about a century, this Dutch Republic, as it was colloquially known, reigned as a world power of great economic and maritime strength. Its center was the province of Holland and its commercial capital, Amsterdam, the hub of worldwide shipping and trading interests. What has been called the first industrial revolution took place north of Amsterdam in the Zaanstreck, driven by a vast wind-powered industry that sprang up there in the early seventeenth century. Between six hundred and seven hundred windmills in the area drove mills that produced flour, dyes, timber, and hundreds of other commodities. Foreign powers could order a complete navy here, fully equipped, armed, and manned.

In the seventeenth century, the Dutch East and West India Companies established a far-reaching colonial empire, with settlements and trade stations from Japan to Indonesia, India, Ceylon, and the Cape of Good Hope in the

East, to West Africa, Brazil, the Caribbean, and North America in the West. Aside from Amsterdam, a host of other towns in Holland, such as Haarlem, Leiden, Delft, Dordrecht, Rotterdam, and many smaller towns, formed a solid industrial and mercantile base for the Dutch Republic's growing wealth, making it the richest country in the world. Although the country always remained a republic constitutionally, the stadtholders from the house of Orange-Nassau, descendants of William the Silent, reached almost kingly status. Indeed, stadtholder William III (1650–1702) was also crowned king of England after the Glorious Revolution of 1688.

The rest of the original Spanish Netherlands, later known as Belgium, remained in the hands of the king of Spain until the Peace of Utrecht of 1713, when the land came into the possession of the Austrian emperor. Liège, on the Meuse River, always a separate bishopric, maintained close commercial ties to Holland.

As the eighteenth century unfolded, the Dutch Republic suffered a long economic standstill, in many respects a decline, coupled with an ossification of its governmental structure. Although Amsterdam remained the financial capital of the world, Great Britain overtook the Netherlands in virtually every other area. In 1795 the French revolutionary armies easily overran the republic's weak defenses and helped set up a new Batavian Republic in accordance with the principles of the French Revolution. Gradually this republic was made more dependent on France, until in 1810 Napoleon incorporated the Netherlands into his large but short-lived French Empire.

When the battle of Waterloo put an end to Napoleon's grand dreams, the northern Netherlands, the former Dutch Republic, declared itself independent under King Willam I. He was the son of the last pre-revolution stadtholder, William V of the house of Orange-Nassau, a descendant of the line that had overseen the affairs of the republic since the sixteenth century. The Congress of Vienna of 1815, set up by the victorious Allied powers, then decided that the power of France should be curbed for good by setting up a strong state at its northern border. The southern Netherlands—Belgium—were added to the new kingdom of William I, which became the United Kingdom of the Netherlands.

Almost nobody was happy with this reunion. During the preceding two centuries, the northern and southern Netherlands had grown apart. The mercantile and predominantly Protestant North had little interest in acquiring an area inhabited by Roman Catholic Belgians, some of whom even spoke French, while the Belgians did not want to be governed from The Hague by a Protestant king and his Dutch servants. The South was already more industrialized, chiefly in Wallonia with its coal mines and in the Liège area along the Meuse River, where John Cockerill had set up his first ironworks with the direct help of King William. High tariff barriers were required to protect this young industry from English competition, whereas the North favored a low tariff because of its commercial interests.

King William did his best to unite the two countries, but the Belgians revolted in 1830, set up an independent government in Brussels, and acquired a king of their own in Leopold of Saxe-Coburg. King William tried to subdue the insurgents with military force, with some success, until French troops intervened to protect the young Belgian state. A stalemate resulted, lasting until the Treaty of London of 1839, which formally ended the war. The key fortress town of Maastricht, on the Meuse River, a Dutch-held enclave, was returned with a large part of the province of Limburg to King William, and the land and river connection between Maastricht and the North was reestablished.

As a result of these political upheavals, the southern borders of the Kingdom of the Netherlands were redrawn, and they have not changed since. Amsterdam remains the formal capital, and The Hague is the seat of government. Belgium went its own way under King Leopold I, with Brussels as its capital and Antwerp, on the Scheldt River, as its chief port city.

THE KINGDOM OF THE NETHERLANDS

The Netherlands, then as today, was a country of water. Situated on the broad delta of the Rhine and Meuse Rivers, whose branches crisscross the country, the greatest of its many fine harbors were, as now, Amsterdam and Rotterdam. Inland lakes dotted its 32,000 square kilometers, today larger by 1,000 square kilometers, the result of large-scale drainage of the former South Sea.

More than a third of its 2.5 million people lived in towns and cities. (Less than a quarter century later the population reached 4 million; in 1900, 5.1; 1940, 8.8; 1950, 10; and today the country's nearly 16 million make it one of the most densely populated in the world.) Until expansion took hold after 1850, fortifications dating to the seventeenth century still confined most towns, including Amsterdam, easily the largest with 200,000 people.

The country's ten provinces included Holland in the west, the old economic heartland of the Dutch Republic and still the most populous and most important province economically. (The province was split in 1840 into North and South Holland, making eleven provinces, with Haarlem and The Hague as the new capitals.) In the Southwest, Zeeland, with its capital, Middelburg, was largely an island province straddling the Scheldt estuary, with some agriculture and much fishing. (Today, as a result of the great flood of 1953, all the province's sea arms and rivers, with the exception of the Western Scheldt, have been dammed off and all its islands connected by dams and dikes.) In the center of the country lay the populous and prosperous province of Utrecht, whose capital, also Utrecht, was a university town. To the east, largely agrarian Gelderland was home to some paper-making industry and old established iron foundries; its capital was Arnhem.

To the north lay two poor counties—the largely agricultural Overijssel with its capital, Zwolle, and Drente, mostly wasteland and the poorer of the two, with its capital, Assen. In the far north were agrarian Friesland and its capital, Leeuwarden, as well as many small fishing ports, and Groningen, largely agricultural, whose capital, also Groningen, was home to an old university.

South of the great rivers, the textile industry had settled in the fairly populous North Brabant (called "north" to avoid confusion with the Belgian province of Brebant), whose capital was 's-Hertogenbosch. Farthest south is Limburg, whose capital, Maastricht, was an old Roman city; the wedge-shaped province lies between Germany and Belgium. Its extensive coal fields, though known, were left almost untouched until the end of the nineteenth century.

Geologically, the Netherlands can be divided into western, eastern, and southern land types. The west is mostly low-lying peaty soil, generally below sea level, that still requires constant artificial draining; in the 1800s, such draining relied wholly on windmills. In the east, higher sandy or clay soils predominate. The highest land—just over three hundred meters above sea level—lies in the far south, near Vaals, close to the Belgian and German borders.

But it was the waterways that distinguished the country, where railways were concerned. In countries with no or few waterways of importance, the railways would impose an almost absolute transportation monopoly, but in the Netherlands, competition from the waterways prevented such a monopoly from ever establishing itself.

Since the seventeenth century, a system of canals had been dug to connect and complement the many natural waterways. Around the country, regular barge services, including night boats with sleeping accommodations, provided a fairly sophisticated, cheap, and comfortable way of traveling. Complementing this network of natural and artificial waterways was a system of paved highways, begun by Napoleon to connect all the outlying districts of his empire, and expanded under William I. New shipping canals constructed in both the North and the South made it possible to transport the industrial products of Wallonia to the port of Amsterdam entirely by water.

FIGURE I

The mile-long Moerdijk Bridge, opened in 1872 and for a time the longest bridge in Europe, ample illustration that the Kingdom of the Netherlands is a land of water.
(Photo NS, Collection NVBS)

The province of Holland in the early 1800s was the site of many inland lakes. The largest, the Haarlemmermeer, stretched between Amsterdam, Haarlem, and Leiden and expanded with every storm. After many abortive attempts to drain the lake by windmill, steam power finally accomplished the task in the 1850s, and the reclaimed land was converted into arable soil. (Schiphol, Amsterdam's airport, is today situated on this land, about five meters below sea level.) Other inland lakes lay in southern Holland, near Rotterdam and Gouda, and east of Leiden. Although most were finally drained in the 1840s and 1850s, engineers in the late 1830s charged with building the first railways still had to reckon with these lakes, which often lay in the path of the most direct routes between cities.

Both Amsterdam and Rotterdam depended on the Rhine and Waal Rivers to connect them with their natural hinterland, the Prussian Ruhr area, by 1830 heavily industrialized. Complaints about the navigability of the Rhine and its extensions multiplied with the growth of shipping. Narrow locks, sandbanks, low water, sharp bends, droughts in summer, and ice barriers in winter all contributed to the navigational problems. A trip from Amsterdam to Cologne by water—some three hundred kilometers—often took two weeks or more, and from Rotterdam upstream the situation was much the same. In summer, boats could carry only half loads to avoid getting stuck on shoals, and in winter, swift currents presented another hazard. It would take most of the nineteenth century to regulate these rivers and make year-round traffic possible.

Despite these hindrances, transportation by water was the generally accepted means of carrying freight and passengers, creating stiff competition for the new railways. The railways' superior speed soon won over the passengers, but freight continued to go by water, even when railways covered the same routes.

The war with Belgium from 1830 to 1839 burdened the new Kingdom of the Netherlands with an enormous public debt. The debt had been high since the closing years of the eighteenth century, and the French wars had only made matters worse. Forced bond exchanges and deferment of interest payments had helped somewhat, but the Belgian war required more loans, and by 1840 the debt amounted to 1.3 billion guilders, about 0.5 billion U.S. dollars— for a country of just over two million people, quite a large sum. (During the nineteenth century and as long as the gold standard and its system of fixed rates of exchange existed, one U.S. dollar was worth about 2.50 guilders.) Until 1850, more than half of the annual budget went to paying off interest.

Still, the colonies represented an important asset. During the time of the Dutch Republic, its East India Company had managed to acquire not only the East Indian archipelago (modern Indonesia), but also the island of Ceylon (Sri Lanka), settlements and factories on the Indian coast, a factory in Japan on an island in the Bay of Nagasaki, and the area of the Cape of Good Hope in South Africa. The West India Company had acquired a couple of forts on the African West (Gold) Coast, islands in the Caribbean such as Curacao, Aruba, and Saint Eustatius, and Surinam on the South American mainland. During the Napoleonic wars, Great Britain took possession of all these Dutch colonies except

Nagasaki. In 1815 it restored the East Indies, the Gold Coast, Surinam, and the Caribbean islands to the Netherlands but retained the rest.

Only in South Africa did a permanent settlement of Dutch farmers and artisans spring up, the nucleus of the Afrikaans speakers of today. In the Indies, the small number of Dutch lived chiefly on the island of Java, with some military and trading establishments elsewhere. The thousands of other islands, although officially under Dutch rule, were largely left to themselves until the end of the nineteenth century, when law and order were imposed in the whole archipelago by treaty with local rulers where possible, by military force when necessary. The sale of agricultural products from the East Indies made up an important share of the Netherlands national income, but market fluctuations and tropical diseases made their contribution undependable. Only from the 1850s onward did the annual sales of coffee, tea, sugar, and other cash crops produce an important and reliable revenue for the Dutch state.

Early Railway Projects, 1834–1860

The English phenomenon of the railway with propulsion by steam locomotives had not gone unnoticed in the Netherlands. William Archibald Bake, a Dutch artillery officer, was among the spectators in 1830 at the opening of England's Liverpool-Manchester Railway, the world's first modern railway. Bake, who was Dutch despite his English-sounding name, was in England to buy guns for the army and supervise their construction. Enthusiastic about the potential for railways as a means of transportation, back in Holland Bake developed plans for a railway line to connect Amsterdam, by way of Amersfoort and Arnhem, with the Prussian railways then under consideration in the Rhineland. King William, with economic foresight, viewed Bake's plans favorably and ordered Bernard H. Goudriaan, one of the top engineers at the Waterstaat, the Board of Public Works, to draw up a formal project. Until then, the Waterstaat had supervised all works of national importance, including rivers, canals, highways, and defenses against the sea. Soon the railways would also become its responsibility. (Then part of the Ministry of the Interior, the Waterstaat became a separate ministry in 1877.)

The detailed plans for Goudriaan's project, published in 1833, brought a positive reaction in Amsterdam's commercial circles but faced strong opposition as well around the country. Not only did the usual prophets of doom predict horrible disasters, but also respected technicians and engineers questioned the advisability of building railways in the soft Dutch soil and found fault with the proposed direction of the line. Loud complaints came from barge masters, coachmen, innkeepers, and others who foresaw the railways taking bread off their tables. The most influential of these was Gerhard M. Roentgen of Rotterdam, owner of a shipyard there and director of the Netherlands Steamboat Company, which operated a steam tug service on the rivers. Although unlike many of his contemporaries Roentgen did not oppose steam propulsion—he had in fact improved steam technology, inventing the system of compounding in steam machinery—for obvious reasons he advocated improving the rivers instead of building railways.

Competition from Belgium made producing a railway from Amsterdam to Cologne a matter of some urgency. The Belgians, independent since 1830 and locked out of the Dutch waterways throughout the conflict with the North, had instituted a commission in 1831 to study the possibility of an Iron Rhine, a railway from Antwerp to the Prussian Rhineland by way of Liège. The commission acted quickly, and with help and advice from George Stephenson, the father of railways, Belgium opened its first railway in 1835. While technical problems in the descent of the steep Meuse valley near Liège delayed the connection with the Prussian Rheinische Eisenbahn for eight more years, the North, especially Amsterdam, viewed a direct connection between Antwerp and the Rhineland as a threat.

Despite the opposition of the Rotterdam shipping interests, in 1834 William Bake invited subscriptions to a loan of twelve million guilders for his railway. The bond drive was a dismal failure. Bake had asked for a down payment of 20 percent immediately, even before the company had been incorporated legally and before the government had approved the course of the line. Capitalists were not eager to sink money into such an insecure venture, and moreover, a crisis in Spain had led to severe losses for Dutch investors, causing them to shy away from any risk at all.

The railway seemed farther away than ever, but King William, who never lost interest in the project, ordered a government commission to study the feasibility and desirability of a railway between Amsterdam and the Rhineland. In 1836, this commission concluded that such a railway should indeed have a high priority, for it might stop the decline of Amsterdam trade. If not enough private capital were forthcoming, the government should build the line. However, the interior minister's proposal early in 1838 to construct this line failed in the Second Chamber of Parliament, chiefly because he suggested financing it with the profits from East Indian cash crops. At that point, by a royal decree on April 30, 1838, the king, persuaded of the railway's necessity, simply ordered its construction by the state. (Until the revised Constitution of 1848—a year of revolution in Europe—the powers of the king, while not absolute, went far.) King William guaranteed from his personal property the interest payments on a loan of nine million guilders, which then easily drew subscribers, and the Rhine Railway was born. Bake withdrew from the project but set up an iron foundry at Leiden that produced rails and other ironwork for the railways. The Waterstaat engineer Bernard Goudriaan and his assistant L.J.A. Van der Kun were charged with building the Rhine

Railway; when Goudriaan died in 1842, Van der Kun took over as supervisor of construction.

THE HOLLAND IRON RAILWAY COMPANY

While the government was considering whether to build the Rhine Railway, construction had already begun on another line, which would be the country's first. Two well-respected Amsterdam merchants, L.J.J. Serrurier and R. le Chevalier, together with an army engineer, W. C. Brade, set up the Holland Iron Railway Company in 1836 to build a railway from Amsterdam to Rotterdam by way of Haarlem, Leiden, and The Hague. Unofficially, the railway soon became known as the Holland Railway Company. The 1836 government commission recommended the line's construction, and in the same year, the Holland Railway received a formal government concession to build the first experimental stretch, Amsterdam-Haarlem.

Brade, one of only a few railway experts in the country, drew up the plans for the line but soon fell out with his fellow directors and was replaced as engineer-director by Frederik Willem Conrad, Jr., another engineer of the Waterstaat, who was loaned to the company until 1855. Conrad became the

FIGURE 2

Reconstruction of the Holland Railway's broad-gauge track, first used in 1839. (Photo NS, Collection NVBS)

leading Dutch engineer of his time. A member of the respected English Institute of Civil Engineers beginning in 1843, he in 1847 cofounded the Dutch equivalent, the Royal Institute of Engineers. As advisor to many governments on matters of canals, polders, and civil engineering in general, Conrad was a member and for a time chairman of the International Suez Canal Commission and in fact died in Munich in February 1870 on his way home from the opening of the Suez Canal.

The Amsterdam-Haarlem line opened on September 20, 1839, an immediate success. Work began at once to extend it south to Rotterdam by way of Leiden, The Hague, and Delft. A major problem arose in the shape of a law dating to 1810 that granted companies like the Holland eminent domain. (A new expropriation law would pass in 1841, too late to do the Holland any good.) Under the 1810 law, landowners could exact outrageous concessions from the company, and to avoid endless litigation, the directors generally gave in. An exception came in the case of an insignificant little lane south of Delft that the railway had to cross and for which the owners asked an exorbitant price plus other concessions. Conrad instead bought and leased enough land to construct a temporary loop line around the contested property, and the railway was opened triumphantly. The owners, lampooned in the press for their obstructive attitude, gave in and presented the lane to the company free of charge. The next day, Conrad gave orders to straighten the line and remove

FIGURE 3

A somewhat exaggerated artist's impression of the loop south of Delft, built to avoid the disputed lane. (From *Nederlandsche Stoompost,* June 6, 1847, author's collection)

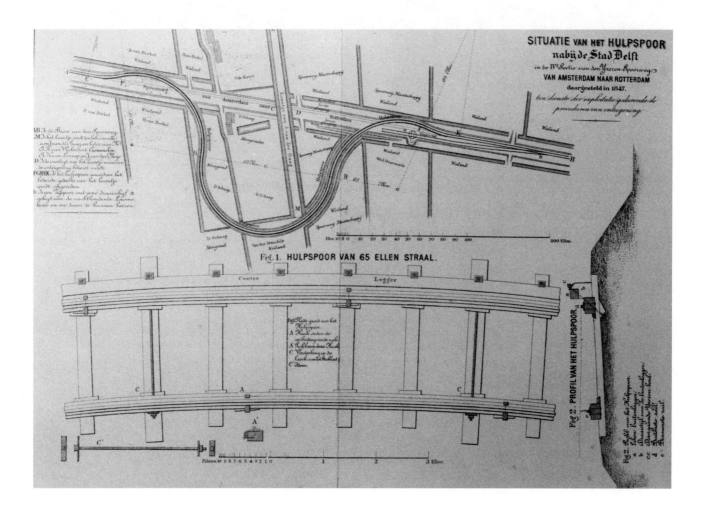

FIGURE 4

View to scale of the temporary loop south of Delft, designed by Conrad. (From *Hollandsche IJzeren Spoorweg-Maatschappij 1839–1889*, author's collection)

the temporary loop. The railway finally reached Rotterdam in 1847, nine years after the first rails were laid.

Financing the Holland Railway proved easy, despite Bake's earlier disappointment. Unlike Bake, Le Chevalier and Serrurier were well-known in Amsterdam business circles and had no problem persuading their friends and associates to buy shares in their new venture. Moreover, the prospectus of the Holland Railway was more carefully written than Bake's, spelling out more financial details, so that investors felt sure of where their money was going and believed the prospectus's confident promise of yields of around 8 percent. Capital was not scarce in the Netherlands, and although Dutch investors willingly speculated in Russian and Austrian—and, later, American—railways, they reserved enough for the home railways, although these investments never reached the same high levels, because the Netherlands required less construction capital than did other countries. On the other hand, a generous amount of German, English, and Belgian capital, attracted by the promised high yields, found its way to the Dutch railways.

The Holland Railway's first stock offer, 1.3 million guilders, was bought up quickly in Amsterdam, and when in 1837 the capital needed grew to 6.5 million, the new stock again sold without problems, mostly to the original shareholders. About 1844, it became known that a majority of the company's shares were held in Germany. International banking houses such as Bisschoffs-heim and Königswarter, which had branch offices in Amsterdam, had subscribed to large blocks of the original shares, and they had gradually sold their holdings to German investors. Dutch shareholders had also started to sell off their holdings, disappointed in their dividends, a meager 4.4 percent in the first distribution in 1840, which would drop to 2 percent later. (After this low, dividends rose slowly to top 5 percent in 1858 and reached a high of 7.25 in 1865, a record that would stand until the 1880s.)

Apart from enlarging its own capital to fifteen million guilders in several stages in 1866, 1874, and 1890, the Holland issued bonds. The first, in 1839, carried 5 percent interest, but bonds sold in 1889 offered only 3 percent. The company met no real problems in placing these bonds on the Amsterdam Stock Exchange. Any temporary setbacks usually resulted from influences outside the company—wars in Europe, worldwide economic crises, or bankruptcies of foreign governments.

—— THE RHINE RAILWAY ——————————————————

While the Holland Railway was being built, the Rhine Railway got under way in 1838 under the direction of Goudriaan and Van der Kun, who ran into the same problems with the 1810 land law. One landowner demanded that all trains forever stop at a station near his home, somewhere in the fields between Amsterdam and Utrecht. Later, as trains grew faster and ran more often, this landowner had to be bought off at great cost. Other problems arose with the land itself and the construction workers, or navvies (for navigators). East of Utrecht in 1843, the hilly country required some deep cuttings, which called for a large number of navvies. When bad weather made work impossible and no wages were paid, the army had to be called in to quell the disturbances among them, as the rural area had no police force. (The line would not reach its temporary end, at Arnhem, until 1845, and the extension to connect with the railways in Prussia was finished only in 1856, after the Rhine Railway had been narrowed to the European standard gauge.)

Apart from the railway's unfinished state, which prevented the earning of significant revenues, constructing the line had cost more than the nine million guilders originally anticipated and covered by King William's personal pledge. The state had built the line, and should revenues prove insufficient, the king had promised to contribute enough to make up the 4.5 percent interest on the loan, which he did. Because of this royal guarantee, the loan was heavily oversubscribed, chiefly by the Amsterdam *haute finance*. After King William I abdicated, in 1840, his son William II was willing to honor his father's obligations, but not forever. A state commission advised in 1845 that the railway must be transferred completely either to the state, without royal guarantees, or to a private company.

State railways did exist in some European countries: in part in Belgium, and in Hanover, Braunschweig, Baden, and Bavaria, but the Netherlands pub-

FIGURE 5

The modest terminus of the
Netherlands Rhenish Railway
at Arnhem, reached in 1845.
(Contemporary drawing,
Collection NVBS)

lic was not ready for this kind of government involvement, and the Rhine Railway was transferred to a private company, the Nederlandsche Rhijnspoorweg Maatschappij (NRS), or Netherlands Rhenish Railway Company. The railway actually had two official names, one in Dutch and the other in English, as English investors held a majority of its stock from the start. Capital was set at twenty-four million guilders, in shares of Dfl (Dutch florins) 240 or £20, again reflecting the English influence. All 100,000 shares sold easily, with about 65 percent of them ending up in Britain. None of the original Dutch holders of the royal first loan appeared on the list of new shareholders. Later issues, in 1868 and 1873, of Dfl 6 million each, were bought up only in London, expanding the British influence. British investor interest in the Rhenish Railway may be explained by the fact that the railway mania in Britain had peaked. The enormous floating capital available could find no profitable employment in Britain's home railways—hence the interest in European companies.

Shareholders expected the railway to show a high profit, certainly after linking up with the Prussian lines. What the British could not foresee was that it would be ten more years before this connection was made; Dutchmen may have been more cautious, reluctant to sink their capital in the Rhenish. Initial yields were indeed disappointing. The first dividend, less than 1 percent, was paid only in 1853. Interest on the former royal loan always had preference, and only after 1858 did dividends climb above 1 percent, reaching a high of 8.8 percent in 1868, with later yields generally between 7 and 8 percent, and falling again, to 4 percent, after 1885.

— TECHNOLOGY —

The English dominated railway technology in those first years. Great Britain was the cradle of the steam railway, and British influences appear in both the Holland and Rhine Railways. The Holland Company's intended gauge was the standard Stephensonian 4 ft 8.5 in, or 1435 mm. Brade had already ordered parts for this gauge, such as timber for the stringers and ties, when the Dutch government, advised by Goudriaan, prescribed a broad gauge of 1945 mm. In England, Goudriaan had visited Isambard K. Brunel, the chief engineer of the Great Western Railway and a great believer in a broad gauge of 7 ft. Goudriaan judged this broad gauge to be technically superior to anything else and expected it to become the standard, even though the neighboring countries of Belgium, Hannover, and Prussia had already opted for the Stephenson standard gauge.

Other countries, such as the Grandduchy of Baden and Russia, had also opted for a wider gauge than the standard, although only 5 ft in these cases. In the end, both the Holland and the Rhenish found themselves the lone supporters of the broader gauge and were obliged to change over to the standard gauge—narrow gauge, as it was then called—so as not to lose the connection with the European railway network. The NRS changed over to the standard gauge in 1855, with a government subsidy, while the Holland Railway did the same in 1866, entirely at its own expense.

The structure of the track itself was clearly inspired by Brunel's Great Western. Iron bridge rails, of the so-called hat profile, of 20 kg/m were spiked down on wooden longitudinal stringers, with wooden ties to keep them in gauge. The roadbed consisted of sand, covered with a layer of seashells to keep down the dust.

Conrad, Goudriaan, and Van der Kun had little trouble building the roadbed. The peat soil in some places threatened to create an unstable foundation for the railway, but centuries-old Dutch experience with building dikes on layers of faggots pulled them through. Railway bridges were something new, however. Small road bridges abounded in the country, but bridges able to withstand the much heavier weights and higher speeds of trains did not exist. Conrad proved to be an expert in their construction, however: For the Holland Railway line between Amsterdam and Rotterdam (84 km, mostly single track, with passing loops), he had to build ninety-eight bridges, twelve of them of drawbridges. He tried every design available, English, American, and domestic, swing bridges, rolling bridges, and crane bridges, the latter his own later popular design. The swing bridge across the Spaarne River, just east of Haarlem, had cast-iron girders of 22 m, weighing some 110 tons altogether. They were cast by the Amsterdam firm of John

FIGURE 6

A contemporary wooden model, now housed at the Netherlands Railway Museum at Utrecht, of the opening bridge across the Old Rhine south of Leiden, designed by F. W. Conrad. Note the broad-gauge double track. (Photo NS, Collection NVBS)

Dixon, an expatriate Englishman who had set up a foundry and machine shop in Holland. This job was no mean feat for the early 1840s, and envious competitors maintained that Dixon had imported the girders ready-made from England.

South of Haarlem, in 1842 Conrad built a double-track timber-lattice girder bridge of 54 meters, easily the longest span in Holland. He used a design patented in 1830 by the American engineer Stephen H. Long. In the damp Dutch climate, however, the wood proved to rot quickly, and it was never again used as a building material for major bridges.

While Conrad relied primarily on his own fine engineering capabilities, the design of the IJssel River bridge of 1855, east of Arnhem on the Rhine Railway, showed a direct foreign influence. The then engineer-in-chief of the Netherlands Rhenish Railway, W.C.P. baron van Reede van Oudtshoorn, had designed a double-track iron swing bridge patterned after a bridge across the Shannon in Ireland. The English and Dutch directors of the railway and the Netherlands government approved his design, but the predominantly English shareholders demanded a second opinion from an English engineer. Edwin Clark, who had been supervising the construction of Robert Stephenson's Brittannia Bridge across the Menai Straits in Wales, changed Van Reede's design only slightly, substituting plate girders for Van Reede's lattice girders

FIGURE 7

The double-track iron swing bridge across the IJssel River near Westervoort, opened in 1855, designed by W.C.P. van Reede and Edwin Clark and built by Thomas Brassey. (Contemporary lithograph, author's collection)

and retaining the swing bridge in midstream. This bridge would remain an isolated example of its type.

A well-known English railway contractor, Thomas Brassey, built the IJssel bridge with ironwork from the Butterley Iron Works. Brassey also built the Utrecht-Rotterdam branch of the Netherlands Rhenish Railway, which opened the same year. Joseph Locke, the famous English railway engineer, reviewed the plans for the branch and even walked the whole line, but Dutch engineers designed and built the Holland Railway and the later lines with little foreign influence.

STEAM LOCOMOTIVES AND ROLLING STOCK

While building the lines went smoothly enough, the Dutch engineers had problems acquiring locomotives and rolling stock. Steam propulsion was stipulated from the outset, but Conrad, Goudriaan, and Van der Kun lacked personal experience in this field. For guidance, they went not to England, but to Belgium. Despite the official state of war with that country until 1839, Pierre Simons, one of the leaders of the Belgian railway program, advised the Holland Railway in 1837 and 1838 about locomotives.

The Holland ordered the most modern engines, patterned after Stephenson's Patentee type, from the foundry of Longridge and Company of Bedlington, near Newcastle. (The better-known factory of Robert Stephenson and Company of Newcastle was so busy that it could not promise delivery soon enough.) The Patentee type had one powered axle, with two carrying axles in front and behind—the 2-2-2 type, as it became known. The engines weighed between 12 and 13.5 tons and with a light load could reach speeds of more than 80 km/h. Conrad, apparently not easily scared, tried them out himself, which must have qualified him as the fastest traveler in the country for a long time. In normal service, the engines moved much more slowly. As elsewhere, the early engines all burned coke, and coke ovens were established in several places convenient for loading.

Dutch coach makers built the carriages, of three classes, following an example of each delivered by Belgian, German, and English factories. (How a

FIGURE 8

A contemporary large-scale model, now at the Utrecht Railway Museum, of one of the first engines of the Holland Railway, either *De Hoop* or *De Snelheid*, in spite of the *Hercules* nameplate. (Photo NS, Collection NVBS)

Belgian factory managed to sell a coach to the "enemy" remains a mystery.)

The Rhine Railway also ordered its early engines in England, from Sharp, Roberts and Company of Gorton, near Manchester. The Netherlands government, then still responsible for the railway, loaned some of these engines to Dutch firms to be copied. Christiaan Verveer was the first to adapt his existing Amsterdam factory, which mostly made nails and other small ironwork, to the construction of steam locomotives for both the Holland and the Rhine Railway. John Dixon followed suit some years later. A third Amsterdam firm, Paul van Vlissingen and Dudok van Heel (much later famous under the name Werkspoor), soon joined them.

Conrad bought Verveer's equipment for the Haarlem works of the Holland Company, then built two locomotives at that works in 1848 and 1850. However, the railways continued to prefer foreign-built engines over the home product, the result partly of existing prejudices, partly of the English machines' better workmanship. The Netherlands Rhenish Railway was to remain faithful to Sharp, Roberts, its early supplier (later Sharp, Stewart and Company), until that company cofounded the North British Locomotive Company of Glasgow. The Holland Railway, after some deliveries from Robert Stephenson, switched to the German firm of August Borsig of Berlin-Moabit (later Berlin-Tegel).

The Netherlands suffered from an almost total lack of heavy industry, yet attempts to change this state of affairs failed until the later years of the nineteenth century. Shipyards were slow to switch to both iron construction and steam propulsion, at least for seagoing ships. The domestic and colonial sugar and textile industries had to import most of their machinery until the 1850s, when some Dutch firms began making it, at first with licenses from foreign factories, later from Dutch designs as well. A few early firms did make railway supplies on a small scale. Besides Bake's foundry at Leiden, another Leiden firm, D. A. Schretlen and Company, supplied iron rails and switches. John Dixon's factory of Amsterdam, after 1841 known as De Atlas, built iron bridges, station roofs, and such, soon joined by the rolling mill Pletterij Enthoven and the iron foundry De Prins van Oranje, both in The Hague, a city not typically associated with heavy industry.

On the other hand, Dutch firms made passenger coaches and freight trucks from the outset. J. J. Beijnes of Haarlem entered the field in 1855 and soon became the leading supplier of rolling stock, as well as an exporter; the company shipped its products to markets around the world.

STATIONS

Station buildings had not only to give passengers comfortable ingress and egress from the trains, but also to inspire confidence in this new mode of transportation. As the new city gates, stations should suggest new and unlimited opportunity. Amsterdam Willemspoort Station built in 1842, designed by Conrad's assistant Cornelis Outshoorn, looked like a Greek classical temple; long covered galleries enclosed the tracks. Haarlem (1841), Leiden (1842), and The Hague (1843), all designed by Conrad himself, were also built in the popular neo-classical style. For Rotterdam Delftsche Poort (1848), Outshoorn chose a neo-Tudor style. Three colossal arches over the tracks provided a fitting frame for the vehicle of the future, the steam train. A group of German shareholders, taking this grandiosity amiss, judged these buildings far too costly.

FIGURE 9

The first permanent station of the Holland Railway at Amsterdam (Willemspoort), designed along reassuring classic lines by C. Outshoorn and opened in 1842. The upper part of the De Koe windmill is just visible behind the building. (Author's collection)

The conflict was hushed up, but later station buildings were indeed somewhat simpler and cheaper.

The government-built stations for the Rhine Railway were also designed on a smaller scale. The terminus of Amsterdam Weesperpoort originally consisted only of two low buildings, one on either side of the tracks. Not until much later would an iron roof stretching over both buildings, along with other additions, make it a station worthy of the capital. Utrecht's and Arnhem's buildings were both somewhat larger, still fairly simple, in a pleasant neo-classical style.

The first line of the Holland Railway was intended for passenger traffic only. No freight trucks had been ordered, no connection with the port of Amsterdam or Rotterdam had been envisaged, and no rates for the carrying of freight had been established. At the outset, in 1839, the royal stables and well-heeled customers used flat trucks for their private carriages. Horse vans and cattle trucks were in service by 1840, but closed vans for smaller shipments did not appear until 1847.

The emphasis on passenger traffic at once killed off all competing coach and barge services along the same routes. A third-class railway ticket cost the same as a ticket for the barges, effectively putting an end to that popular mode of transportation. Many new coach services sprang up, however, to connect outlying towns and districts with the new railway stations.

In 1840, 97 percent of the total income of the Holland Railway came from passenger traffic, and one year later, 98 percent. Only after 1843 did freight traffic begin to increase the company's total revenue. The opening of the Eastern railway—Amsterdam-Amersfoort-Zutphen and on to the German Ruhr—in the 1870s would alter the proportion of passengers to freight, but passenger

FIGURE 12

Holland Railway locomotive *Holland* in broad-gauge days in Haarlem station circa 1865, shortly before the narrowing of the gauge.
(Photo A. Jager, Collection NVBS)

traffic would always remain the mainstay of revenue for the Holland Company, as indeed it is for its successor, Netherlands Railways.

The Rhenish Railway took a different path. Bake had drawn up his plans and designed his railway to carry freight; passengers were secondary. In 1845, even before the line connected with Prussia, freight traffic brought in 25 percent of all revenues. The through line to Cologne in 1856 increased freight traffic enormously, and by 1866 it accounted for 45 percent of the company's income. Passenger traffic contributed another 45 percent, and the rest came from miscellaneous sources, such as cattle, coaches, and corpses. Coal from the Ruhr was by far the most important freight, and for this traffic the Rhenish Railway ordered six-coupled engines as early as 1857. (The Holland took this step only in 1871.) The Rhenish made a big business of coal traffic; the fuel served domestic and industrial purposes, as well as the growing number of steamships in the docks of Amsterdam and Rotterdam.

—— SAFETY AND ACCIDENTS ——————————————————————

Railroad speeds were much higher than people were accustomed to; engines weighed more than anything else on land; and steam boilers required high pressure, the dangers of which were hardly known. Accidents were unavoidable.

Based on accidents that had already happened in France and England, some predicted, in lurid language, the same for the Netherlands. Yet the Holland and Rhine companies established a fair safety record, even with virtually no signaling system and no brakes. Not more than four daily trains in both directions ran on the Holland, and only two on the Rhenish Railway. Both lines were single track with passing loops, and policemen stationed at regular intervals announced the coming trains with disc signals and trumpets.

The electromagnetic telegraph made these policemen redundant. Eduard Wenckebach put up the first wires along the Amsterdam-Haarlem line, and by 1847 the telegraph reached Rotterdam. At first the company kept the invention for its private use but soon opened it to the public. The telegraph was an immediate success, and in 1852 the government took over all existing services, although the railway companies continued to use their own system for their service dispatches.

Although the tender of the engines was equipped with a handbrake, and the guard of the train had a handbrake in his van, no braking system existed. In emergencies, the driver could reverse his engine, but this practice could easily damage the engine. Some carriages and freight trucks were later equipped with handbrakes operated by brakemen. In their little brake huts on the roofs, the brakemen acted on whistle signals from the driver.

The first recorded railway accident in the country happened in 1843 on the Holland Railway, when the engine *Vesta,* running light, derailed on the bridge across the Warmonder Leede north of Leiden, which had not been closed properly. The young engineer A. D. Teyler van Hall, a nephew of the assistant engineer-director C. C. van Hall, was killed instantly. Similar accidents with

open bridges or bridges not properly closed became all too common, partly the result of Netherlands' extensive waterways.

Thirteen years passed before the first accident involving passengers took place, in 1856. On a dark night, near Schiedam (just west of Rotterdam), a passenger train hit another passenger train from behind that had stopped after colliding with an empty carriage blown onto the line by high winds. The driver of the second train saw the red taillight of the first too late. Three passengers were killed outright and five others injured. In 1868, in a similar accident on the Rhenish Railway, a passenger train that had broken down between Breukelen and Maarssen, on the Amsterdam-Utrecht line, was rammed from behind by a freight train. One passenger was killed and several others injured.

This accident was responsible in large part for the introduction of the block system the next year by the Rhenish. Under this system, a line was divided into sections that were protected by semaphore signals and other equipment brought from England; only one train at a time could run in each section. The Holland Railway and others later introduced similar systems, generally using German equipment.

Although double-track lines were much safer than single-track lines, the small number of trains in the Netherlands did not warrant the extra cost. By 1864, only Utrecht-Arnhem on the Rhenish Railway and the short Vogelenzang-Veenenburg stretch (between Haarlem and Leiden) on the Holland were double tracked. The single-track lines everywhere else had passing loops, but only at the stations.

Apart from the Holland and the Rhenish, several other companies operated railways in the Netherlands. In the far south, the Aachen-Maastricht Railway Company opened a line between the Prussian city of Aachen and the Dutch city of Maastricht in 1853. This company was a mixed Dutch-Prussian enterprise whose engineer-in-chief was J. A. Kool, a Dutch army officer; Kool's name crops up again later in Netherlands railway history. In 1856, the company extended the railway westward to Hasselt in Belgium, crossing the Meuse River at Maastricht. The lattice girder bridge built across the river was the first railway bridge designed by a Dutch engineer—J. A. Kool.

A Belgian company, the S. A. des Chemins de Fer d'Anvers à Rotterdam, opened a line from Antwerp to Moerdijk, with a branch to Breda, in 1855. Now one could travel from The Hague to Paris in one day or visit the Antwerp bourse and return on the same day. However, the journey could be trying in bad weather, as the stretch between Moerdijk and Rotterdam required switching to a steamboat. Bridging the Hollands Diep estuary north of Moerdijk was considered impossible.

Engineering the Dutch section of this Belgian railway was the Dutchman J. W. Fijnje van Salverda. Delays during construction of the swing bridge across a small river northwest of Breda jeopardized the opening of the line on schedule. Fijnje's assistant J. J. van Kerkwijk used the newly invented electric light to allow work on the bridge to proceed at night. Inside a huge wooden shed erected over the whole construction site hung a single carbon arc lamp (System Jaspar) fed by a forty-cell wet battery. On December 5, 1855, the last

FIGURE 14

Testing the new swing bridge across the Gent-Terneuzen Canal near Sluiskil (Dutch Flanders), February 22, 1907, with the old bridge of the Belgian Chemin de Fer de Gand à Terneuzen in the background.
(Photo General State Archives, author's collection)

29-m girder was delivered from the Pletterij Enthoven of The Hague, and seventeen days later the bridge opened for traffic, the result of a splendid combination of technological ingenuity and organizing ability.

A second Belgian company, the Compagnie du Chemin de Fer de Liège à Maestricht, opened a railway line in 1861 between its two namesake cities. In Maastricht, it shared the station of the Aachen-Maastricht Company.

In Zeeuws Vlaanderen (Zeeland Flanders in northern Flanders, Dutch for centuries), a third Belgian company, the Société du Chemin de Fer de Gand à Terneuzen, opened service between Terneuzen and Sas van Gent into Belgium in 1869. Two years later came the Société du Chemin de Fer International de Malines à Terneuzen. The two companies, subsequently under one management, would remain in Belgian hands until 1948. Foreign ownership created no real problem, as the line did not connect with the rest of the Dutch railway network.

——— THE NETHERLANDS CENTRAL RAILWAY ———

Another newcomer was the Netherlands Central Railway Company, incorporated in 1860 by a number of Dutch individuals. They planned to build a railway between Utrecht and Zwolle by way of Amersfoort and had found financial support in France. The stretch from Utrecht to the IJssel River at Hattem opened in 1863, and the next year the bridge across the IJssel itself was finished, which brought the line into Zwolle. The line reached Kampen, the ancient Hanseatic town at the mouth of the IJssel, in 1865.

The French contractor of the line, the Paris firm of Delettrez, Père et Compagnie, which played an important role in attracting French capital, had to accept a large block of shares of the Central Railway in part payment, which contributed to the French company's subsequent bankruptcy. Another French contractor, Vitali, Picard et Compagnie, finished the line. A British supplier of rolling stock was also paid off in shares and bonds, a financing system unknown in the Netherlands but widely used elsewhere in Europe and in America. Numerous foreign investors held shares in the Central until 1881, when the Rhenish Railway acquired a majority of its stock.

The Central, although eventually an important link to the North, was in financial trouble from the start. The company could not pay the interest on its outstanding loans for many years. Only the opening of the connecting lines to the North by the State Railways Company between 1866 and 1870 brought some relief. Stockholders received no dividends until 1881, nearly twenty years after the line opened, when a paltry 0.1 percent was distributed. Until 1890 dividends remained below 1 percent, and they never reached the level of returns of the other Dutch railway companies.

One nuisance remained from the early days. The town of Kampen had subsidized the construction of the line on condition that every train from the South would continue to Kampen from Zwolle. Built by the state as a through station for the North, Zwolle was the terminus for the Central's trains. To get

FIGURE 15
Netherlands Central Railway No. 18 leaving Utrecht with a train for Zwolle, about 1910. The engine, originally a 2-4-0 named *Sumatra,* is one of a series of three bought in 1874 from Georg Egestorff of Hanover, here rebuilt into a 4-4-0. (Author's collection)

these trains to Kampen, they had to reverse, with another engine placed at the end. Only much later was Kampen's condition modified, and eventually the town was bought off; the Central then offered connecting trains to Kampen. In Utrecht, the Central never built its own station but instead contracted to use that of the Rhenish.

The State Builds the Missing Links, 1860–1870

THE ROLE OF GOVERNMENT

Until the 1850s, the government stayed out of the business of running railroads, apart from the brief involvement in the Rhine Railway discussed earlier. In concessions granted to the private companies, the government made stipulations about their rates, safety, rights, and duties. These were generally elaborated on and subsequently regulated in more detail in a set of working rules to be approved by the minister of the interior. To limit the number of applications from concession hunters in the 1850s, the government required a security deposit, which was forfeited if a railway line was not built before the stipulated date.

The government also loaned engineers from the Waterstaat to the private companies. Even after the state transferred the Rhine Railway to private owners, engineers of the Waterstaat remained in charge. Some of them returned to the Waterstaat after many years with a private company. F. W. Conrad, engineer of the Waterstaat, for example, served the Holland Railway from 1839 until 1855 as engineer-director and returned to government service until he retired.

The need for more government supervision of the several private railways became apparent only gradually. In 1859, the first railway law introduced and approved by Parliament gave the minister of the interior more

RAILWAY NETWORK 1860

Legend

Holland Railway	broad gauge	
Netherlands Rhenish Railway		standard gauge
Antwerp–Rotterdam Railway		
Aachen–Maastricht Railway		
State boundary		
Provincial boundary		
Rhine Important watercourse		

Dick van der Spek 8-2000

FIGURE 16

The primitive Oudewater
Station of the Rhenish Railway,
post-1890 and part of State
Railways. The mail pickup and
delivery equipment has been
removed.
(Postcard, Collection NVBS)

control over the companies than was laid down in the various concessions. As a result of this law, a supervisory railway board, Raad van Toezicht op de Spoorwegdiensten, was set up in 1860. Charged with approving all matters related to safety and with inspecting rolling stock and locomotives, its functions were comparable to the English Railway Inspectorate of the Board of Trade. (Its functions would compare in the United States first to those of the Interstate Commerce Commission, today those of the Surface Transportation Board.) Christian Schanze, a German engineer who had been chief of the works of the Rhenish Railway Company at Utrecht, became the board's first inspector. In 1863, a general set of rules that related mainly to matters of safety (maximum speeds, and so on) was made mandatory for all companies. These rules were elaborated and modernized as needed to keep up with technological progress.

Trains carried mail almost from the outset, at first only closed mailbags accompanied by a postal officer. After 1850, the government required newly established private railway companies to carry this mail in special closed compartments of their trains free of charge. For the existing railways, a transitional arrangement was devised that in some cases included indemnification. The mails traveled free until 1925.

The original mail-by-rail system soon outgrew existing facilities, especially railroad cars, and the government started building its own special mail vans in 1856. Later the railways built their own mail vans as well, fitted out as traveling post offices—well lit, heated, and equipped with sorting racks and such, plus amenities for the staff in the way of toilets and stoves.

In 1859 the Rhenish Railway, always innovative, introduced the system of transferring mail bags from train to station on the run. Because the new Amsterdam-Cologne expresses did not stop at smaller stations, local mailbags were hung from a pole and caught by a device on the mail van of a passing train. In a similar way, mailbags could be transferred from the moving train to a hook on the pole. While not perfect, this equipment, already much in use in England, was used for many years. Several smaller stations between Amsterdam and Arnhem, and also Oudewater between Gouda and Woerden (South Holland province), used this apparatus to ensure fast and frequent mail deliveries for their small towns.

STALEMATE AND THE LAW OF 1860

By 1860, it became obvious that the system of privately built railways had left large gaps in the railway network. The Netherlands Central Railway, the last of the major companies incorporated, never grew beyond its one Amersfoort-Zwolle line, despite grandiose plans for connections with Germany. The Holland Railway, which ran from Amsterdam to Rotterdam on its antiquated broad gauge, seemed to have fallen asleep. The Rhenish Railway, on the standard gauge since 1855, ran its trains from Amsterdam and Rotterdam to Emmerich, where the Cöln-Mindener Eisenbahn continued to Cologne and beyond. In the south were only the Aachen-Maastricht and the Antwerp-Rotterdam railways.

In 1860, altogether not more than 335 km of lines existed, negligible compared to Belgium's 1,729 km in an area roughly the same size. Even Switzerland, a smaller country with a later start, had 1,058 km of railways by the end of 1860. The German states, especially Prussia, had also forged ahead.

A kind of all-pervading lethargy seemed to have made itself felt all over the country and the Dutch were fast becoming the laughing stock of Europe in railway matters. Furthermore, with Antwerp's rail connection to the Rhineland in operation since 1843, German commerce was shifting from the Dutch ports to the Belgian port and to Hamburg and Bremen.

Meanwhile, foreign and Dutch investors were clamoring for concessions for the best possible routes, with no thought of a coherent network. The government was afraid of foreign concession hunters, especially Belgian and English, who threatened to bring the railways of the Netherlands under foreign influence to the possible further detriment of the commercial interests of Amsterdam and Rotterdam. A major stumbling block for all private enterprise, foreign and domestic alike, had been the high cost of bridging the great rivers. After seeing the Waal River at Nijmegen full of drifting ice, the English engineer Sir John Rennie had at one time declared that bridges could not be built across such rivers at all. But by the mid-1800s, bridges over most major rivers seemed feasible; the question that remained was whether they would be profitable.

A slow change in the attitude of the government became noticeable after 1856. The financial situation had improved enough to enable the state to bear at least part of the expense of the river bridges. Van der Kun, now advisor to

FIGURE 17

Construction of the
government line near
Enschede, close to the
Hanoverian border, with a
contractor's tank engine,
with clean British lines,
on a work train.
(Photo General State Archives,
author's collection)

the minister of the interior and the government's foremost authority on railway matters, was charged with designing two networks, one north and one south of the lines of the Rhenish Railway. Private parties were to construct and run these lines, but the state was to participate in capitalizing the companies and was to pay for the great bridges. Although Van der Kun himself favored railway building by the state alone, he saw this solution as the best possible at the moment, when the prevailing liberal party precluded the state from taking any active role in industry and infrastructure apart from the rivers and canals. A bill to this end narrowly passed the Second Chamber of Parliament in 1859 after lengthy and heated debate. The First Chamber then discussed the proposals again at length, and to everybody's surprise rejected them, twenty to seventeen. The ministry stepped down in February 1860, and a completely new start had to be made.

A new ministry under F. A. van Hall and S. van Heemstra proposed that the state construct a network of 800 km of rail lines, for which ten million guilders (four million dollars) annually were to be set apart over a period of ten years. The money would come from the East Indian revenues, which flowed more richly into the government coffers every year.

Van Hall was a financial wizard and an old hand at the railway game, having been the attorney for the Holland Railway. With the help of Van der Kun, he had made certain the new network gave almost every electoral district in the country its coveted line. No elected representative could afford to oppose such a proposal. Moreover, people were getting tired of the endless and fruitless debates about railways. Despite opposition from the liberal minority in Parliament, the act passed the Second Chamber on July 27, 1860, forty-nine to twenty-three. The First Chamber subsequently passed the act with an even greater majority, thirty-four to six, on August 17. Although the decision about who would work the new network was left for a future ministry, the stalemate was over.

—— CONSTRUCTION BY THE STATE ——

The network as enacted comprised the following lines:

> Arnhem–Zutphen–Zwolle–Meppel–Leeuwarden
> Harlingen–Leeuwarden–Groningen–Nieuweschans–German border
> Zutphen–Hengelo–Enschede–German border
> Maastricht–Roermond–Venlo–Eindhoven–Tilburg–Breda
> Roosendaal–Bergen op Zoom–Vlissingen (Flushing) Venlo–
>   German border
> Maarsbergen (halfway between Utrecht and Arnhem)–
>   Tiel–'s-Hertogenbosch, later changed to Utrecht–Culemborg–
>   Zaltbommel–'s-Hertogenbosch
> Rotterdam–Dordrecht–Moerdijk–Breda
> Amsterdam–Zaandam–Alkmaar–Den Helder

At the request of the Second Chamber, a Meppel–Hoogeveen–Assen–Groningen line was added. The result was an ambitious and far-reaching program, the more so because all great river bridges were included. Only the crossing of the Hollands Diep just south of Dordrecht, the estuary of the Meuse River and about two miles wide, was left out for the time being. A bridge across the estuary was still seen as impossible; steam barges or floats to ferry complete trains were envisaged instead.

An office set up in the Ministry of the Interior would execute the plan. Van der Kun, as chief, would have several engineers, both military officers and civilians, serving under him. Some of these had previous railway experience, others none at all. Fijnje van Salverda, former construction chief of the Antwerp-Rotterdam Railway line, was made responsible for the northern network, everything north of the West-East Rhenish Railway. When he retired in 1863, he was succeeded by J.A.A. Waldorp, a civil engineer with no railway experience. In the South, Kool was made chief, and he had plenty of railway experience as engineer-in-chief of the Aachen–Maastricht Railway.

Section engineer for the lines north of Amsterdam was N. Th. Michaëlis, while G. van Diesen had to tackle the difficult Utrecht–'s-Hertogenbosch line, which would cross three great rivers—the Lek (Lower Rhine), Waal, and Meuse. M. Simon first got the easier Breda–Tilburg and Breda–Moerdijk lines, but he subsequently took on the very difficult Zeeland line to Flushing, which crossed two sea arms. Finally, J. G. van den Bergh, experienced in railway building under Kool but with no formal technical training, was charged with constructing Maastricht–Venlo–Breda and later would add to his responsibilities

FIGURE 18

Gerrit van Diesen's Culemborg Bridge near completion, 1868, then the longest span in the world, lacking only the ornamental lanterns on the balustrades. (Photo P. Oosterhuis, author's collection)

the problematic Dordrecht-Zevenbergen line, with the mile-long Moerdijk Bridge.

The engineers had little trouble building 800 km of railway lines over soft ground and marshy areas, but the great bridges presented a formidable challenge. Weak dikes, lots of drifting ice in winter, high water in spring from the melting snow in Switzerland and Germany, and shallow places in summer, all contributed to the difficulty. Every hindrance in the navigational channel endangered not only shipping but also the dikes. Rivers regularly froze over (hard to imagine in these days of thermal and chemical pollution). When a thaw set in, a drifting mass of ice flowed downstream; and if an obstruction blocked this slow-moving mass, allowing it to build up, the dikes were in immediate danger.

In 1861 the Bommelerwaard, between Waal and Meuse, and another region west of Nijmegen had been inundated after crushing walls of ice had demolished the dikes, with great loss of life and property. As late as 1891, after many river improvements and widenings, the Waal and its connections with the Hollands Diep (called the Merwede River) had become so completely clogged with ice in only eleven days that steam tugs, powerful icebreakers, and even dynamite could not break up the ice barrier.

The Waterstaat authorities and local water boards imposed almost impossible requirements at the crossing of the Lek River, the northernmost branch of the Rhine, near Culemborg: No piers in the river, and no obstructions anywhere. Gerrit van Diesen was compelled to design a bridge that would cross the river in one long span. His bold design spanned the main channel with one bridge of 154 meters, the longest single span anywhere in the world for many years to come, supplemented with one girder of 80 and seven of 57 meters over the overflow meadows. The bridge was high enough to obviate the need for an opening span, and the piers, solidly built of stone and masonry, also served as icebreakers. German engineers had developed this type of bridge in theory, but it had not yet been tested in practice. It was a truss girder bridge with a curved top chord, constructed in wrought iron, later a common design. Van Diesen's Culemborg Bridge, considered one of the new wonders of the world, opened in 1868.

Van Diesen's other bridges for the same line were smaller: At Zaltbommel, he used three spans of 124 meters and eight of 60 meters to cross the Waal River, while at Hedel he bridged the Meuse with one span of 110 and ten of 60 meters. German contractors built all these bridges based on the Dutch designs.

For these bridges, van Diesen and his colleagues mainly used wrought iron. Steel, made with the Thomas or Bessemer process, was lighter and stronger but too brittle to be trustworthy. Only with the development of the Siemens-Martin process at the end of the 1860s would steel become the major material for bridge construction.

An even greater challenge than bridging the Lek was crossing the Hollands Diep, the tidal estuary of the Waal and Meuse Rivers. In spite of its two-mile width, shifting sandbanks, and strong currents, engineers prepared to tackle it with the confidence gained from the successful completion of so many other bridges of unheard of dimensions. In 1866, Waldorp, Kool, Michaëlis, and Van den Bergh advised building a bridge rather than relying on cumbersome and expensive steam ferries. Michaëlis and Van den Bergh, assisted by the young engineer J. L. Cluijsenaer, then designed a single-track bridge of fourteen spans of 100 m each, with a swing bridge on one side and long approach dams at both ends. In July 1867, with government approval, work on the mile-long bridge began. For the hundreds of workers on this project, a whole new town was constructed on the north bank, complete with houses for workers and their families, stores, schools, churches, and a hospital.

Soundings in the estuary had shown that most of the thirteen piers and two bridgeheads could be built on ordinary foundations of long piles driven into the layers of hard sand that lay under the muck and unstable sand. At three places where these stable layers occurred at depths of twenty-two meters and more, piles could not be driven; the newly invented pneumatic caisson was used instead. French contractors did that part of the job, while Dutch firms built the rest, including all the ironwork. The first rivet was driven in October 1869, and on the first day of 1872, the bridge opened for traffic. It was to remain the longest bridge in Europe for many years.

Bridges near Dordrecht and in Rotterdam, together with a long iron viaduct through the heart of Rotterdam, were finished in 1876. The line was ready for through traffic.

FIGURE 19

Members of the Royal Institute
of Engineers inspecting the
works of the line to Flushing,
1870, behind an ancient
contractor's engine.
Top hats were apparently
de rigeur for gentlemen.
(Collection NVBS)

The Zeeland line to the planned packet station of Flushing involved not
only the technical challenge of crossing two arms of the tidal Scheldt River but
also negotiations with the Belgians. Under the 1839 treaty with Belgium, the
Netherlands had guaranteed free and unhindered shipping from Antwerp
through the Zeeland waters into open sea. The railway needed two embank-
ments constructed through the Eastern Scheldt and the Sloe, another branch
of the Scheldt River, that would block these waters. Even though the Netherlands would dig two new canals to replace the natural waterways, the Belgian
government was not satisfied. After many abortive conferences, foreign,
chiefly British, pressure compelled Brussels to agree to the Dutch plans. Work
trains brought in millions of tons of sand from the high Brabant shores and
dumped them in the deep waters until a stable foundation was laid. The railway to Flushing finally opened in 1872.

Meanwhile, hot debate continued over who would work the new railway
network. The imminent opening of the first lines of the state-built network in
1863 forced a choice. The ministry, now led by liberal politician Johan R. Thorbecke, considered several options, but state working was not one of them. The
Rhenish Railway, the Antwerp-Rotterdam, and others all declared themselves
willing to work the lines. In the end, Thorbecke opted for a new combination:
the rolling stock company Damlust of Utrecht (a new company set up for the
construction of rolling stock) and an Amsterdam financial group led by the
banker F. van Heukelom. Together they founded the Maatschappij tot Exploitatie van Staatsspoorwegen (Company for the Exploitation of the State Railways), usually abbreviated to Exploitatiemaatschappij or, more often, simply
Staatsspoorwegen (State Railways), as it will be in this book. Despite its title,
State Railways was always a private limited company, *not* a government insti-

tution. With royal approval obtained on September 7, 1863, the first line, Breda-Tilburg, opened on October 5, soon followed by other sections. Only the line from Amsterdam to Den Helder in the province of North Holland would be worked by the Holland Railway.

STATE RAILWAYS STATION BUILDINGS

The railway construction office drew up a number of standard designs for the stations of the new network. K. H. van Brederode was the architect responsible for the smaller buildings, which would serve the smallest towns. These pleasant buildings reflected in their round arches a style made popular by the French architect Durand. Apart from this French influence, they resembled contemporary stations and other railway buildings in the neighboring Kingdom of Hanover. The smallest, which cost only Dfl 8,700 ($3,480), were solidly built; some are still in use.

Although the architect of the large first-class stations in Zwolle and Dordrecht is unknown, van Brederode was probably at least consulted. On an even grander scale, his Rotterdam Delftsche Poort Station, which replaced the 1847 Holland Railway station, was part Holland Railway terminus, part State Railways through station. Apparently some stylistic variation was permitted, as van Diesen used a design of his own on his Utrecht-'s-Hertogenbosch line and later in finishing the station at Middelburg on the Zeeland line. Only Zwolle and Rotterdam sported large and impressive iron overall roofs over the tracks. Other large stations provided awnings over the platforms, while the smaller ones offered no shelter at all for passengers outside.

FIGURE 20
The new station of the State Railways at Zwolle, 1868, also used by the Central Railway, with a State Railways 2-4-0, later NS series 700. Protection for the engine crew was still minimal. (Author's collection)

FIGURE 21

The State/Holland Railways joint station at Rotterdam (Delftsche Poort), 1913, destroyed on May 14, 1940, by the German bombardment of the city.
(Photo State Railways, Collection NVBS)

The many fortress towns still extant could have no permanent station, because in the event of war, all buildings had to be demolished quickly to give the artillery a clear range of fire and offer the enemy no brick buildings for cover. The cities of Bergen op Zoom, Breda, 's-Hertogenbosch, Venlo, Maastricht, Deventer, and Groningen, therefore, all got unimpressive stations, long and low wooden buildings. When the Fortress Act of 1874 put an end to all fortified towns, they were allowed to level the sometimes antiquated bastions and earthworks. (The defense of the country then lay with modern fortified lines, such as the Holland Water Line east of Utrecht, the works around Amsterdam and the naval base of Den Helder, and the coastal fortresses of IJmuiden, Hook of Holland and Flushing.)

STAFF AND EMPLOYEES

Finding staff was a challenge for the first railway companies. Virtually everyone had to be trained on the job. Few foreigners served in the early years. In the higher ranks, Conrad, Outshoorn, Van der Kun, and Van Reede were well-qualified, and only the Rhenish Railway had a non-Dutch engineer, the German Christian Schanze, who served as chief of its works at Utrecht. For the lower ranks the demobilization of the army in 1839, after the Dutch-Belgian treaty of that year, turned out to be a great boon. Subaltern officers were gladly employed by the Holland and Rhenish Railways. They were literate, were used to a line of command and to working in a large organization, were careful dressers, and could be counted on to behave decently toward the trav-

FIGURE 22

The only wing built of the Utrecht terminus of the State Railways line from the South, 1866. The company moved its operations to the city's Rhenish/Central Railways station, on the site of today's Utrecht Central.
(Photo P. Oosterhuis, author's collection)

eling public. Many former subaltern officers became career conductors and station staff.

Enough Dutch farm boys and navvies signed up for track maintenance and other unskilled labor, but skilled technical personnel were almost impossible to find. Some Englishmen hired on as the first engine drivers, but they tended to claim special treatment and high wages, so Conrad trained Dutchmen to replace them as soon as possible. The railway workshops employed a number of foreign technicians, such as Schanze on the Rhenish or the Walloon Taskin (who could barely speak Dutch) on the Holland Railway, but they too were soon replaced by Dutch staff.

Only the State Railways was forced to hire a number of foreign staff as a result of its late start and need for a large workforce quickly. Among the many Germans hired was Herr Prüssmann, a well-known technician of the Hanover State Railways, who was first appointed as chief mechanical engineer of the State Railways. Even before he started work, however, he handed in his resignation and was replaced by a Dutchman, J. W. Stous Sloot, hired away from the Rhenish Railway. Another German, Friedrich Oberstadt, became chief of the Tilburg works. A number of French-speaking Belgians hired on as station workers.

A great drawback for the State Railways was the division of its lines into northern and southern networks separated by the Rhenish Railway, with separate workshops—Tilburg in the South and Zwolle in the North. The central directorate at Utrecht found itself faced with regional managers and engineers who expected to wield independent authority. One result of this lack of central direction was insufficient maintenance of the rolling stock. In 1868 the boiler of a locomotive standing in Harlingen (Friesland) Station exploded because it had not been inspected, killing the fireman and injuring the driver. The company would not manage to bring order out of this chaos for many years.

The Network Nears Completion, 1870–1890

── NEW CONSTRUCTION BY THE STATE ──

The law of 1860 created a more or less coherent network, but the lack of a connection of its own between the State Railways' northern and southern systems remained a nuisance. To remedy it, a law in 1873 called for an Arnhem-Nijmegen line bridging both the Rhine and the Waal, and therefore astronomically expensive for the relatively short distance. J. G. van den Bergh, backed by his experience with the Moerdijk Bridge, designed both bridges, and in 1879 the line opened to traffic. Nijmegen, since 1865 connected with Cleve in Germany by way of a small private company worked by the large (Prussian) Rheinische Eisenbahn, now also was linked up to the Dutch network.

Nijmegen, on the banks of the Waal, got an even greater boost in 1875 with the third railway law, which ordered the construction of the following lines:

> Nijmegen-Venlo
> Zwolle-Almelo
> Dordrecht-Gorinchem-Kesteren-Elst
> Amersfoort-Rhenen-Kesteren
> Zaandam-Hoorn-Enkhuizen
> Stavoren-Leeuwarden

The Second Chamber of Parliament, which passed this law almost unanimously, then added three more lines:

Schiedam–Hook of Holland
Lage Zwaluwe–Waalwijk–'s-Hertogenbosch
Groningen-Delfzijl

The State Railways was to work all these lines except Schiedam–Hook of Holland, Zaandam–Hoorn–Enkhuizen, and Amersfoort–Kesteren, which went to the Holland Railway. Although the State now had a fully connecting network, it still lacked an entry to Amsterdam over its own rails.

THE HOLLAND AND RHENISH RAILWAYS AFTER 1860

Concurrent with the construction of the State network, the Holland Railway—although still operating on outdated broad-gauge track—reentered the competition. The company tried hard to obtain the Leiden-Woerden project, but Parliament awarded it to the Rhenish. Then the Holland applied for a subsidy to narrow the gauge of its existing line, as had earlier been granted to the Rhenish, but Parliament voted down this proposal as well. The company then narrowed its line at its own expense and doubled the tracks at the same time,

FIGURE 23

Alkmaar Station on the North Holland government line, worked by the Holland Company, 1865, with a Borsig 2-4-0 in the distance. (Author's collection)

efforts completed in 1865, when the North Holland State-built line and Holland's own short Haarlem-Uitgeest connecting line both opened.

Despite these improvements and extensions, the Holland only really became a competitor with the opening of the Eastern Railway. In 1870 the company had obtained a concession for this line, which ran from Amsterdam (Oosterdok) to Hilversum, where it branched south to Utrecht (Maliebaan Station, the present-day Railway Museum), with a connection to the State Railways line to 's-Hertogenbosch. The main Holland line continued on from Hilversum east to Amersfoort, connecting there with the Central's north-south line, and from there farther east to Zutphen. The line reached Utrecht in 1874 and Zutphen two years later; from there, the Netherlands-Westfalian Railway continued southeast to Winterswijk. This company, nominally independent, had obtained a subsidy from the state and was worked from the outset by the Holland Railway. At Winterswijk the Prussian Bergisch-Märkische Eisenbahn made two connections to the coal fields of the Ruhr; both opened in 1880.

Under the energetic leadership of A.K.P.F.R. (Robert) van Hasselt, who had started his career as engineer in charge of construction of the Eastern Railway, the Holland became a strong presence in the country. Besides its monopoly in North Holland, it also worked the state-built Zaandam-Enkhuizen line and its own Velsen-IJmuiden branch, which opened in 1883.

FIGURE 24

The stately terminus of the Rhenish Railway at The Hague, with the company's connecting steam tram to Scheveningen Beach, 1881. This station was one of few with a royal waiting room.
(Collection A. D. de Pater/ NVBS)

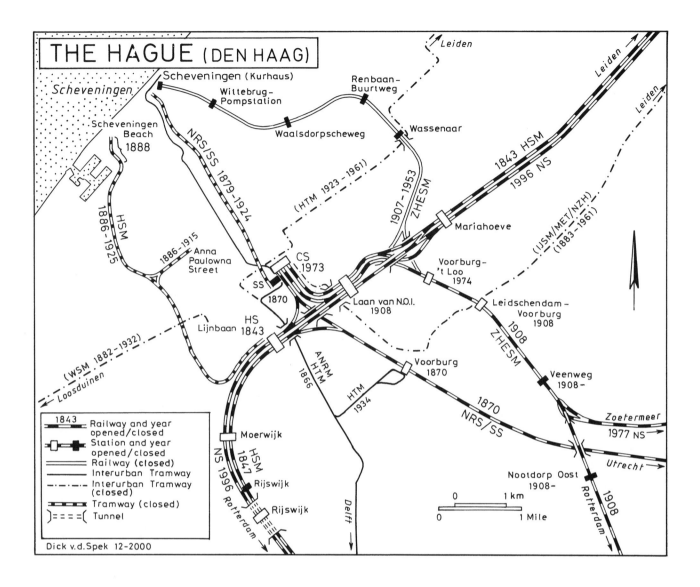

The Rhenish Railway, encircled by the new State Railways system, and in the Eastern line of the Holland Railway facing vigorous competition for German traffic, also found new life. It opened a branch off the Utrecht-Rotterdam line from Gouda to The Hague in 1870, and the connecting Harmelen-Breukelen line in 1869, enabling the company to compete directly with the Holland for the important Amsterdam-Rotterdam traffic. These trains also served—in a peculiar way—The Hague, equally important as the center of government. The direct Rotterdam trains did not stop in Gouda, where the line to The Hague branched off; instead, a slip carriage was dropped off the moving train and braked to a stop at Gouda, where a separate locomotive took it to The Hague. This practice, common in England, was new to the Netherlands.

In 1879, the first steam tramway opened between The Hague (Rhenish Railway station) and its fashionable beach resort, Scheveningen, after some negotiating between the Rhenish and the city of The Hague. Because a large number of railway passengers to The Hague wanted to continue their journey to Scheveningen, the Rhenish had applied for a concession for a railway line to the resort. The Hague city council was willing to grant the company a concession only for a standard-gauge horse tramway between its railway station and Scheveningen-Bath. Meanwhile, the Rhenish was experimenting with a new mode of transportation, the steam tramway, trying out English Merryweather tram locomotives on the line between The Hague and Voorburg. These proved so successful that the company applied for a license to use them on the projected horse tramway to Scheveningen. The city agreed, and the line was opened with steam traction, the first of many steam tramways in the country.

Another success for the Rhenish was connecting with England by steamer in 1863. Although several steamboat services ran from Rotterdam to London and other ports before 1863, travelers on the Rhenish had to take a cab or walk from the Rhenish station to reach them. On the English side, the Eastern Union Railway (EUR) had run from London to Harwich, the traditional packet station in England, since 1854. In the next decade, no steam packet service established regular passage to the Continent. Not until the Great Eastern Railway took over the EUR was the link completed with a nightly Harwich-Rotterdam service in 1863; steamers for England departed conveniently from the wharf in front of Rotterdam's Rhenish station. The service had a virtual monopoly for twelve years, until the Zeeland Packet Company opened a Flushing-Queenborough service in 1875, strongly supported by State Railways.

A somewhat ironic footnote to this competition concerns James Staats Forbes. Forbes was not only the director of the London, Chatham, and Dover Railway, which handled the Queenborough side of the Zeeland service, but also (since 1857) a director of the Rhenish Railway. By fostering the growth of his English company, he damaged the interests of his Dutch railway.

The Rhenish also had its disappointments, for example, with the Leiden-Woerden project awarded to the railway by Parliament. After an independent company built the line and opened it in 1878, the Rhenish bought up the majority of the stock and worked the line. The poor returns from the project, however, constituted a permanent and severe drain on the resources of the Rhenish.

TWO SMALLER RAILWAY COMPANIES

The short-lived Netherlands South Eastern Company, a highly speculative British enterprise, opened a line between Tilburg and Nijmegen in 1881 as the first part of an international line from London to Berlin and beyond via the Flushing packet station. But the Netherlands government did not look favorably on this new foreign influence, and the State Railways, safely settled in at Flushing, refused to cooperate fully. As a consequence, the South Eastern languished and sold out to State Railways in 1883.

Five years later, a second small company tried for a share of the lucrative London-Flushing-Berlin traffic. The Noord-Brabantsch-Duitsche Spoorweg Maatschappij (NBDS, North Brabant–German Railway) in 1878 opened a Boxtel-Gennep-Goch-Wesel line as part of the North German direct line.

Again the State Railways, which was hauling trains from Flushing to Boxtel anyway, preferred to haul them all the way to its own border station at Venlo. Although the North Brabant Company, under the vigorous leadership of its president J. M. Voorhoeve, succeeded in winning over some passengers, from the viewpoint of its bondholders and shareholders it was a dismal failure. While emperors, kings, queens, and members of the European nobility rode its trains and lent some glamour to its shabby stations, the company could not even pay for its own rolling stock. Instead, separate partnerships were set up to buy rolling stock, then rent it out to the NBDS. With no local traffic to bolster its revenues—that part of the North Brabant countryside was sparsely populated—the company never paid a dividend and could rarely pay its debt service.

RAILWAYS IN AMSTERDAM

Before the State Railways built an Amsterdam-Zaandam line, the Holland Railway terminus in the capital was the old Willemspoort Station on the west side, just outside the city walls. Then the State built the line to Zaandam, and

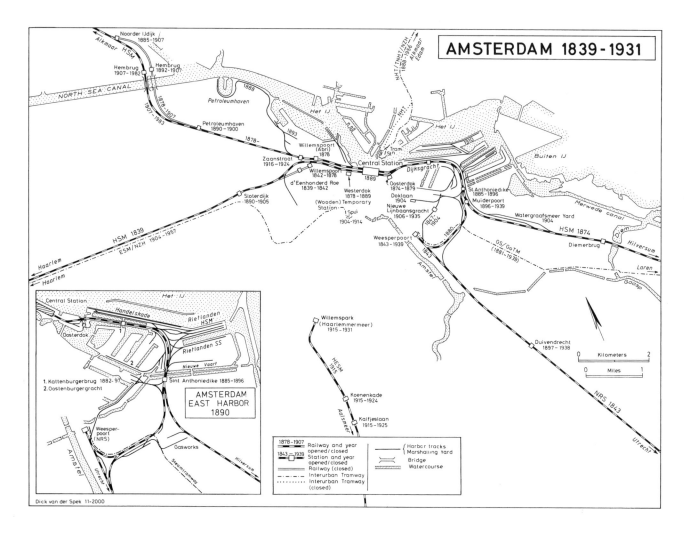

the Holland connected with it and built a new, temporary, wooden station at the Westerdok, which opened in 1878 on the northern outskirts of the old city, close to the old harbors in the open IJ. This body of water, formerly linked with the South Sea and the open ocean, was now confined within locks in conjunction with the new North Sea Canal to IJmuiden.

Plans to build a grand new Central Station on artificial islands in the open harbor of the IJ near the Westerdok Station brought howls of protest. The huge new station, many complained, would permanently block the view from the old city over its old harbors and the countryside beyond. Still, a central station required a central location, and the harbor front met that criterion. Despite the opposition, the city council approved the plans. The islands were built with sand dug out for the North Sea Canal then under construction. A temporary line was laid from the Westerdok Station across the site of the future Central Station to the Oosterdok and the terminus of the Eastern Railway, also in the hands of the Holland Company—another temporary wooden building, in place since 1874. When the Oosterdok Station burned to the ground in 1879, just a year after the temporary line was laid, the whole service was transferred to the Westerdok. The wooden station there served as a makeshift Central Station for the next decade, until the magnificent new station opened in 1889. Designed by architect P.J.H. Cuypers, the building is still in operation.

The Rhenish Railway entered Amsterdam from the southeast and had its terminus at the Weesperpoort Station, but in 1880 the company opened a

FIGURE 25

Gennep Station of the North Brabant–German Railway Company, opened in 1873, with an international train hauled by a small 2-4-0 locomotive, series 1–5. (Collection NVBS)

connecting line to the Westerdok. International and other expresses were routed over this line only after first stopping at the Weesperpoort, a terminal station. This cumbersome setup necessitated placing a second locomotive at the rear of each train.

Apart from a Rhenish Railway line built in 1847 to a coal transfer wharf, no lines connected the railways to Amsterdam's harbors until the 1870s. (The Rhenish's so-called dock line included a spur to the bonded warehouse's Entrepot dock.) Large seagoing ships had trouble reaching the harbors anyway, as the Noordhollands Kanaal to Den Helder was too narrow and too shallow in places. These ships were unloaded at Den Helder and their cargoes transferred to barges that could pass through the canal until the North Sea Canal to IJmuiden opened in 1876, giving even the largest steamers access to the harbor.

In 1877, when the Holland Railway was about to open its connecting lines into Prussia, it also laid tracks to the wharves in that old part of Amsterdam. In that same year the State began building extensive new docks in the Rietlanden, east of the old city, and the city council itself ordered the laying out of new installations. All these harbors were served by the Holland Railway, and to a lesser extent by the Rhenish. (In the twentieth century, harbor develop-

FIGURE 26

Amsterdam (Weesperpoort), the terminus of the Rhenish Railway, circa 1913, then part of the State Railways. *At left,* a tank engine coupled to the rear of an international train just arrived from Germany via Utrecht that will take the train over the belt line to the Central Station. The station master, *left,* in plain long coat and uniform hat, talks with a young rail fan; on the platform, *right,* men admire No. 701, the first of the State's new 4-6-0s. (Photo Staatsspoorwegen, Collection NVBS)

HANDELSKADE - AMSTERDAM

FIGURE 27

Part of the new harbor
installations of Amsterdam,
circa 1910, with a Holland
Railway 0-4-0 saddle tank
switcher (ex-Rhenish Railway)
at work.
(Postcard, Collection NVBS)

ments to the west were in the hands of the Holland Company from the out-set.) Amsterdam became the nucleus and operations center of the Holland Railway under the direction of Robert van Hasselt; the company's headquarters were housed just across the street from the Central Station.

RAILWAYS IN ROTTERDAM

In Rotterdam, the Holland left its monumental Delftsche Poort station in 1877 to share a new station of the same name with the State Railways. The Holland used the terminus portion, while the State used the through tracks. International trains and other expresses had to change engines here, as the companies had not yet agreed to run on each other's lines.

The Rhenish Railway had opened its first temporary station in 1855 at the Plantage, east of the old town, then transferred its operations to its new but still temporary Rotterdam-Maas Station closer to the city center. In 1876 the company built a permanent station on the same spot, which stood until destroyed in the 1940 bombing of Rotterdam. It was at the quay in front of this station that the Harwich steamers of the Great Eastern Railway moored. A Rhenish innovation here was a large shed for the transfer of freight between ship and rail, an idea other Netherlands railways did not take up until many years later.

Rotterdam's harbor in these years was accessible only via the canal through the island of Voorne, and only smaller vessels could navigate even this passage. Digging on the New Waterway began in 1866. The waterway

FIGURE 28

Rotterdam (Maas) terminus
of the Rhenish Railway shortly
before World War II. German
bombs destroyed the station
on May 14, 1940.
(Photo NS, Collection NVBS)

would dramatically improve the situation, but the largest steamers would be unable to reach the harbor until the 1890s. With the construction of the State Railway line from Dordrecht, it became possible to open new and better-equipped facilities (wharves, warehouses, steam cranes, and so on) on the south bank of the New Meuse River, which runs through Rotterdam. The State Railways, the town council itself, and private parties all opened new installations there in 1878 and 1879. (Among the private companies was the Rotterdam Trading Company, headed by Lodewijk Pincoffs, whose fraudulent dealings came to light only after Pincoffs himself had fled abroad.) The State Railways dominated the movement of freight in the Rotterdam harbor. The Holland Railway acquired a share in the rapidly expanding business only toward the end of the nineteenth century, by serving new docks built on the north bank of the river to the west. (Rotterdam would develop into the world's biggest port after the Second World War.)

INTERNATIONAL COOPERATION

The Verein Deutscher Eisenbahnverwaltungen (Association of German Railway Companies) was a group that banded together to help establish uniform working rules, safety measures, bookkeeping, and such, and to act as a clearinghouse for its participants. Although founded as a German business, the association included the Aachen-Maastricht from the start, and several Swiss, Austrian, Belgian, and Russian companies soon joined. The Rhenish in 1860 was the first of the entirely Dutch railways to become a member, followed by the State Railways; the Holland was to join in 1873. With all these non-German members, the name of the group was modified to the Association

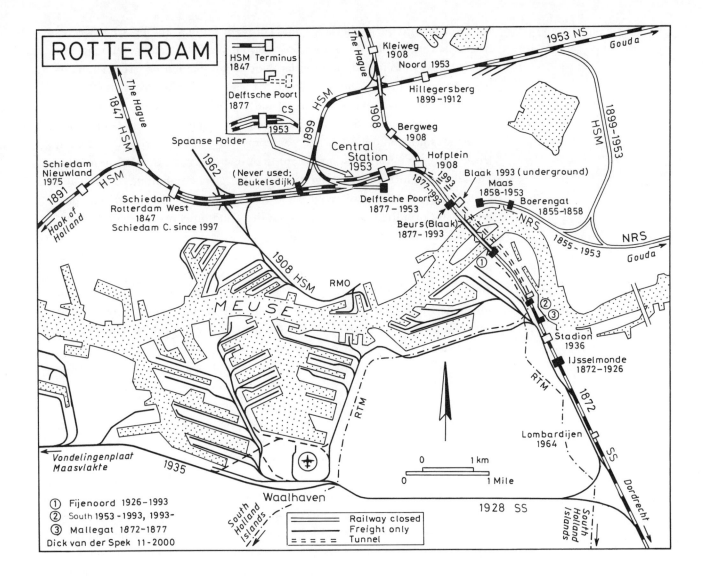

ROTTERDAM

HSM Terminus 1847
Delftsche Poort 1877
CS 1953

The Hague
1847 HSM

1847 HSM
1891 HSM

Schiedam Nieuwland 1975

Schiedam Rotterdam West 1847
Schiedam C. since 1997

Hook of Holland

Spaanse Polder

1962

1908 HSM

(Never used: Beukelsdijk)

Kleiweg 1908
Noord 1953

The Hague
HSM

1899 HSM

1908

Hillegersberg 1899–1912

Bergweg 1908

Central Station 1953

Hofplein 1908

Delftsche Poort 1877–1953

Beurs (Blaak) 1877–1993

1877–1993

1993

Blaak 1993 (underground)
Maas 1858–1953

Boerengat 1855–1858

NRS 1855–1953

1953 NS
Gouda

1899–1953
HSM

NRS
Gouda

RMO

① Fijenoord

① ② ③

Stadion 1936

IJsselmonde 1872–1926

MEUSE

RTM

RTM

1908 HSM

1872

SS

Lombardijen 1964

0   1 km
0   1 Mile

Vondelingenplaat Maasvlakte
1935

Waalhaven

South Holland Islands

① Fijenoord 1926–1993
② South 1953–1993, 1993–
③ Mallegat 1872–1877
Dick van der Spek 11–2000

Railway closed
Freight only
= = = = = Tunnel

1928 SS

South Holland Islands

Dordrecht

of Middle European Railway Companies. Its clearinghouse in Berlin became an important venue for settling the accounts of the growing international railway traffic.

The Verein was most visible through its two publications: the *Zeitung des Vereins,* general railway news published biweekly beginning in 1861, and the *Organ für die Fortschritte des Eisenbahnwesens* (Journal for Railway Development). Founded by German engineer Edmund Heusinger von Waldegg in 1845 as a technical journal, the *Organ* was taken over by the Verein in 1864. It soon became the leading technical journal outside the British-American world. Dutch mechanical engineers such as G.A.A. Middelberg (Holland Railway), J. W. Stous Sloot (State Railways), and C. W. Verloop (Rhenish Railway) became regular contributors to the *Organ.*

Dutch engineers adhered to the Technische Vereinbarungen (technical regulations) published in the journal: Dutch rolling stock was to run through on foreign rails; Belgian, German, French, and other coaches and freight trucks came into the Netherlands; and couplers, buffers, and braking systems had to be compatible. When these regulations were not detailed enough, the Dutch railways followed the Prussian Normalien (Standards). The neighboring Königliche Preussische Eisenbahn Verwaltung (Royal Prussian Railway Administration) was easily the largest railway organization in the world. (As of 1913, the organization had almost 40,000 kilometers of line, more than 20,000 steam locomotives, 45,000 passenger cars, just under 500,000 freight trucks, 559,817 employees, and more than one billion passengers annually.) The Prussian Normalien couplers, brakes, axles, wheels, lighting fixtures, and so on became the standard, resulting in very Prussian-looking freight and passenger stock on the Dutch railways. At the same time, many Dutch locomotives were patterned after the British.

Apart from technical compatibility, international agreement regarding finance and jurisprudence also proved necessary. For instance, a conflict might arise over who was responsible for goods damaged or lost in transit somewhere between Holland and Italy—the Dutch railway company that had contracted with the shipper, or the German or Swiss railway company on whose line the damage had occurred. And what of cases in which it was unclear where and when the damage had been done? Regulations about liability in such cases differed from country to country, and suits against the railways could become stuck in a morass of litigation.

The Swiss took the lead in 1878 and convened a conference in Bern to regulate this thorny issue. In 1890 the governments of Switzerland, the German Empire, Austria-Hungary, Russia, Italy, France, Belgium, Luxembourg, and the Netherlands finally reached agreement on the Bern Railway Convention. The convention laid out precisely all matters of international freight traffic between the participating countries. An office set up in Bern would oversee the agreement, paid for by all participants in proportion to the length of their railway lines. Later other southern European and Scandinavian countries joined the group, and the Bern office became a highly successful tool for international cooperation.

GOVERNMENT AND RAILWAYS

In practice, the too narrowly worded railway law of 1859 gave the Netherlands government only restricted powers to cope with the fast-growing railway traffic. A new law introduced in 1875, strongly influenced by German railway laws, laid out a framework to be filled in by successive government measures. This law, with later amendments, remained on the books until 1945. The details of the original law were worked out in the Algemeen Reglement voor de Dienst op de Spoorwegen (ARD, General Regulations for the Railway Service) of 1875 and the Algemeen Reglement voor het Vervoer op de Spoorwegen (ARV, General Regulations for Railway Traffic) of 1876. The ARV was an almost literal translation of the German Betriebs-Reglement für die Eisenbahnen Deutschlands (Regulations for the Service on Germany's Railways), another indication of the strong German influence on Dutch railways.

Both the ARD and ARV were changed and amended regularly, sometimes even annually, to keep them in line with developments in railway technology. Some articles of the ARV sound especially odd in these days of the Eurodollar. Article 6 in the ARV of 1887, for example, governed the acceptance at Dutch ticket windows of all current gold and silver specie of the surrounding countries: Because an almost universal gold standard fixed the rate of exchange among guilders and Reichsmark, Belgian and French francs, and so on, every station clerk had a list of accepted foreign currency and the rate of exchange.

The ARD mostly covered technical matters. Article 75 of the 1887 ARD, for instance, limited the maximum speed of passenger trains to 60 km/h, and of expresses, when equipped with air brakes, to 75 km/h. Express trains of first- and second-class coaches only could travel at 90 km/h. Freight trains, most of which had no brakes, could not exceed 45 km/h. Running tender first (that is, the locomotive running backward) was prohibited, apart from some well-defined cases, and speed in those cases was limited to 25 km/h. Passenger trains were not to number more than one hundred axles; with the mix of six-wheelers and four-wheelers then in use, this worked out to between thirty-three and fifty coaches, a number rarely reached. Freight trains could not exceed two hundred axles, which meant one hundred wagons at the most, as contemporary freight trucks were generally four-wheeled.

The ARD also laid down rules about safety measures, signaling installations, movable bridges, inspection of locomotives and rolling stock, and all kinds of other technical matters, which meant that the text had to be changed frequently to keep it up to date. Railway technology developed quickly in the nineteenth century, and the necessary international collaboration meant that new foreign improvements and inventions found their way almost at once to the railways of the Netherlands.

CHAPTER

4

Railway Operation
before 1890

— THE STATE RAILWAYS

The State Railways Company's difficult start resulted in part from its cumbersome corporate structure, five directors whose opinions and management styles often clashed. The company's corporate headquarters in The Hague had no physical connection to the State Railways system. In 1870, the company moved its offices to Utrecht, in the center of the country and directly connected to its own network, to resolve one problem at least.

The lack of cohesion between the several parts of the network produced revenues that lagged far behind the original optimistic estimates, aggravating the situation, which would be remedied only in the late 1870s. Although the company's first stock offering of 6 million guilders in 1863 went smoothly, the public responded less enthusiastically to a second offering in the same amount in 1866; only an advance from the government of 2.5 million guilders kept the company afloat. Foreign banking houses, such as the Belgian-French Bisschoffsheim and Hirsch with its extensive railway investments across Europe, showed an interest, but the Netherlands government was loath to open the door to any large foreign influence in the State Company.

The long overdue reorganization took place in 1868: A single director-general, F. 's Jacob, replaced the five directors. After many abortive attempts, 's Jacob in 1870 obtained a sufficient loan on reasonable conditions. A German-Netherlands consortium—Lippmann, Rosenthal and Company, and Wertheim and Gompertz, both of Amsterdam, and the Bank für Handel und Industrie of Darmstadt, Germany—floated a large convertible 5 percent loan that rescued the company. Most bonds were soon converted into shares, in the hope that dividends would be higher than the 5 percent bond interest, a hope rarely realized. In 1874 the stock paid no dividend at all because of that year's poor earnings, and until 1890 dividends hovered around the 5 percent mark.

The first shareholders were mostly Dutch bankers, merchants, shipowners, and other private persons; 35 percent of the original capital came from out of the country. As with the other railways in the Netherlands, the shares slowly spread over a large number of small holders, as the great banking houses and merchants gradually disposed of their large holdings when prices were good. Shares of the Holland, the Rhenish, and later the State Companies were generally quoted over par at the Amsterdam Exchange, certainly in the period 1870–1890, so shares of these companies sold with little difficulty. The Central's shares did badly compared to those of these three railways, generally only between 65 and 80 percent of par; they rarely rose to par. Only the North Brabant–German showed worse results.

The first lease contracts between the government and the State Railways had proved disadvantageous for the company. One of the first acts of 's Jacob as director-general was to open negotiations for better terms with the government; the result was a much better position for the State Company. And as the network moved toward completion, the revenues from the increase in traffic moved the State Railways out of the danger zone toward the end of the 1870s.

The original five directors had cherished high hopes of international connections. Without consulting his fellow directors, one of them, the Belgian F. de Brouwer van Hogendorp, in 1866 contracted with the Belgian Compagnie du Chemin de Fer Liégeois-Limbourgeois et des Prolongements (the Liège-Limburg Railway) to work its Eindhoven-Hasselt-Liège line. (It was probably no coincidence that van Hogendorp had private interests in the Liégeois-Limbourgeois.) Traffic on the line remained disappointing, even after it connected with the State line to Utrecht, and operating trains up and down the steep slope into the Meuse valley near Liège was difficult and costly. The Liégeois-Limbourgeois was to remain a drain on the State Company's resources for many years.

The directors spotted another international opportunity in the Twente region (Overijssel), in the Northeast. The State-built line to the town of Enschede ended at the border, awaiting the German connection there. In 1861, the independent Almelo-Salzbergen Company had obtained a concession for a line between its two namesake cities, and another line already connected Salzbergen (Hanover) and Berlin via Rheine. The State Railways contracted in 1865 with the Almelo-Salzbergen Company to work its line, but through traffic remained disappointing. The State Railways still depended on the Rhenish Railway at Arnhem to connect with Holland's major cities, and the Rhenish was not disposed to boost a competitor and lose part of its own German traffic in the process.

Oudenbosch
Station

FIGURE 29

The State Company's Oudenbosch Station on the former Grand Central Belge Antwerp-Roosendaal-Moerdijk line, whose architecture sets it off from other State stations. (Postcard, Collection NVBS)

Another disadvantage for State Railways through traffic was that a foreign company owned the Roosendaal-Breda stretch, part of the most important Flushing-Venlo line. The section had been built by the Antwerp-Rotterdam Company, now part of a larger Belgian body, the Grand Central Belge, which had also taken over the old Aachen-Maastricht. The State Railways managed to negotiate running rights for Roosendaal-Breda but forfeited the revenues that would have come with ownership. In 1880 the Netherlands government, after protracted negotiations, bought all the old Antwerp-Rotterdam lines on Dutch territory, giving the State Railways full control of the Flushing-Venlo route.

Unlike the Holland Railway, the State Railways relied on freight traffic right from the start. Initial revenues from freight were about 37 percent of its total income, but this figure soon climbed to over 45 percent, with passenger traffic contributing between 46 and 48 percent.

After the opening of Arnhem-Nijmegen and Dordrecht-Rotterdam in 1877, the State Railways' general position improved dramatically. It had established a near monopoly of the fast-growing traffic through the port of Rotterdam, and the revised contracts with the government in 1876 allotted a larger portion of the revenues to the company. Successive directors-general—'s Jacob until 1879 and W.K.M. Vrolik until 1889—carried on a running battle with the Holland and the Rhenish Companies, but contracted alliances where necessary. Although the State Railways had the advantage of several connections with foreign railways, its one major handicap was its lack of its own lines into Amsterdam. The Holland Railway agreed to carry State Railways trains from the South via Utrecht-Lunetten (just southeast of Utrecht-Central, the joint station of the Rhenish and Central Railways) and Hilversum to Amsterdam. The Holland Company also hauled State Railways trains from the South from Rotterdam-Delftsche Poort to Amsterdam via Leiden and Haarlem, giving travelers two options between Amsterdam and Brussels and beyond. The State Railways route from Roosendaal via Tilburg and 's-Hertogenbosch to Utrecht was circuitous, and it gave the Holland only the relatively short stretch Utrecht-Amsterdam, while the more direct route from Belgium to Amsterdam by way of Rotterdam gave the Holland a longer and more profitable haul. And if the Rhenish Railway offered the State Railways better conditions, it could haul those same trains from the south from Utrecht to Amsterdam over its line. In light of all the necessary negotiations, small wonder that the State Railways kept aiming at an entry of its own into Amsterdam.

The Utrecht factory of Damlust, one of the constituents of State Railways, built hundreds of passenger and freight cars for the company in its first years, until the factory was converted into a repair shop in 1867. Other domestic and foreign suppliers then took over.

FIGURE 30
Rotterdam (Beurs) Station on the elevated line through the heart of the old city, shortly after opening, 1877. The train includes through coaches to Belgium. (Photo J. Baer, author's collection)

Meanwhile, Vrolik and van Hasselt, the undisputed leaders of the State and the Holland, cutthroat competitors in business, had been close friends since their days at the Delft Polytechnic. Every year they still went on vacation, with their wives, to Switzerland or Germany, climbed mountains and took long walks, and discussed everything but railways.

THE RHENISH RAILWAY COMPANY

The Rhenish Railway had moved its corporate headquarters from Amsterdam to Utrecht in 1861, and under its president H. Ameshoff it concentrated on through traffic with Germany. Former secretary of the International Rhine Navigation Commission, Ameshoff knew the ins and outs of freight traffic by water and how to bring it on the rails. One of the Rhenish directors, the Britisher James Staats Forbes, was specifically charged with developing this freight traffic. Under the inspirational leadership of this duo, the Rhenish quickly became the darling of both investor and traveler.

Gradually the Rhenish introduced more express trains, some of which ran into Germany, where they were hauled from Emmerich to Cologne by the Cöln-Mindener Eisenbahn. One handicap for the Rhenish was that all trains, even the Amsterdam-Utrecht expresses, still had to stop at Nieuwersluis, the result of that unfortunate right obtained by a local landowner during the original construction of the line.

The Rhenish main line between Amsterdam and Breukelen, where the Rotterdam connection branched off, in the 1880s carried no fewer than twenty-three passenger trains in each direction daily, plus some freight trains, mak-

FIGURE 31

A Rhenish Railway freight train at Elten (Prussia) Station circa 1880, hauled by 0-6-0 No. 54, an 1867 Sharp, Stewart product. On the platform, *right*, an armed border patrol. (Collection A. D. de Pater/ NVBS)

ing the doubling of the line necessary. Among local trains, Utrecht-Maarsbergen carried a frequent suburban service, and intermediate stations such as Driebergen-Zeist, east of Utrecht, developed a healthy commuter service. Small towns such as Oosterbeek and Wolfheze, just west of Arnhem, became favorite destinations for Sunday outings by city dwellers.

The Rhenish Railway pioneered not only the block system described earlier but also automatic brakes. Until the 1870s only handbrakes were in use, operated by conductors and special brakemen; in 1877 the Rhenish equipped two of its newest express engines plus a number of carriages and conductors' vans with the newly invented Westinghouse air brake for the express trains between Amsterdam and Cologne. Albert Kapteijn, an independent Dutch engineer, was the driving force behind their introduction. Kapteijn went to work for the Westinghouse Brake Company in 1878 and was to become director of its European branch in London in 1882. In this capacity he contributed materially to the success of the air brake and made a large number of important improvements to Westinghouse's original design. He also managed to interest the State Railways in his system, and that company soon opted for Westinghouse too.

Gradually both the Rhenish and State Railways equipped their modern passenger stock with the new continuous brake. Holland Railway's management shared in the widespread fear that the air brake would make the engine drivers less attentive, but as its success became clear, the Supervisory Railway Board pressed for its mandatory use. The government hesitated, expecting companies to introduce air brakes on their own. When the Holland, and also the Central, still held out, the government in 1883 ordered them to equip all passenger rolling stock used in trains with speeds of 60 km/h and higher with the automatic continuous air brake. Thus the country avoided the proliferation of different brake systems that plagued operations in such countries as Great Britain.

Freight trains continued to depend on the brakes of the locomotive and caboose, plus handbrakes on some freight cars. Only in 1934 was an air brake system—the German Kunze-Knorr brake—introduced for freight trains. Dutch railways did not use the vacuum brake developed in England, although some of the regional light railways later introduced it, which necessitated equipping some locomotives with both systems.

For a while, some Rhenish's Amsterdam-Cologne trains crossed the Rhine between Spyck and Welle, just east of the Dutch-German border, by ferry. Unhappy with the Cöln-Mindener Eisenbahn's cooperation, especially regarding rates, the Rhenish in 1862 took up the offer of another German company, the Rheinische Eisenbahn, to complete its Amsterdam-Cologne run. The Rheinische was building a branch to Cleves at the time and extended this line toward the south bank of the Rhine at Spyck. The Rhenish built a new line from Zevenaar that ran alongside its existing line for some miles, then branched off to Welle, opposite Spyck on the river. For economical reasons, a ferry service was chosen over a bridge; it operated via a cable on the river bottom. Beginning in 1865, some regular Amsterdam-Cologne through trains—but not the locomotives—rode the ferry over the Rhine, but it remained a cumbersome and time-consuming arrangement.

Political circumstances intervened with the founding of the German Reich in 1871. When German chancellor Otto von Bismarck instituted a policy of buying up all Prussian private railway companies, both the Cöln-Mindener (in 1879) and the Rheinische (in 1880) became part of the Royal Prussian Railway system. Local trains continued to use the ferry service until World War I finally put an end to this remnant of early competition.

— THE HOLLAND RAILWAY —

The Amsterdam-Hilversum-Utrecht stretch of the Holland Railway's new single-track extension into Germany completed in 1874, the Eastern Railway, carried nine passenger trains daily, with one connecting Hilversum-Amersfoort train. Around 1877 traffic had so increased that five daily Eastern Railway trains connected with the State Railways line to the South at Utrecht-Lunetten, just east of Utrecht Central. Five other daily trains were divided at Hilversum, one section going on to Utrecht and another to Amersfoort and Zutphen. Two daily through trains ran Amsterdam-Zutphen. In 1880 the Holland added two daily trains to Amsterdam-Winterswijk, with connections into Germany via

FIGURE 32

Holland Railway station at Baarn, circa 1900, had a royal waiting room. The locomotive on the train departing for Amsterdam is one of Middelberg's Runners. (Collection NVBS)

the Bergisch-Märkische Eisenbahn. For a new line—all single track—this was a sizeable amount of traffic. The villages in the Gooi, the pleasant sandy area east of Amsterdam, began to grow quickly now that rail transportation to Amsterdam was available. The middle classes much preferred to live in the green villages of Baarn or Bussum than in the crowded and dirty city.

Freight traffic was modest during the Holland Railway's first years, but as soon as the connecting lines into the Ruhr coal area opened, coal traffic grew so fast that the coal trains had to run at night, as the single-track line was already crowded with passenger trains during the day. By 1889, twenty passenger trains were running daily between Amsterdam and Hilversum in each direction.

On the North Holland line, leased from the government, traffic remained more modest. One daily Amsterdam-Den Helder freight train and some passenger trains sufficed for many years. On the old Amsterdam-Haarlem-The Hague-Rotterdam line, only two daily freights ran in each direction, but passenger trains abounded. In 1877, eleven through trains were running Amsterdam-Rotterdam, in addition to some locals running Amsterdam-Haarlem and The Hague-Rotterdam. In 1887 the Holland introduced a nonstop express (maximum speed, 90 km/h) that traveled the eighty-five kilometers between Amsterdam and Rotterdam in only seventy-five minutes, and a year later, only seventy. (Today, the fastest electric trains between the two cities run by way of Schiphol Airport, eighty-six kilometers, in sixty minutes with two stops.) After 1880 the Holland carried through carriages Amsterdam-Brussels four times a day and passed them on to the State Railways at Rotterdam; two went all the way to Paris. Flushing-Amsterdam mail trains, connecting with the packets to Queenborough, were also run in cooperation with the State Company.

By 1889, the Holland had fifteen Amsterdam-Rotterdam daily trains and fifteen Rotterdam-Amsterdam, plus some local trains on shorter stretches of the line. All these trains could easily be accommodated, as the Old Line had been doubled when the gauge was narrowed after 1866. Adding a parlor car of the Wagons-Lits Company to some of the trains in 1886 did not attract the traveling public, however, who evidently did not find the luxury worth the extra fare.

Despite their ongoing antagonism, the Holland and the State Companies cooperated in other foreign connections, among them Amsterdam-Berlin expresses run by the Holland to Zutphen, from there by the State Company to Salzbergen, and from there by the Prussians to Berlin (Hanover had been annexed by Prussia in 1866). The Holland leased the government-built Amersfoort-Kesteren line in 1886 and ran an Amsterdam-Cologne express as far as Kesteren. From there the State Company hauled the train to Nijmegen, where the Holland took over again for Cleves. (That year the Holland bought the Nijmegen-Cleves line—built by the Nijmegen Railway Company and formerly worked by the Rheinische Eisenbahn.) From Cleves the Rheinische, or its successor, the Royal Prussian Railways, took care of the last leg of the journey to Cologne. Even though each of these connections required a time-consuming change of locomotives, the system worked.

FIGURE 33

Holland Railway freight trucks from Friesland arrive in Enkhuizen's harbor on a steam ferry, circa 1900. (Collection NVBS)

Like the Rhenish Railway, the Holland operated a ferry service. In 1886 a private shipping company had opened a steamer service between Enkhuizen in North Holland and Stavoren in Friesland. Heavily subsidized by the Holland Railway, which ran connecting Amsterdam-Enkhuizen trains, the line was only partly successful, as the Stavoren-Leeuwarden line at the other end was not a priority for the State Railways that worked it. The State preferred the longer haul over its own lines in the northern and eastern part of the country to this nautical shortcut that gave the Holland and its shipping subsidiary a larger share of the revenues.

After 1890, when the Holland took over working the Friesian line, the company introduced special ferryboats for freight traffic that could accommodate about fourteen four-wheel wagons. Long trains of Friesian cattle traveled over the steam ferries, but passengers had to detrain and board one of the steamers for a pleasant journey of several hours. Although the steamers were luxurious and comfortable, crossing the Zuiderzee on days of choppy seas and heavy swells presented a challenge.

Locomotives and Rolling Stock

5

RHENISH RAILWAY LOCOMOTIVES

When the Rhenish Railway went to narrow gauge in 1855, it sold off most of its broad-gauge engines for scrap iron. (Some of the better ones went to the Holland Railway, which continued to operate on the broad gauge for ten more years.) New engines for the Rhenish came chiefly from its regular supplier, Sharp, Stewart and Company of Manchester. Most of the engines were designed by the factory, not by C. W. Verloop, the chief mechanical engineer (CME) of the Rhenish since 1853. Any visible unique influence is not Verloop's but that of William Martley, CME of the London, Chatham, and Dover Railway, one of several connections between the two companies. James Staats Forbes was a director of both the LCDR and the Rhenish, and in 1861 the LCDR even took over some Rhenish engines not needed in Holland, which would provide many more years of service in England.

Most Rhenish engines were of the 2-4-0 configuration, with outside frames and inside cylinders and motion. (The 2-4-0 configuration denotes one [forward] carrying axle and two driving axles with four wheels.) They had the typical clean, British lines, were painted green with red and black trim, and had lots of gleaming brass work. Apart from the 2-4-0s the Rhenish also ordered six 2-2-2 singles, intended for light express trains. When they proved too light, most were later rebuilt as tank engines for shunting duties. Relative outsiders were six inside-framed, outside-cylindered 2-4-0s built in 1857–1858 by Henschel of Cassel and intended for the railway's increasingly important freight service. Henschel had been building steam locomotives since 1848 but had found it difficult to enter an already crowded market and aggressively sought new customers—these six locomotives was its first foreign order, works numbers 27–32. In service the engines did not last long and were relegated to shunting duties, and after 1865 superseded in freight service by twelve heavy 0-6-0s, again from Sharp, Stewart. The last of these was delivered in 1881.

For shunting the remunerative dock traffic in Amsterdam, the Rhenish in 1880 ordered five 0-4-0 saddle tanks from Sharp, Stewart, with outside cylinders and very short wheel bases that could negotiate the sharp curves in the harbor tracks and go anywhere. After 1890, when the Holland had taken over these five, that company ordered many more, the last as late as 1915.

The connecting line between the Rhenish's Amsterdam-Weesperpoort Station (Rhenish Railway) and the Amsterdam-Central, a joint station, needed something new to bring the Rhenish trains around. Between 1869 and 1871, Sharp, Stewart delivered seven outside-cylindered 2-4-0 tanks that could run forward and backward with the same ease and speed. This was one of Sharp, Stewart's standard designs, and many were in service on English railways.

FIGURE 34

Holland Railway No. 336,
built by Sharp, Stewart in 1855,
an ancient 2-4-0 of the
Rhenish Railway here doing
some switching at Dordrecht,
circa 1905. The engine
remained in service until 1914.
(Photo Tabernal,
Collection NVBS)

FIGURE 35

State Railways No. 1075, a Rhenish Railway 2-4-0 tank for the Amsterdam belt line traffic, Amsterdam (Weesperpoort), 1898. (Photo L. Derens, Collection NVBS)

The company supplied six more of the same type, slightly heavier, soon afterward, and these mostly handled the suburban traffic east of Utrecht.

For the twelve years between 1877 and 1889, the Rhenish needed no new express locomotives, its fairly antiquated stock apparently still able to fulfill all duties. In 1889 the Rhenish ordered from its regular supplier nine inside-framed inside-cylindered 4-4-0 express engines, of quintessentially British style. These elegant engines, nicknamed "Rhine bogies," were the first with this wheel arrangement in the Netherlands and greatly admired. With their large driving wheels—2,000 mm—they excelled in express service. Again the Rhenish had set a new standard. The Holland Railway, which later inherited the engines, was so happy with them that it ordered fifty more.

HOLLAND RAILWAY LOCOMOTIVES

Soon after the gauge conversion of 1866, and after accommodating its 2-2-2 convertibles from Robert Stephenson to the standard gauge, the Holland Railway needed new engines. Stephenson delivered twenty 2-4-0s in the years immediately after the conversion, fairly light machines (29.4 tons) with 1,860 mm coupled wheels and slightly inclined outside cylinders. Besides numbers, they also bore colorful names—from classical antiquity, such as *Xanthippe*, Socrates' wife, and from nature, stars, and animals to Dutch heroes and Dutch and Flemish painters. In day-to-day practice, the Holland Railway administration always used the names, not the numbers.

FIGURE 36

A German-looking
Holland Railway 2-4-0, No. 119,
Cats, built by Borsig of Berlin
in 1883 and named for a
famous poet of the Dutch
Golden Age, circa 1900.
(Photo L. Derens,
Collection NVBS)

A technical innovation was the use of the injector to keep the boilers filled with water. A French inventor, Henri Giffard, had patented this device in 1859, and Stephenson had used it in 1864 in his last convertible engines for the Holland. In 1866 an owner of a shipyard and engineering firm in Haarlem, H. Figée, Sr., bought the Dutch rights to this invention and started to make the equipment under license. Despite some initial disbelief on the part of the engineering fraternity, the injector soon made itself indispensable and was used all over the world.

While Stephenson was still delivering the 2-4-0s, Borsig of Berlin-Moabit was building other engines of comparable dimensions, named after Dutch provinces, for the Holland. Whether or not the railway placed this order with Borsig to placate its many German shareholders, Borsig was one of the largest locomotive builders in the world and built cheaply and swiftly. Hundreds of similar engines were running on almost every European railway, and the German company continually added improvements and innovations that benefited the Holland along with the rest of its clients. Borsig was to remain the sole supplier of engines to the Holland Railway until 1890.

Between 1874 and 1877, Borsig delivered twenty-six engines of a slightly larger type, still 2-4-0s and again with outside cylinders. Chiefly for the Eastern Railway traffic, the last of these was delivered as a new chief mechanical engineer took charge of the Holland's works at Haarlem. Gerrit A. A. Middelberg, son of a Protestant minister and with an imperfect technical education, was to prove the leading Dutch railway engineer of the nineteenth century. He had started his career with the State Railways and become chief of their works at Zwolle, then moved to the Holland in 1876. He was a prolific inventor and inveterate tinkerer who took out scores of patents and wrote numerous articles in the European technical press.

Middelberg's first engines came from Borsig, heavier editions of the earlier 2-4-0s, twenty-nine delivered between 1878 and 1883. Middelberg named his engines after Dutch heroes of the Golden Age of the Dutch Republic. His magnum opus came in 1883, with the first of his Snellopers (Runners), enormous 2-4-0s with outside cylinders and 2,150 mm driving wheels, and weighing no less than 44.6 tons (empty, engine only). The first came with ugly wooden cabs that looked more like outhouses, but later examples had elegant steel cabs with large side windows. They were the heaviest and most powerful 2-4-0s in Europe, and complete masters of anything put behind them. These were the engines that hauled the nonstop Amsterdam-Rotterdam expresses, with an average speed of 73.4 km/h and probably occasionally exceeding the legal maximum of 90 km/h.

For freight service the Holland in 1871 had ordered from Borsig two six-wheelers with outside cylinders, whose names, *Trade* and *Shipping*, indicate their intended use. Unfortunately their short wheelbase made their concentrated weight too large for the IJssel bridge at Zutphen, which prevented their intended use on the Eastern line into Germany. In 1877 Middelberg therefore designed a larger 0-6-0 with a much longer wheelbase suitable for the Zutphen Bridge. Between 1877 and 1883, Borsig built twenty-nine of them in two slightly different versions.

For all railways, the price of coal was of supreme importance. Most steam locomotives were voracious coal eaters, and any measure to bring down coal consumption could count on a favorable hearing from the management. One such measure was the compound system: Steam was first expanded in a small high-pressure cylinder, then further expanded in a larger low-pressure cylinder before being exhausted through the blastpipe and chimney. G. M. Roentgen, the Rotterdam shipbuilder and shipowner, had

FIGURE 37
Holland Railway No. 193, *Simon Stevin*, one of Middelberg's impressive but disappointing compound 2-4-0 express engines, built by Borsig in 1888. (Author's collection)

introduced compounding in his steam tugs in the 1830s, but the equipment was difficult to install in a fast-moving and relatively small machine like the railway locomotive. After the Swiss engineer Anatole Mallet demonstrated the practicability of compounding in 1878 in France, several systems were tried out in Germany and England. Middelberg followed these experiments closely and in 1886 converted his freight engine *Donder* (Thunder) to a primitive system of compounding. When the results were satisfactory, he ordered Borsig to equip with his unique system four of his big 2-4-0 Snellopers then being built. The two outside cylinders had the same diameter, but different strokes, 400 and 800 mm respectively. Coal savings were impressive, some 17 percent, but at speed the engines oscillated so badly because of the unequal stroke that they damaged the track and even bent or broke their connecting rods. Consequently, they were taken off the fast trains and relegated to secondary duties.

Middelberg left the Holland Railway in 1889 to become director of the Netherlands–South African Railway Company, which was building a railway in Transvaal, the South African republic, from Johannesburg to the Indian Ocean at Portuguese Lorenço Marques. This line was intended to make President Paul Kruger's republic independent of the British-controlled Cape and Natal railways. In the process, Middelberg earned the nickname "Terror of South Africa" because of the ferocity with which he negotiated with the British. He nevertheless managed to build a railway of more than one thousand kilometers through difficult terrain in a remarkably short time.

—— STATE RAILWAYS LOCOMOTIVES ——

The State Railways engineers in charge of the construction of the State network had also given some thought to the best equipment for the new railways. Gerrit van Diesen, on a tour of inspection in East Prussia to examine the railway bridges at Marienburg and Dirschau, had been impressed by the performance of the Prussian Eastern Railway's big Crampton express engines with a single giant driving wheel behind the firebox. Although he deemed something along these lines eminently suitable for the flat stretches of the Dutch State network, no action was taken, and when the new State Railways Company needed locomotives, there was no time to shop around or to have something built to specification. Beyer, Peacock and Company of Gorton, near Manchester, however, could deliver more pedestrian engines from stock, and Richard Peacock himself drove the first train from Breda to Tilburg with State Railways No. 1 on October 5, 1863. His company was to build hundreds of engines for the State Railways over the years.

The first four engines were 2-2-2s, part of a large order in hand for Sweden and ready for delivery. They were smallish engines but well built. Later rebuilt as 0-4-2s by the State Company, they had long and useful lives.

Five 2-4-0s also came from Beyer, Peacock stock. Locomotive builders were wont to construct engines for stock in slack times, to keep their skilled employees in work. These five engines were somewhat disappointing in serv-

FIGURE 38

State Railways' first engine, No. 1, built by Beyer, Peacock in 1863, renumbered No. 251, Dordrecht, circa 1900. This machine remained in service for fifty years. (Photo Staatsspoorwegen, Collection NVBS)

ice and did not have very long lives. Another small 2-4-0 design proved most satisfactory and lasted well into the twentieth century. Beyer, Peacock built seventy of these elegant engines between 1865 and 1872. All had inside frames and inside cylinders, and the first few were delivered without cabs, only spectacle plates to give the engine men some protection against the elements. All were more or less standard designs of Beyer, Peacock, and it is improbable that the chief mechanical engineer of the State Railways, J. W. Stous Sloot, who had started his career on the Rhenish, had much to do with them.

The takeover of the Liège-Limbourgeois had brought in some engines of French and Belgian provenance, a feeble and badly maintained lot that gave Gerrit Middelberg, then still regional superintendent of the State Company at Liège, a lot of trouble. In 1871 improvement came in the shape of six so-called mountain crawlers from Beyer, Peacock, powerful small-wheeled 0-6-0 engines of the popular Bourbonnais type, with a very short wheelbase and outside cylinders. These strong haulers could take sharp curves but were unsteady at higher speeds. Yet they served their purpose well; the State Company ordered three more in 1880.

The next series of fifty 2-4-0 engines also came from Beyer, Peacock, beginning in 1872, but here the hand of Stous Sloot appears. The CME specified outside cylinders, a somewhat unfortunate choice, as the engines were unsteady at speed and the cylinders tended to work loose. In his next design, Stous Sloot returned to inside cylinders and double frames. Working with

FIGURE 39

An elegant State Railways Great Green One designed by Stous Sloot and Beyer, Peacock, Rotterdam (Delftsche Poort), 1895. (Photo L. Derens, Collection NVBS)

FIGURE 40

Testing a bridge in Groningen, 1880s. Two 0-6-0 freight engines of the State Railways, *left*, face two ancient contractor's engines, the one in front a 2-4-0 built by Cockerill of Liège for the Cöln-Mindener Eisenbahn in 1848. (Author's collection)

Hermann Lange, the chief draughtsman of Beyer, Peacock, he evolved a big 2-4-0 express engine. Nicknamed "Grote Groenen" (Great Green Ones), these were the final development of a common British engine, with big 2,150 mm driving wheels and a weight of forty-two tons empty, with thirty-three more tons in the six-wheeled tender. The first, in 1880, was so successful that over the next fifteen years 176 were built.

Despite their large size, these engines were among the most elegant on Dutch rails, painted light green with reddish brown frames and with much gleaming brass work. English railway historian C. Hamilton Ellis described them as "green as spring grass, lovely as Aphrodite rising from the Aegean."

Other contemporaries called them "a Parisienne dressed to kill." A resounding success, they even hauled freight trains, despite their large driving wheels. Coincidentally, Middelberg's contemporary Snellopers, with their austere, boxy, German lines and somber dark green paintwork, had almost exactly the same dimensions as the Grote Groenen of Stous Sloot. Each represented the final development of a well-tried type of locomotive, one of German and the other of British lineage, each a success in its own right.

Before the big 2-4-0s arrived on the premises, the State Railways had ordered a series of forty-six 0-6-0 engines for freight service of the common British double-framed type with inside cylinders. Beyer, Peacock delivered them between 1865 and 1878, but the Grote Groenen obviated the need for more special freight engines.

—— LOCOMOTIVES OF THE SMALLER RAILWAYS ——

The Antwerp-Rotterdam began operations in 1854 with nine small British 2-2-2 and 2-4-0 engines. Business was not good, apparently, in the first years, for later machines were bought used from English railways, chiefly from the London, Brighton, and South Coast. Only in 1863 and 1864 did four modern 2-4-0 engines built by Tubize (Belgium) reinforce the locomotive stock. These four served well and were the forerunners of a successful Belgian type. When in 1880 the railway line was bought up jointly by the Netherlands and Belgian governments, the engines continued to serve their new owners, the Grand Central Belge.

The Aachen-Maastricht had only eighteen engines, mostly from Borsig of Berlin and Cockerill of Seraing, near Liège. Singles (2-2-2s) hauled the passenger trains, and the small-wheeled 2-4-0 type was favored for freight. The Grand Central Belge (GCB), which worked the line beginning in 1867, used these engines for many years, and even the Belgian government, which bought up the GCB in 1897, found a use for some of these antiques.

Smaller still was the Liège-Maastricht Railway. When the Belgian government took it over in 1899, it had only eleven engines, all of common Belgian types. Only three very light—eighteen-ton—0-6-0 tank engines, built in 1883 and 1884, deserve special mention. Comparable to the Dutch light railway engines to be discussed later, these pulled light trains consisting of a couple of four-wheelers that halted at every level crossing and small stop.

Two other Belgian companies, Gand-Terneuzen and Malines-Terneuzen, operating in Dutch Zeeland Flanders south of the Scheldt River, between them owned a hodgepodge of new and secondhand engines. Some were new Dutch State Railways small 2-4-0s; others were used 4-6-0 tanks, originally from the Liège-Limbourgeois but sold off when the State Railways took over that line; others were used machines from French, Belgian, and even English railways.

The Netherlands Central Railway Company, always short of cash, paid for its first engines partly in shares and bonds, a practice then unusual for the Netherlands but common elsewhere. These engines were not French, as might have been expected on a railway built by French engineers with French capital, but twelve small and long-lasting 2-4-0s from Neilson and Company of Glasgow. The last—old Central No. 10, named *Kampen*—remained in service until 1934, having been rebuilt as a 2-4-0 tank long before.

The Central acquired three bigger 2-4-0s with outside cylinders from Stephenson's in 1872 and bought three somewhat similar engines cheaply in 1874, when a German railway that had ordered them from Georg Egestorff of Hanover-Linden went bankrupt and refused them. The Central apparently was so happy with them that it ordered three more in 1876. They had long lives that included many rebuildings, and the last—by then a 4-4-4 tank engine—did not go to the scrapper until 1927.

Although even poorer than the Central, the North Brabant–German Railway in its early years bought only engines of proven quality. It started its service in 1873 with five Beyer, Peacock 2-4-0s, exact copies of those built for the State Railways. After 1881 even these good engines could no longer pull the heavy Flushing mails alone and had to be used in pairs. The company then ordered from Hohenzollern of Düsseldorf-Grafenberg two English-looking 2-4-0s, smaller versions of the contemporary Grote Groenen of the State. The company ordered a third a few years later, but when in 1892 it again needed stronger engines, it ordered a real Grote Groene from Beyer, Peacock and two more some years later, when there was money in the till.

Freight traffic was important to the North Brabant–German, and because it did not reach Rotterdam over its own rails, it organized a steamboat service between Veghel and Rotterdam. The service proved fairly successful, despite the nuisance of transshipment from rail to boat at Veghel. For the railway segment of this traffic, the company bought in 1878 from Hohenzollern four standard 0-6-0 engines with small wheels and outside cylinders. Two more were ordered much later, in 1902 and 1907. By that time the design must have been

FIGURE 41

One of a series of three engines bought from Georg Egestorff of Hanover in 1874, here in its last guise as 4-4-4 tank No. 20 for the Central Railway's suburban service, Utrecht, 1920.
(Photo L. Derens, Collection NVBS)

FIGURE 42

Veghel (North Brabant)
Harbor, where the North
Brabant–German transferred
its freight to boats for the trip
to Rotterdam. A 2-4-0 of the
first series is shunting the
trucks, mostly Prussians,
on the quayside, circa 1900.
(Collection NVBS)

antique, but these small engines sufficed for the relatively light trains of the North Brabant–German.

PASSENGER CARS

The passenger cars of all Dutch railways looked very much alike. There had been three classes of cars from the start—the so-called diligence, charabanc, and wagon, for first, second, and third class respectively. The early Belgian influence is clear. Only the diligence was completely enclosed, with glass windows. The second-class charabancs had a roof and waist-high sides; the opening above could be closed with curtains. The third-class wagons had only a roof, low sideboards, and slatted wooden seats, as opposed to the upholstered seats of first and second class.

Most of these cars rode on four-wheel underframes, although the Holland Railway experimented for a short time in 1845 with six-wheelers. Regular six-wheelers for the standard gauge were introduced by the State Railways in 1871, and the Holland followed suit three years later. Four-wheelers were generally favored because of their light weight and low internal resistance; their uncomfortable ride was taken for granted. After 1880 the German railways refused to allow four-wheelers for international travel, forcing the Dutch railways to switch to the heavier but better riding six-wheelers for these trains.

For purely domestic service, they continued to use four-wheelers for many years. In 1886 Middelberg tried out two long bogie carriages, the first in the Netherlands, but when their tracking qualities proved to be below standard, they were sawed in two and placed on four-wheeled underframes.

After the first hesitant use of the Westinghouse air brake, the process of converting the rolling stock did not take long. In 1888, 99 percent of all mainline passenger stock of the State Railways was equipped with the new brake, and the Rhenish had converted all of its main line cars; the laggard Holland had equipped only 83 percent of its stock. Conductors' vans scored a bit lower, but here also the State Railways was first with 96 percent equipped with continuous air brakes, and the Rhenish and the Holland followed with 76 and 59 percent respectively. The Central and North Brabant–German lagged far behind in this respect.

All rolling stock was provided with screw couplings, superseding the first primitive link-and-chain couplers. Side buffers were universal, and after some confusion, rolling stock in the Netherlands and elsewhere in Germany adhered to the Prussian standards and could move freely around Europe.

Most passenger cars were of the traditional British compartment model, with an outside door opening onto each compartment and no central corridor. The conductors walked along the footboards of the moving train—on the outside of the cars, just below the doors—to check tickets, until this dangerous practice was abolished in 1875. After that year, ticket platforms were constructed just outside the major stations for checking the ticket of every passenger, after which a train moved to the station proper, where passengers would have free access to the platforms.

Heating was gradually introduced but at first only in the first and second classes. Foot warmers—flat metal containers filled with hot water—placed in the carriages lasted for some time. Later a preheated solution of soda acetate filled the foot warmers, and they stayed warm much longer. On the light railways, where most cars consisted of only one compartment, coal stoves provided heat. Steam heating, using steam from the locomotive, was slowly introduced after 1888 and soon became universal.

Candles lit the cars, again in the superior classes first. About 1847 kerosene lamps were introduced, serviced and lit from the roof. Lamps burning oil gas were a great improvement over kerosene because of their superior lighting qualities and their lack of soot and odor. Introduced in the 1880s, they soon came into general use all over the country. The railways themselves produced the gas, which was stored under high pressure in steel tanks under each carriage. Special gas trucks filled the tanks at the terminus.

Lavatories were nonexistent at first, even in the higher classes, and only slowly introduced after 1888. The use of compartment carriages required elaborate internal corridors if lavatories were to be provided, and some first-class carriages had a toilet for every two compartments.

The first passenger cars rode on wooden underframes with iron wheels and axles. Iron frames came into use in 1863, which meant a much stronger and longer-lasting assembly. Superstructures of all vehicles remained wooden, even into the twentieth century. Most Dutch railway companies painted their passenger cars dark green, with lots of gold striping and scrollwork on cars in the superior classes. The firm of J. J. Beijnes built many of the Dutch cars; its works lay just opposite the Holland Railway's station in Haarlem. Although Beijnes became the favorite supplier of the Holland and other Dutch railways, Belgian and German firms also competed successfully in this market.

—— FREIGHT STOCK ——

Generally wooden, again with iron frames coming in use slowly, freight stock had less elaborate exteriors than passenger stock and was less well maintained. Four-wheeled stock predominated all over Europe, and the Dutch railways were no exception. Boxcars, the most common type, were used for almost everything; coal trucks were low-sided and open.

Some German lines experimented early with all-iron coal trucks, as wooden cars disintegrated too fast in this rough service. These iron trucks also showed up on the Dutch railways; industry and households in the Netherlands, as well as the railways, used a lot of German coal. Domestic coal was almost unknown in the Netherlands until the opening of the Limburg coal fields in the early years of the twentieth century.

CHAPTER

6

Light Railways
and Tramways

CHANGES IN THE NETHERLANDS, 1875–1900

A late starter in industrial development, the Netherlands around 1870 was still largely an agricultural and mercantile nation, but change was in the air. The textile industry, especially the cotton manufacturers in Twente (Overijssel province), was booming, chiefly through export to the Dutch East Indies. Tilburg, in North Brabant, was a center for the woolen industry. New docks at Rotterdam and Amsterdam, now able to serve the largest steamships afloat, gave a boost to shipping and shipbuilding. The opening of the Suez Canal late in 1869 shortened by weeks the sea journey to the Indies. Even before Dutch shipping lines understood the Canal's possibilities, Prince Henry, brother of King William III, bought prime land at Port Said. When the two Dutch shipping companies, one in Amsterdam and one in Rotterdam, opened weekly steamer lines to the Indies in 1871 and 1875 respectively, the Port Said land was a ready site for their coaling stations. Other companies opened regular steamship lines to New York and to South America and covered European waters with dense shipping networks. These lines ordered most of their steamships from British builders until 1900, when Dutch shipyards could supply the majority of new ships.

Old manufactures, such as cigar making, gained new life when the tobacco leaf from Dutch Sumatra proved excellent for cigars. Production and exports soared. Other older industries, such as gin distilling, were concentrated in a few big companies. When Napoleon's Continental System stopped the import of cane sugar, modern factories undertook beet sugar refining. (Government fiscal decisions directed the export of most of the cane sugar from the Indies to England and other countries, and only small quantities reached the Dutch market.)

Agriculture thrived until the 1870s, when American and later Russian grain flooded the European markets, and prices plummeted. The resulting widespread poverty led some Netherlanders from agricultural areas to emigrate to America. Others found solutions in modernization, in diversifying and growing crops other than wheat, and in government-sponsored education. Cooperative creameries and cheese factories sprang up in the grassland areas of Holland and Friesland, and cooperative mills and farina (potato flour) factories in the sandy areas of Groningen and elsewhere. Butter and cheese became major exports.

Of less importance was the machine industry, although it was always part of the scene and played a role in the construction of early steam locomotives and bridges. After 1870 its contribution to the economy began to grow. Existing factories, such as Van Vlissingen and Dudok van Heel of Amsterdam, concentrated on manufacturing machinery for the sugar and textile industries, and pumps and related apparatus for the growing number of steam-powered pumping stations that replaced the old windmills. For all these products there was a large and fast-growing market. New factories, such as Stork in Hengelo (Twente), built complete steam plants for all sorts of other factories and in the late 1800s also built the first stations to generate electric power. The number of installed steam engines, large and small, in Dutch factories grew from only 364 in 1853 to 1,815 in 1872 and to 4,728 in 1895. The numbers continued to increase, although from about 1895 gas, oil, and electric plants competed with steam power.

Capital for the new developments was never scarce. The more speculative Dutch investors tended to favor high-yield and high-risk bonds and shares over more solid domestic ventures that brought lower returns. American railroad shares and bonds were popular at the Amsterdam Stock Exchange, and international economic crises like the ones of 1873 and 1893 cast a temporary pall over the Bourse. Modern banks willing to invest in new industry sprang up beginning in the 1860s, ideal vehicles for funneling capital into industry and enterprise.

All factories with steam plants needed coal in ever increasing quantities, and the railways carried this fuel from mines in the Ruhr, Belgium, and Great Britain. For bulk goods like coal, however, the waterways were generally cheaper, if slower, posing an omnipresent threat to the railways. The ongoing process of straightening and deepening the great rivers, and the gradual opening of the Merwede Canal in the 1890s, gave Amsterdam at long last a deep-water connection to the Rhine and Waal Rivers and increased the threat. Rotterdam became the chief port for freight to and from Germany. The Rhine was the main artery of central Europe, with Rotterdam the heart that kept its blood pumping. The city is still the chief port for a large part of Europe.

During the last quarter of the nineteenth century, Dutch society also changed profoundly. From a largely agricultural and mercantile country with a population concentrated on about half of the available land, it became an industrialized country with a factory proletariat in the big cities of the West, and with more land than ever serving agricultural-economic purposes. Although agricultural production skyrocketed, industrial production rose higher and faster, and more people than ever worked at something other than agriculture. New industries in their infancy around 1900, such as the electrotechnical and chemical factories, and mining and related branches, would dominate the next century. Integral to the country's industrial growth and development, the railways would prosper until new modes of transportation challenged them in the 1920s and 1930s.

—— TECHNICAL DEVELOPMENTS IN THE RAILWAYS ——

The materials that went into building railroads changed in the last quarter of the nineteenth century. Since the 1870s steel had become available in larger quantities, and the original somewhat brittle steel of the first years had been developed into a suitable material for bridges, locomotives, and rails. On the main lines, steel rails replaced the fast-wearing soft iron rails. Yet, side tracks and yards continued to use the cheaper iron rails well into the twentieth century. A domestic steel industry did not exist until after World War I, and all rails had to be imported, chiefly from Germany and Belgium, but also from England.

Wooden ties, called "sleepers" in England, did not last long in the damp Dutch climate, and experiments to strengthen them with kyanizing or superficial burning met with no great success until the development of pressure-impregnation with creosote. Meanwhile, engineers tried their hand at developing iron or steel ties. The State Railways used iron ties of a design by Cosijns on a large scale beginning in 1866. In the same year, J. W. Post, of the Permanent Way Department of the State Company, invented a system of steel ties and bolts that saw use not only by the State, but also by the other Dutch and Netherlands-Indies railways and those in some foreign countries.

With the growth of rail traffic, some lines had been doubled by 1890. The Old Line, the Amsterdam–Haarlem–Rotterdam line of the Holland Railway, was doubled in 1865 and 1866, and the Eastern line was double tracked as far as Utrecht and Amersfoort in the 1880s. The Rhenish doubled all its lines except Leiden-Woerden, which is single track to this day. On the State network, double tracks ran between Rotterdam and Breda—the Moerdijk Bridge excepted—and between Flushing and Venlo. Utrecht–'s-Hertogenbosch had double track as far as the Waal River Bridge near Zaltbommel. The great Culemborg Bridge, was converted to two tracks, as was Nijmegen–Arnhem–Zutphen, but the IJssel River Bridge at Zutphen had only one set of rails. The rest of the national network had single tracks, and the Central and North Brabant–German Railways had no double tracks at all.

By the early 1870s, a reasonably interconnected network crisscrossed the country, although worked by different companies. Yet, the main lines still hardly touched some regions. Especially in the provinces of Overijssel, Drente, Groningen, and Friesland, large areas remained many kilometers from the nearest railway station. Yet these areas were developing with the modernization of agriculture, the setting up of cooperative creameries, and the growth of small-scale cottage industries into full-fledged industrial enterprises. All of these needed raw materials and coal, and an outlet for their products. The solution would be a system of light railways.

The railway companies needed to lower the cost of railway building to match an anticipated drop in revenues. In Germany, guidelines for Secundär Bahnen (secondary railways) had been published in 1869 in the widely read *Zeitung des Vereins Deutscher Eisenbahn-Verwaltungen*. The Netherlands' Royal Institute of Engineers published a translation the next year under the title "Fundamentals of Regional Railways." The standard on this new kind of railway would be simple, light construction, low speeds, simplified safety measures, and smaller staffs. But Dutch engineers could reach no consensus on whether their gauge should be narrow or standard. Narrow gauge was cheaper, but it created a problem for transshipment at stations that connected with the main lines. Using standard gauge would resolve this problem. In the end, most Dutch regional railways were built on the standard gauge, which

FIGURE 43

A train on the single-track Haarlem-Zandvoort light railway, before it was upgraded to main line standards in 1902, headed by one of the numerous 4-4-2 tanks of the Holland Company, running bunker first. In the distance, *right*, the Bavo Church of Haarlem.
(Collection NVBS)

made through freight traffic possible and made them feasible transportation for longer than those in countries that had chosen the narrow gauge.

A law was passed in 1878 to create a legal framework for these new-fangled light railways, or locaalspoorwegen (local railways). Their speeds were not to exceed 30 km/h, and their maximum axle loads were ten tons. They did not need continuous brakes. Other simplified rules related to the protection of level crossings and the signaling system. The new law did not apply to railways with a maximum speed of 15 km/h, which were now classified as (steam) tramways. Revisions of the law raised the maximum speeds, until by 1917 60 km/h was allowed, with the use of an air or vacuum continuous brake.

In 1879, the Haarlem-Zandvoort Railway Company obtained a concession for the first of these light railways. Zandvoort, on the North Sea, was a favorite watering place for rich Germans, and the initiative for this venture came from Rudolph Sulzbach, a well-known banker in Frankfurt am Main, together with a group of interested German bankers and merchants. The line opened in 1881, and its trains used the Haarlem station of the Holland Railway from the start. In 1889, the Holland took over the railway, including rolling stock, and it doubled and upgraded the line to main line standards in 1902.

FIGURE 44

Light railway around the turn of the century. Holland Railway 0-4-0 tank, *Monkey*, at Hengelo-GOLS with a train of light four-wheelers to Ruurlo. (Collection NVBS)

THE GELDERSCH-OVERIJSSELSCHE LIGHT RAILWAY

In 1881 the Geldersch-Overijsselsche Locaalspoorwegmaatschappij (GOLS) obtained the second concession under the new law, for a network of standard-gauge light railways in the eastern part of Gelderland province and the adjoining area of Overijssel, in the Twente region. J. Willink, a Winterswijk textile

mill owner, and nobleman-landowner J.G.H. baron van Nagell tot Ampsen founded the company to bring coal from the German Ruhr to Twente's flourishing textile industries. They viewed passenger traffic as secondary.

The men envisaged lines from Winterswijk and the connection with the German railways to Hengelo and to Doetinchem, with branches to Ruurlo and Enschede. A later Ruurlo–Doetinchem line would bring the total to 134 km of track. Both the State Railways and the Holland Railway were willing to work these lines, and the State even had plans to use the GOLS as part of a new connection between Rotterdam and northern Germany. The Holland, however, was the victor and worked the whole network, which was opened gradually in 1884 and 1885, with its own staff, locomotives, and rolling stock. Revenues were somewhat disappointing in the beginning, but at least the area was safe from competition, and traffic developed satisfactorily after some years. The short Enschede–Oldenzaal line joined the GOLS network in 1887, owned by a separate company but also worked by the Holland.

THE KONINKLIJKE NEDERLANDSCHE LOCAALSPOORWEG WILLEM III

The next company to build light railways was the Nederlandsche Locaalspoorweg Maatschappij of 1880, soon granted the designation Koninklijke (Royal) because the company planned a network of light railways around Apeldoorn, residence of King William III. The king even permitted the company to use the line from Apeldoorn's Holland Railway station to his palace, Het Loo, nearby. The KNLS Willem III as it was soon known, built lines from Apeldoorn to Hattem to the north, on the Central Railway's line to Zwolle, to Almelo to the northeast, and to Dieren to the southeast, 110 kilometers altogether. By 1888, all lines were up and running, worked by the Holland Railway.

At the request of the military authorities, the Apeldoorn-Dieren and Apeldoorn-Hattem lines were built to main line standards, to make military traffic possible even if an enemy had taken the IJssel River, cutting off the existing Zutphen-Deventer-Zwolle main line on the right bank. All lines were worked as light railways, however. The government provided a welcome subsidy of 800,000 guilders for the large IJssel River Bridge at Deventer. Many factories and industries got their first rail connection over these lines, and the line to Almelo proved so successful that it was later doubled and rebuilt to main line standards.

Connecting the GOLS or the KNLS Willem III with the main lines at stations the Holland owned or worked was simple, but Vrolik, president of the State Company, refused point-blank to have connections laid at his stations and threw up obstructions at every turn. At Hengelo, he even had a ballast train run continuously across the planned site to make it physically impossible to lay a crossing. The GOLS had to resort to the courts, where Vrolik fought all the way to the Hoge Raad, the Supreme Court of the Netherlands. He lost, was fined heavily, and had to allow the laying of the connecting switches at Hengelo. The State Railways of course paid his fine.

FIGURE 45

Wierden Station, the junction of the Zwolle–Almelo main line of State Railways and the original Holland Company light railway from Apeldoorn, here upgraded to main line standards, circa 1910.
A Holland Railway 4-4-0, series 350–408, heads a train to Deventer, circa 1910. (Collection L. J. Biezeveld/ NVBS)

OTHER LIGHT RAILWAYS

In a different part of the country, the Holland Railway in 1887 undertook the working of a Hoorn–Medemblik line built and owned by the Locaalspoorwegmaatschappij Hollands Noorderkwartier. This line formed a nice addition to the State-built line to Enkhuizen, already worked by the Holland. (Today, the Hoorn–Medemblik line is famous as the museum line, worked by the Stoomtram Hoorn-Medemblik with vintage rolling stock.)

Compared to the success of the Holland Railway in the light railway field, the Rhenish Railway lagged behind. It added only two standard-gauge steam tramways to its network during these years: The Hague–Scheveningen of 1879 mentioned earlier, the first steam tramway in the country, and the Ede (west of Arnhem)–Wageningen line of 1882. The Rhenish probably had some influence on another early steam tramway, the Rijnlandsche Stoomtram, with a line, on the standard gauge, from Leiden to the fishing village of Katwijk on the North Sea coast. The Rhenish's president, H. Ameshoff, was on the board of the Rijnlandsche, but in 1883 the tramway went to the Holland Railway, when this company started to amass a network of tramway feeders. Other Holland Railway tramways were Beverwijk–Wijk-aan-Zee of 1882, Bussum–Huizen of 1883, and Rijnsburg–Noordwijk of 1885, all built on the standard

FIGURE 46

Roodeschool, the
northernmost station in the
Netherlands, with a State
Railways light train to
Groningen, shortly after the
opening of the line, circa 1896.
Chickens on the rails mark
the pleasant rural atmosphere.
(Collection L. J. Biezeveld/
NVBS)

gauge, but not all meant for the interchange of freight trucks with the main
lines.

The most successful was the steam tramway from The Hague's Holland
Railway station to the beach resort of Scheveningen, in direct competition
with the Rhenish tramway. This Holland line opened in 1886, and between
1890 and 1907 it even carried through carriages from Scheveningen to Rotterdam in the summer for the benefit of businessmen commuting daily between
the city and their families at the beach. The line also carried fish from the
Scheveningen harbor and coal to the harbor. (Today, this is line 11 of the electric city tramway network of The Hague, still on the same right-of-way.)

After its defeat over the GOLS, the State Railways had to be content with
the crumbs left by the Holland Railway. It operated Groningen-Delfzijl in the far
North and in 1893 added a branch to Roodeschool, the northernmost place in
the country reached by rail. Only later in the nineteenth century and early in the
twentieth could the State Company add more light railways to its network.

ROLLING STOCK

For the new light railways, the law prescribed light rolling stock. The Haarlem-
Zandvoort started its service with three six-coupled tank engines from Borsig,
weighing twenty-seven tons, well under the limit of ten tons per axle. The

State Railways, when it still had visions of working the GOLS, had ordered twelve twenty-ton machines from Hohenzollern of Düsseldorf—one of these four-couplers was even delivered with the inscription GOLS No. 1. When the Holland Railway got the contracts for working the GOLS lines, the State used these engines chiefly on its light railways in Groningen province.

The Holland's chief mechanical engineer, Gerrit Middelberg, had little time to come up with suitable engines and passenger cars for the GOLS lines. Typically, he did not buy something off the shelf in Germany or Belgium but designed something new and unusual. In 1883 Borsig delivered the first of his "stoves" or "donkeys," as they came to be fondly called. These were four-wheeled tank engines with inside cylinders, and with a rather peculiar exterior—steel disc wheels, long square water tanks up to the front buffer beam, and a tall, narrow smokestack. The cab was half open at the front, enabling the crew to walk forward between the tanks and the boiler, and more important, enabling the conductor to reach the foot plate in case of emergencies, a feature pre-scribed by law when only one driver was present. A door in the back of the cab served the same purpose. The engines were a bit too heavy, between 21 and 22.5 tons, but no one seems to have objected. All had the mandatory steam bell on the cab roof to warn traffic at the many unguarded level crossings.

Until 1889 Borsig built forty-two of these "stoves," all named after ani-mals—many a vacation trip in Gelderland or Overijssel started and ended behind the *Donkey, Dove,* or *Fox.* The engines also saw service on the tramways between The Hague and Scheveningen and elsewhere.

Passenger coaches on the light railways were generally four-wheeled boxes on wheels, with open platforms at the end, and with oil lamps and no heat. They weighed around ten tons. Second class seated twenty-four in two

FIGURE 47

State Railways tank engine No. 505, one of a small series built by Hohenzollern of Düsseldorf, is the equivalent of Middelberg's light 0-4-0s on the Holland. The drive mechanism has coupling rods on long crank pins to clear the cylinders between the wheels. (Photo L. Derens, Collection NVBS)

FIGURE 48

One of Middelberg's charming "stoves," the small 0-4-0 tanks for light railways, Holland Railway No. 172, *Polar Bear*, on the turntable at Dordrecht, 1895.
(Photo L. Derens, author's collection)

big compartments, one smoking and one nonsmoking, and third class seated forty; there was no first class on the light railways.

For years, a hand brake on one of the platforms sufficed. Continuous brakes came much later, generally the Westinghouse air brake, when the maximum speed was raised. The Holland preferred the vacuum brake for its steam tramways, so many of the "stoves" were equipped with both air and vacuum brakes, plus a steam brake (the Middelberg system) for the engine only. The elaborate braking arrangement indicates the versatility of these small engines.

THE STEAM TRAMWAYS

Although the steam tramway, a very Dutch phenomenon, falls outside the scope of this book, it played an important part in opening up the countryside to rail travel. Moreover, the distinction between a steam tramway and a light railway is sometimes difficult to draw, and some tramways were indeed later upgraded to light railways and incorporated into the railway network.

The light railway act provided dependable transportation to outlying regions that could not support a main line railway. But for some regions, even light railways would never be economically viable. There were also towns and villages that had been passed by when the main lines were built, either with no stations of their own or stations several kilometers away. Horse tramways, in use in the Netherlands since 1864, were mostly big-city affairs. The solution lay in something between a light railway and a horse tramway, and the steam tramway seemed to fill that gap nicely.

The Rhenish led the way with its line to Scheveningen, operated by light four-wheeled steam dummies, completely enclosed so as not to frighten horses and pedestrians on city streets. The next steam tramway was in Brabant, between Breda and Oosterhout, where a narrow-gauge line opened in 1880. The success of these pioneers encouraged the building of steam tramways all over the country.

There were many gradations of the steam tramway. Some simply followed existing roads, their tracks laid on the shoulder. These touched every village and town and stopped on request; consequently speeds were slow and travel times long. Others acquired their own right-of-way and were built with heavier rails. On these lines, speeds were higher and the level of comfort generally higher too. Gauges differed widely: In Gelderland a fairly dense network of lines on the 750 mm gauge was successfully operated for many decades, while in Brabant several companies built another extensive network on the 1,067 mm (3 ft 6 in) gauge, with connections into Belgium. Others operated on the meter gauge (1,000 mm), and one or two primitive lines on gauges as narrow as 600 mm. In Friesland, Groningen, and Drente, the Nederlandsche Tramweg Maatschappij (NTM), controlled by the Netherlands Central Railway, constructed an extensive network on the standard gauge that connected to the main lines at several places, making through freight traffic possible. Nearly all provinces had steam tramways, which brought many small communities out of isolation and contributed to the development of the agricultural areas of the country.

Around the turn of the century, government subsidies became available for tramway companies in areas that still had no modern means of communication, such as the South Holland and Zeeland islands. As a result, the Rotterdamsche Tramweg Maatschappij (RTM) built a number of interconnected lines on these islands, with Rotterdam as their focal point. Steamboats connected the islands and ferried freight trucks over; passengers had to detrain and board another tram on the other side. In this way, connections reached even Brabant, where the tramways had the same 1,067 mm gauge. Major cargoes included sugar beets in season and coal for dealers all along the line. Rotterdam vacationers used the trams to Oostvoorne in summer in large numbers; the line ended on the beach.

Another latecomer was the Limburgsche Tramweg Maatschappij in the far South, which constructed a standard-gauge line from Maastricht to the East in the 1920s. Heavy freight traffic was anticipated on the hilly line, and for this purpose the LTM bought a fifty-six-ton 0-6-0 + 0-6-0 Garratt locomotive, a type more familiar in South Africa and Rhodesia than in the Limburg hills. Unfortunately, the traffic never materialized, and the impressive machine was used for only a few years.

Some steam tramways were later converted to electric traction, especially in North and South Holland and Utrecht, which generally meant that they remained in service until long after 1945. One—The Hague–Delft, which began as a horse tramway in 1866 and converted to steam traction in 1884— survives as an electric interurban line of the city network of The Hague. Most other steam tramways were closed between the wars as a result of unlimited road competition, with a few lingering on into World War II. The standard-gauge NTM in Friesland and Groningen survived for freight only until the 1960s, and the narrow-gauge tramways in Gelderland managed to survive until 1956 as well, largely as a result of successful conversion to diesel traction in the 1930s. The much loved RTM, almost completely converted to diesel by then, was the last to go. The 1953 flood in that area of the country destroyed a large part of the network, and it was not considered worthwhile to repair the antiquated system. The dike building on an unprecedented scale as a result of the flood connected all former islands with a network of modern roads anyway, making the diesel and steam tram superfluous.

Dutch industry supplied most of the rolling stock for the domestic tramways and even built up a sizeable export market. Firms such as J. J. Beijnes of Haarlem, Allan and Company of Rotterdam, and Werkspoor of Amsterdam developed solid and good-looking passenger cars and freight trucks, well suited to the Dutch tramways. The Breda firm of Backer and Rueb, later known as the Machinefabriek Breda, constructed hundreds of steam dummies, ranging from seven to more than thirteen tons. Their products also found markets in the Dutch East Indies and elsewhere.

D. Verhoop, inspector of the Supervisory Railway Board, designed notable engines around 1910 that included superheaters, feed-water heaters, electric lighting, and other modern appliances, and were quite successful. Even on the 1,067 mm gauge, some of his engines weighed in at eighteen tons and easily reached speeds of more than 60 km/h when the track permitted. Heaviest and strongest were Verhoop's 0-4-0 engines of 1922 for the LTM, with an empty weight of more than twenty-three tons. Some of these Verhoop engines were of the familiar overall cab type, but others looked more like an ordinary locomotive with a cab at the rear, although on some of these, plates still covered the wheels and the moving machinery outside the wheels.

At first no national laws covered tramways as long as their maximum speeds did not exceed 15 km/h; their regulation was left to municipal and provincial authorities. This system resulted in some confusion, especially when tramways crossed from one province into another, which happened quite often after the networks expanded. In 1900, a new law was passed that distinguished three categories: tramways, when speeds did not exceed 20 km/h; simplified light railways, with speeds up to 35 km/h (later 40); and light railways, with speeds not exceeding 50 km/h (later 60). Most modern tramways fell into the second category, and older ones were often upgraded to this level of quality.

CHAPTER

7

The Reorganization of 1890

The prosperous and innovative Rhenish Railway reached its commercial zenith around 1880 with an annual dividend of 8.1 percent, but by 1889 increased competition and the consequent lower rates had reduced dividends to 5.1 percent. The State Railways did not do much better over the same period, with dividends of between 4.5 and 5.7 percent, but their investors could count on fewer financial ups and downs. Of the big three, the Holland was the most prosperous, paying out around 6 percent annually.

More important than dividends was a railway's operating ratio, that is, the ratio of working expenses (excluding fixed costs) to receipts. The State Company spent a remarkably low 47.4 percent of total receipts for expenses (more than half of which went to wages) from 1866 to 1870, but its operating ratio climbed to 67.1 between 1891 and 1895, and to 74.4 percent from 1911 to 1915, which left few funds for depreciation. The Holland showed similar figures over the same period, its expenses rising from 54.1 percent between 1876 and 1880 to 70.8 from 1911 to 1915.

At first glance these figures do not seem too bad, but compared to the Prussian and Belgian railways, for example, they were far too high. Unlimited competition between the big three, and each network's lack of internal coherence, were the major causes of these unsatisfactory results. The State Railways still had no access to Amsterdam, for instance, while the Holland did not reach the docks of Rotterdam. Large areas of the country had no through

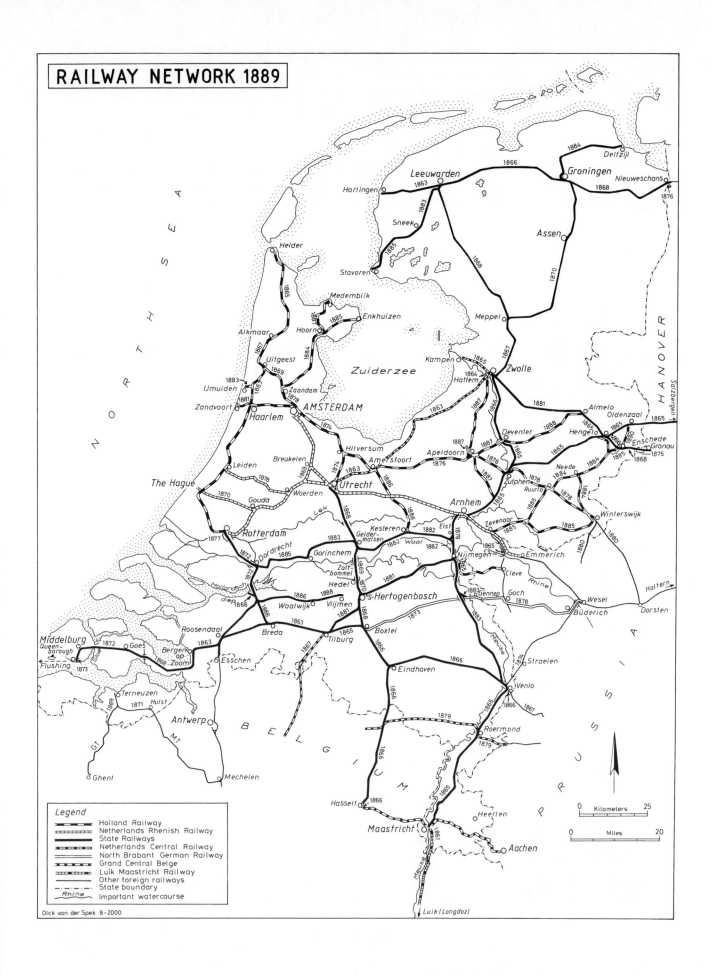

RAILWAY NETWORK 1889

Legend

	Holland Railway
	Netherlands Rhenish Railway
	State Railways
	Netherlands Central Railway
	North Brabant German Railway
	Grand Central Belge
	Luik Maastricht Railway
	Other foreign railways
	State boundary
Rhine	Important watercourse

Dick van der Spek 8-2000

NORTH SEA

HANOVER

Salzbergen

Zuiderzee

BELGIUM

PRUSSIA

Delfzijl
Groningen
Nieuweschans
Leeuwarden
Harlingen
Sneek
Assen
Stavoren
Helder
Medemblik
Enkhuizen
Meppel
Alkmaar
Hoorn
Kampen
Zwolle
Uitgeest
Hatlem
IJmuiden
Zaandam
AMSTERDAM
Almelo
Oldenzaal
Zandvoort
Haarlem
Deventer
Hengelo
Enschede
Gronau
Hilversum
Apeldoorn
Neede
Breukelen
Amersfoort
Zutphen
Ruurlo
Leiden
Utrecht
Winterswijk
The Hague
Woerden
Arnhem
Gouda
Kesteren
Zevenaar
Rotterdam
Geldermalsen
Elst
Emmerich
Waal
Nijmegen
Dordrecht
Gorinchem
Cleve
Rhine
Haltern
Zaltbommel
Hedel
's-Hertogenbosch
Gennep
Goch
Wesel
Hollandsch diep
Waalwijk
Vlijmen
Büderich
Dorsten
Roosendaal
Boxtel
Middelburg
Queenborough
Goes
Breda
Tilburg
Meuse
Straelen
Bergen op Zoom
Flushing
Esschen
Eindhoven
Venlo
Terneuzen
Hulst
Roermond
Antwerp
Heerlen
Ghent
Mechelen
Hasselt
Maastricht
Aachen
Luik (Longdoz)
Lek

0 Kilometers 25
0 Miles 20

FIGURE 49

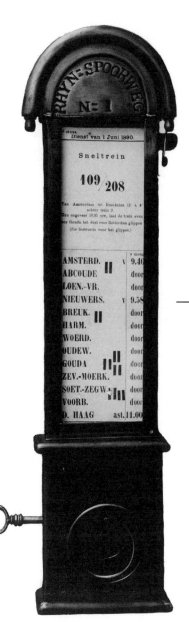

The last timetable for Rhenish Railway train 109/208, Amsterdam—The Hague with a slip portion for Rotterdam, dated June 1, 1890. This train stopped at Nieuwersluis only because of an arrangement with the local landowner in the 1840s.
(Collection NVBS)

connections on any one railway. People from Amsterdam could not travel to Belgium or France over the rails of one company, and Rotterdam had bad connections with the north of Germany. Finally, Germany's new imperial government gave preference to its own ports, Hamburg and Bremen, over Amsterdam and Rotterdam; the disunity among the Dutch railways allowed the lower German rates to endanger Holland's vital rail transit trade in the Dutch ports. Clearly something had to be done. The Netherlands government in 1881 instituted a parliamentary inquiry into the causes of the railways problem.

THE INQUIRY OF 1881

The question set before the parliamentary committee of inquiry was: How should the railways in the Netherlands be managed to adequately meet the requirements of the traffic? In 1882 the committee presented its unsurprising findings: The network should continue to be managed by the big three, as competition was salutary to the public well-being. The smaller companies—the Central, the North Brabant-German, and the South Eastern—should be dissolved and absorbed by the remaining three. The committee further recommended that the big three be placed on a more or less equal footing, without, however, clearly indicating how to accomplish this goal.

As is often the case after official inquiries, nothing much happened. The almost bankrupt South Eastern was indeed snapped up by the State Railways in 1883, while the Rhenish managed to acquire a majority of the shares of the poor Central Railway in 1885. Yet the Rhenish allowed the Central to retain its own corporate identity, and did not integrate the smaller railway into the Rhenish system.

THE TAKEOVER OF THE RHENISH RAILWAY

Although the committee of inquiry of 1881 assumed the continuing existence of the three big railway companies, one of them dissolved. In 1886 the government had reached a provisional agreement with the management of the Rhenish about renewing its concession, set to expire in 1898. But the Rhenish failed to seek parliamentary sanction, and when neither party had taken any action by 1888, the provisional agreement lapsed. The management of the Rhenish believed that the concession was to run for ten more years, and in government circles, the idea of liquidating the Rhenish Railway, the smallest of the big three, had taken hold. In 1889 the government bought the Rhenish, paying 123 percent of par for the shares, altogether some 65 million guilders. This figure was enough to somewhat pacify Rhenish shareholders, as share prices had been quoted at the Amsterdam Exchange shortly before the sale at around 85 percent of par.

The lines of the Rhenish became part of the State Railways, and the locomotives and rolling stock were divided evenly between the State and Holland companies, who had to pay for them at book value. The shares of Leiden-

Woerden and the Central Railway also went to the State Railways Company, but again the Central kept its own corporate identity and some measure of independence.

The Holland came away with 54 locomotives, some 100 passenger cars, and 830 freight trucks. The State Company gained about the same numbers, but as both tramways of the Rhenish also went to the State Railways, that company got all the tramway engines and rolling stock as well. The staff of the Rhenish, some three thousand employees, could transfer to the State Railways at the same rank, but many instead followed their chief mechanical engineer, C. W. Verloop, to Transvaal, where Dutch engineers such as J. L. Cluijsenaer and G.A.A. Middelberg were building the Netherlands South African Railway from scratch. The demise of the Netherlands Rhenish Railway ushered in an era of concentration and competition.

CONCENTRATION AND COMPETITION IN THEORY

The first goal of the railway agreements of 1889–1890—whose accomplishment required the purchase of the Rhenish—was to create equal opportunities for the two remaining railway companies, the State and the Holland. For this purpose, some lines formerly operated by the State Railways were transferred to the Holland, while on some other lines running powers were granted to both companies.

The Holland acquired the State-built lines Stavoren-Leeuwarden and Dordrecht-Elst and thus held the whole Amsterdam-Enkhuizen-Stavoren-Leeuwarden line, including the ferry crossing. A new international connection was also forged for the Holland in Amsterdam-Amersfoort-Kesteren-Nijmegen, whose last section was in the hands of the State Company, but on which Holland held running powers. A Schiedam–Hook of Holland line, yet to be built, was also promised to the Holland, and that company obtained running powers on Rotterdam-Roosendaal-Belgium, Arnhem-Nijmegen-Venlo, Arnhem-Zevenaar-Emmerich (-Germany), Utrecht-Gouda-Rotterdam, and Utrecht-Amersfoort (Central Railway).

The State Railways got running power on the yet to be built beltline around Rotterdam, which was to open in 1899, managed by the Holland. Somewhat unexpectedly, the former Rhenish station of Rotterdam-Maas was handed over to the Holland, even though the State Company used it more, as successor to the Rhenish. At the conclusion of this rearrangement, the State Railways finally had a foothold in Amsterdam over its own rails, while the Holland had access to the Rotterdam docks on the south bank of the Maas along with new international connections. The traveling public now also could choose among the routes of either company, impossible before.

Of course, Parliament had to sanction these agreements, and it turned out that not everybody in Parliament was happy with them. Many thought that the price paid for the Rhenish shares was much too high. Others favored a complete state system, and their number was growing—after all, the big Prussian system just across the border demonstrated the positive results of

Spoorzicht.

SNEEK.

Uitg. R. v. d. Meulen

FIGURE 50

Holland Company train headed by an ancient Borsig engine at Sneek, circa 1905. As a result of the railway agreements of 1890, the Holland Railway took over the operation of the Frisian Stavoren-Leeuwarden line, physically separated from the rest of the Holland network; rolling stock and engines came to the Haarlem shops for maintenance by steam ferry to Enkhuizen. (Collection NVBS)

putting the railways in public hands. Still others were of the opinion that the two remaining companies were too independent. Even though they were obliged to pay a share of their profits to the government when dividends exceeded 4 percent, all bookkeeping remained in the hands of the administration of the railways, which made government auditing impossible. Further, the two companies could end the agreements anytime, at which point the government would have to take over the railways on most unfavorable terms. If forced to buy the railroads, the government had to do so on equally unattractive terms.

A final point that came in for a lot of criticism from members of Parliament was the absence of regulations for the railways' depreciation, except for the rolling stock. Everything else subject to heavy wear and tear was free of mandatory depreciation. The companies' existing reserve funds also went untouched by the agreements; companies might use them to maintain dividends at the 4 percent level, with no one the wiser. The disastrous results of ignoring these issues, many believed, would make themselves felt later. Small wonder that economists and financial specialists of the Second Chamber (equivalent to the U.S. House of Representatives) such as the radical-liberal M.W.F. Treub (later a cabinet minister), were most critical of the railway agreements. The Second Chamber, however, approved them, 48 to 37. On the night of October 14/15, 1890, the new arrangement took effect, and the Rhenish Railway was no more.

Disgusted by the interminable conferences with government officials, W.K.M. Vrolik, director-general of the State Railways, had by 1890 retired in anger, leaving the rest of the negotiations to the chairman of the board, H.P.G. Quack. Vrolik's successor was J. L. Cluijsenaer, who as a young engineer had worked on the Moerdijk bridge back in the 1870s. After that he had taught at the Royal Military Academy of Breda, had constructed railways in the Dutch East Indies, and had served as secretary to Vrolik when he was director-general. Cluijsenaer then had gone to Pretoria, Transvaal, as director of the new Netherlands South African Railway and in 1889 had been called back to Utrecht. (In Pretoria he was succeeded by Gerrit Middelberg, formerly CME of the Holland Railway.)

Cluijsenaer's opposite number at the Holland Railway was still Robert van Hasselt, undisputed leader of the competition. And like Vrolik before him, Cluijsenaer struggled in his dealings with the slick and astute van Hasselt, who was ably seconded by his traffic manager, N. H. Nierstrasz. A former military officer and engineer, Nierstrasz had organized the traffic department of the Holland Railway along the lines of a military unit. (At international conferences about railway schedules, the van Hasselt–Nierstrasz duo was widely feared.) Because of these personal antagonisms, the cooperation between the Holland and State Railways so desired by the government never materialized. J. P. Sprenger van Eyk, a former cabinet minister and an able financier but no railway man, succeeded Cluijsenaer and, despite his good intentions, also failed to improve relations with the Holland. Competition remained as fierce and costly as ever.

Only after Van Hasselt retired in 1907 and after Sprenger van Eyk's sudden death in the same year did things improve. Sprenger's successor as director-general was J. A. Kretschmar van Veen, a nobleman and engineer who had worked under Van Hasselt earlier and who had succeeded Middelberg in Pretoria as director of the Netherlands South African Railway in 1899. With great diplomatic talent, he had guided that railway and its large Dutch and international staff skillfully through the difficult years of the Second Boer War and the occupation of Transvaal by British forces. Now Kretschmar van Veen managed to reach some understanding and even a certain measure of cooperation with van Hasselt's successor at the Holland Railway, F. W. van der Spyck, another nobleman and lawyer. The First World War would speed up this cooperative process.

For the traveling public the new system of concentration and competition was a mixed blessing. Some rates were lowered to draw traffic away from the competition, but the whole structure of rates and schedules was so obscure and complicated that it took serious study to figure out the best, fastest, and cheapest connection. Through services between major cities were not always available, and changing from one company's trains to another's was difficult and certainly not encouraged. Connections were often lacking, sometimes intentionally, and through tickets between the two companies were not available.

At connecting stations, ticket windows labeled "Through Passengers" became a necessary but universal nuisance. Each company had its own tickets, special discounts, and return and season tickets, none of them any good for travel on the other company's trains. Only under strong pressure from government and the public were some improvements introduced in 1898, enabling travelers to buy one ticket for a journey with more than one company. Not until January 1, 1911, was a uniform rate for all railways introduced by all companies. It was a low rate, especially compared with those of foreign railways: 3.25, 2.45, and 1.62 cents per kilometer in first, second, and third class respectively.

For express freight, a more or less uniform rate had taken effect earlier, but for general freight and bulk goods every company set its own rates. Such charges had to be low to compete with the German and Belgian railways, which offered preferential rates in favor of their own ports. In this arena the lack of unity among the Dutch railways cost them dearly and sometimes resulted in ridiculous circumstances, as well. For example, textile mill owners in Twente got together to buy an English coal mine near Newcastle, because the Holland Railway offered such cheap rates to Twente from Amsterdam, where the coal was delivered by collier, that German coal from the nearby Ruhr, hauled by the State Railways by way of Emmerich, was forced out of the market for a time.

NEW LINES

After 1890 the railways added few new main lines, as the network was almost complete. Only the connection with the South was improved materially, with the construction of Eindhoven–Weert in 1913, cutting off the long detour over Venlo. The Schiedam–Hook of Holland line built by the State had opened in 1893, and the Rotterdam belt line, which connected the Maas and Delftsche Poort stations in that town, was finished in 1899. Eindhoven-Weert was managed by the State Railways, the others by the Holland Company.

When the Hook of Holland packet station opened, the traditional Flushing-Queenborough (Folkestone after 1911) day service for the first time faced a strong competitor. The English Great Eastern Railway (GER) ships had been plying the route from Harwich Pier to Rotterdam since 1863, providing a slow but sure night service. At first this service had relied on the tides, but with the opening of the Rotterdam Waterway, the Great Eastern introduced fixed schedules in 1874. The construction of Parkeston Quay near Harwich in 1883 meant better facilities for passengers and freight on the English side, but the real improvement came in 1893, when the Hook of Holland packet station with its connecting railway opened on the Dutch side. The GER introduced fast new steamers for a night service on this route, and the Holland Railway laid in fast trains to Cologne and Berlin. The Holland had taken over the management of the old Almelo–Salzbergen line from the State Railways in 1892 and now ran expresses all the way to Rheine, where the Prussians took charge. The light railway Apeldoorn–Deventer–Almelo suddenly found itself a link in an important international railway and was upgraded to main line standards.

Even when the GER night steamer *Berlin* hit one of the piers at the Hook in a gale and broke in two, February 21, 1907, with great loss of life, the disaster did not long affect this fast, comfortable connection.

Most other new lines constructed between 1890 and 1914 were of the light railway kind. A whole network was built up after 1899 in Overijssel, Drente, and Groningen, owned by the Noord–Ooster Locaalspoorweg Maatschappij (NOLS, North Eastern Local Railway) and worked by the State Railways from the outset. Its lines started in Zwolle and Almelo and ran north and east to the harbor of Delfzijl, with a number of branches.

At the same time, the Noord–Friesche Locaalspoorwegmaatschappij (NFLS, North Frisian Local Railway) was constructing lines in Friesland north of Leeuwarden and Harlingen. In contrast to most other regional railways, this company had its own locomotives and rolling stock and at first managed its lines itself. When revenues were disappointing, it proffered contracts for managing its lines to anyone willing to make an offer. The Holland moved fastest, snapping up the North Frisian before the State Railways could even make an offer. The contract was profitable for the North Frisian's stockholders, it later developed, but not for the Holland's. Traffic remained light and revenues slight, but trains had to be run, passengers or no. Most of the North Frisian and North Eastern Local lines had been built with heavy government subsidies. Minister of Waterstaat C. Lely, himself an engineer, had initiated a program of government subvention for railways and tramways in areas that

FIGURE 51

Holland Railway 4-4-0 express engine No. 434 at the head of a Cologne–Hook of Holland(–London) train at the border station of Kranenburg, 1910. The first car behind the tender carries two containers of the English Great Eastern Railway for registered Cologne-London luggage without customs examination at the borders.
(Collection A. D. de Pater/ NVBS)

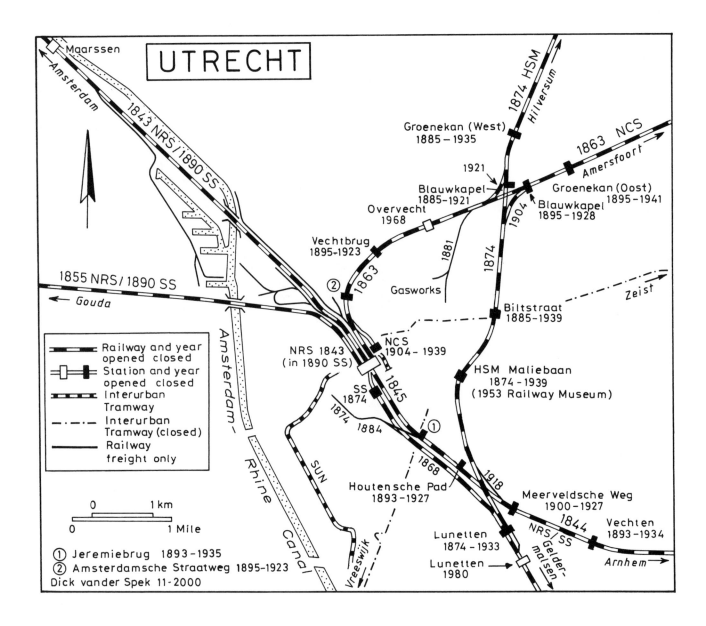

UTRECHT

Maarssen

Amsterdam

1843 NRS/1890 SS

1855 NRS/1890 SS

← Gouda

Amsterdam-Rhine Canal

Railway and year opened closed
Station and year opened closed
Interurban Tramway
Interurban Tramway (closed)
Railway freight only

0   1 km
0   1 Mile

① Jeremiebrug 1893-1935
② Amsterdamsche Straatweg 1895-1923
Dick van der Spek 11-2000

1874 HSM

Hilversum

1863 NCS

Groenekan (West) 1885-1935

1921

Blauwkapel 1885-1921

Overvecht 1968

Vechtbrug 1895-1923

1863

1881

Gasworks

1874

1904

Amersfoort

Groenekan (Oost) 1895-1941

Blauwkapel 1895-1928

Zeist

Biltstraat 1885-1939

HSM Maliebaan 1874-1939 (1953 Railway Museum)

NRS 1843 (in 1890 SS)

NCS 1904-1939

SS 1874

1845

1874

1884

②

①

SUN

1868

Houtensche Pad 1893-1927

Vreeswijk

1918

Lunetten 1874-1933

Lunetten 1980

Meerveldsche Weg 1900-1927

NRS/SS 1844

Vechten 1893-1934

Geldermalsen

Arnhem →

were still underdeveloped. This resulted in a number of other new light railway lines in Gelderland and North Holland, most managed by the Holland Company, and also in the extensive narrow gauge tramway network on the South Holland and Zeeland islands, as discussed earlier.

An acrimonious conflict between the State and Holland Railways erupted over the Hollandsche Electrische Spoorweg Maatschappij (HESM, Holland Electric Railway Company), founded in 1898 by T. Sanders, an Amsterdam architect and tramway promoter, and discreetly supported by the State Railways, which stayed in the background. Sanders had obtained the concession for a number of lines in the Haarlemmermeer Polder, the former inland lake between Amsterdam, Haarlem, and Leiden. One of these lines was to connect Amsterdam and Haarlem (South), in direct competition with the old Holland Railway line between the two towns. At the same time plans were maturing for an electric interurban line between Amsterdam and Haarlem parallel to

FIGURE 52

Station and engine staff at
Anjum on the North Frisian
Local, 1913. The engine,
ex-North Frisian No. 9, is
Holland Railway No. 1059.
(Photo W. Kamminga,
author's collection)

the Holland's main line, and Van Hasselt did not want a second competitor on
this overcrowded route. Sensing the danger, he bought up the majority of the
stock of the HESM in a quick move on the Amsterdam Stock Exchange.
Sanders was furious; he and the State Company's officials withdrew angrily
and were replaced by Holland Railway men. The Haarlemmermeer lines were
built as light railways, but without the planned working with electric accu-
mulator motorcars. The direct Amsterdam-Haarlem line was replaced by a circuitous one by way of Hoofddorp, to further discourage through traffic.
Managing all these lines was unprofitable from the start, and they were to be
a longtime drain on the Holland's revenues. (A similar case occurred some
years later with the Zuid-Hollandsche Electrische Spoorweg; this line will be
described in a later chapter.)

The State Railways, although rebuffed in the HESM case, were more successful elsewhere. The company extended its activities in the area north of
Groningen, and in the far South, in Limburg, it took over the Nederlandsche
Zuider-Spoorwegmaatschappij (NZS, Netherlands Southern Railway Company), incorporated in 1891. NZS was the brainchild of H.L.C.H. Sarolea, a
mining engineer, meant to open up the coal-mining areas then being developed. Its light railway Sittard-Heerlen-Herzogenrath opened in 1896, was
later converted to main line standards, and did indeed form the nucleus of the
extensive network of mine railways in Limburg.

The small and relatively poor Central Railway managed to open some
light railways in Utrecht and Gelderland. The first was the Utrechtsche
Locaalspoorwegmaatschappij (ULS, Utrecht Local Railway) in 1898, whose
Den Dolder-Baarn line connected the Central's own Utrecht-Amersfoort line
with the Holland's Amsterdam-Amersfoort line. Three years later the Nederlandsche Buurtspoorwegmaatschappij (NBM, Netherlands Regional Railway)
followed, a light railway that ran between Bilthoven and Zeist, just northeast
of Utrecht. Both lines were managed by the Central from the start, and a
healthy suburban traffic developed. Well-to-do city dwellers were happy to
move out to the pleasant wooded Utrecht hills, now that commuting was

becoming so easy. A third light railway was the Ede–Barneveld line in 1902, owned by the Spoorwegmaatschappij De Veluwe and also managed by the Central. It connected Ede, on the former Rhenish Railway line west of Arnhem, with Barneveld, on the Holland's Amersfoort–Apeldoorn line, part of the eastern line. It was extended from Barneveld to Nijkerk in 1903 and became known as the "chicken line" because of the many chicken farms in the area.

Apart from these light railways, the Central opened a standard gauge steam tramway, Nunspeet–Hattemerbroek, which followed the main Amersfoort-Zwolle line but ran through the villages and towns along the line instead of passing them by as the Amersfoort–Zwolle did. From Hattemerbroek the steam trams reached Zwolle over the Central's main line. Finally, the Central managed the Spoorweg–Maatschappij Zwolle–Blokzijl that in 1914 opened a narrow gauge tramway between its namesake towns in the IJssel River delta west of Zwolle.

The North Brabant–German Railway, not to be outdone, published a grandiose plan for an extensive network of light railways in the Peel area of Brabant. Nothing came of it, as almost nobody lived there.

In 1898 a few of the Belgian-owned lines were acquired by the Dutch government. The Belgian government at the time followed a policy of purchasing the existing private railways in the country and incorporating them in its state system. It acquired the Grand Central Belge (GCB) Company in 1897, and as this company also owned some border lines in the Netherlands, the Belgian government asked The Hague to cooperate. The Belgians could acquire by compulsory purchase only the GCB lines in Belgium itself, of course, so the Netherlands government obliged by buying the Dutch sections—Lanaken–Simpelveld (part of the old Aachen-Maastricht), Budel–Vlodrop, and Tilburg–Baarle Nassau. When the Dutch State Railways Company was charged with managing these former GCB lines, the Second Chamber of Parliament had some objections, as the move would put the Holland Railway at a disadvantage with regard to the traffic with Belgium. Of course, Holland

FIGURE 53

Voorthuizen Station on the Central's "chicken line," with a small 4-4-0 tank of the series 41–50 and one of the Central's sumptuous American-looking bogie carriages.
(Postcard, Collection NVBS)

FIGURE 54

A State Railways train on the picturesque old Aachen-Maastricht line in the far south of Limburg, near the Oud-Valkenburg stop, around 1905, shortly before the line was double tracked. (Postcard, Collection NVBS)

had running powers over Rotterdam–Roosendaal (–Essen), but the State Company now had Tilburg–Baarle Nassau (–Turnhout) as well. However, these objections were smoothed over, and Parliament confirmed the agreements.

One condition stipulated by the Dutch government was that the two countries also share the Liège–Limbourgeois line. Brussels agreed and bought the LL, which relieved the Dutch State Railways of its onerous 1866 management contracts with the LL, and the line was immediately relegated to secondary status. One year later, in 1898, the Liège-Maastricht Company was similarly purchased jointly by the Dutch and Belgian governments. On the Dutch-German frontier, by contrast, nothing changed.

RAILWAY MANAGEMENT AFTER THE 1890 AGREEMENTS

The major reshuffle of responsibility for managing the railways began at a most unlucky moment, as the severe winter of 1890–1891 caused chaos in the freight sector. The inland rivers and canals froze over for months, bringing water traffic to a standstill. Shippers who usually used the waterways all clamored for rail transportation, which resulted in a serious shortage of freight trucks. Yards were filled to capacity, and although complaints were numerous, many were unfounded, as the railways could not be expected to

FIGURE 55

Holland Railway No. 159, *Van Galen,* steams past Baarn with train D72, Amsterdam-Leipzig, May 1911, one of Middelberg's Runners, still in use for fast but light trains. (Photo L. Derens, Collection NVBS)

keep rolling stock in reserve for such exceptional circumstances. But it was true that the railways for many years had failed to invest enough in new rolling stock.

Chaos ruled in the passenger sector as well. Because of the weather, trains were late or did not run at all; when they did run, they were cold and over-crowded. It was some months before the situation returned to normal and the railway companies could adjust to the new management system.

At first the Holland Company was at a disadvantage because some of its new lines—the Rotterdam belt line and Schiedam-Hook of Holland—were not yet ready. After 1893, however, it entered the competition with a vengeance, running fast, comfortable boat trains to Cologne via Rotterdam-Dordrecht-Geldermalsen-Nijmegen-Cleves, and to North Germany by way of Amsterdam-Amersfoort-Almelo-Salzbergen-Rheine. After the Rotterdam belt line was opened in 1899, these two trains were routed over Rotterdam-Utrecht-Amersfoort, and both services became strong competitors to the State Railways' services by way of Arnhem-Emmerich. The Holland ran its trains from Amsterdam to Belgium and France over Rotterdam-Roosendaal (-Essen), while the State Company preferred Amsterdam-Utrecht-Tilburg-Baarle Nassau (-Turnhout). The Holland inaugurated new through services between Rotterdam/The Hague and Twente, while the State and Central companies jointly developed the service from these Dutch cities to Groningen and Fries-land. The Holland also had some success with its own Amsterdam-Friesland route by way of the ferry service Enkhuizen-Stavoren. Comfortable new steamers crossed the Zuiderzee, the large inland gulf of the North Sea, in about an hour, and passengers generally enjoyed this break from the cramped railway compartments. Special freight boats ferried up to ten freight trucks over in one trip, and traffic in Friesian cattle, butter, and cheese to the markets of Holland boomed.

In season, through coaches from European cities served watering places on the North Sea such as Zandvoort and Scheveningen (Kurhaus, after 1908). Sleeping cars ran to Scheveningen from Altona (near Hamburg), Berlin, and Vienna, while Zandvoort could be reached from Basel and Munich without changing trains. Through carriages also ran in season from Amsterdam and Flushing to transport well-off Dutch to fashionable continental watering places such as Marienbad, Bad Homburg, or Karlsbad.

The State Railways and North Brabant–German carried on a running war over the mail trains London-Queenborough-Flushing-Boxtel-Berlin/Hamburg. The State Company wanted to route them via Venlo over its line, but the North Brabant had the shortest route by way of Wesel and generally managed to keep the mail trains' business. Only between 1888 and 1892 did the State Company persuade Berlin trains to run by way of Venlo, while only the Hamburg/Scandinavia trains still ran by way of Boxtel-Wesel on the North Brabant. The trains to southern Germany, Austria, and Switzerland always took the Venlo route. The Flushing route was a favorite of the European aristocracy and of royalty, sometimes in their own royal or imperial trains. German emperor Wilhelm II preferred this route when visiting his English relatives, and his sumptuous blue and cream and gold train was a familiar sight in Flushing.

The frequency of runs on most main lines gradually increased until on some of the busiest stretches, sixty to seventy trains ran daily. Freight trains were generally banished to the night hours. Amsterdam-Haarlem, Rotterdam-

FIGURE 56

The almost complete joint Holland-Central Railways junction station at Amersfoort, 1901. (Postcard, Collection NVBS)

Schiedam, Utrecht–Amersfoort, and a few other stretches became choked with traffic and should have been widened to four tracks immediately, but the companies were loathe to make the enormous investment required. With the exception only of Rotterdam–Schiedam, the crowded tracks would wait a hundred years before being quadrupled.

NEW STATIONS

In this era new station buildings were erected along most lines. Some of the original stations either were too small for the growing traffic or had fallen into disrepair, and these had to be replaced. The Fortification Act of 1874 meant that most fortress towns could now expand beyond their confining fortifications, with permanent stations replacing their temporary wooden buildings.

Grandest of all the new stations was the Central Station of Amsterdam, designed by architects P. J. Cuypers and A. L. van Gendt. Despite loud protests against locating the station in the formerly open harbor front and against the monumental scale of the buildings, Amsterdam at long last got a station commensurate with its status as capital of the country. The Holland and Rhenish railways used the station jointly until 1890, when the State Railways took over from the Rhenish. Other new stations of the Holland Railway were Leiden (1879), designed by D.A.N. Margadant; Delft (1883), by C. B. Posthumus Meyjes; The Hague (1891), again by Margadant; and Haarlem (1905–1906), also by Margadant, with its magnificent all-sheltering roof. With Haarlem completed, all important stations of the "Old Line" had grandiose new buildings. Apart from Leiden, all still stand, although some have required extensive restoration and rebuilding.

FIGURE 57

Hengelo Station, designed by G. W. van Heukelom, 1899. Although the new buildings, *left*, are finished, the old low platforms are still in use; the iron and glass train shed is some years in the future. (Collection NVBS)

Maastricht
Station

Amersfoort, an important junction station, had a complicated history. Both the Central and the Eastern Railway of the Holland used the same out-dated Central station, while the State-built line south to Rhenen/Kesteren used a separate station some distance away. Travelers changing trains here had to walk from one to the other. During the years 1900–1901 a new station designed by Margadant opened, with new yards and engine sheds. All traffic now flowed through this station, and the others were closed. Not until 1998 would another new station supersede Margadant's 1901 structure.

Along the State Railways too new stations were built, at first cheaper and simpler than those of the Holland. The first important station was Flushing-Harbor (1892), designed by D. H. Haverkamp and T. G. Schill. It exuded some of the grand air that belonged to a meeting place of sumptuous mail trains and mail steamers, where European high society set foot regularly. After Flushing, a series of other important stations was finished, most of them architectural gems. Nijmegen (1892) by C. H. Peters, Groningen (1893) by J. Gosschalk, and 's-Hertogenbosch (1893) by E. Cuypers, are all excellent examples of Dutch Renaissance architecture. Only Groningen survived the Second World War, and it has been restored to its former glory.

G. W. van Heukelom, an engineer and architect who would end his career as chief of the permanent way and buildings of the State Railways, left his mark on contemporary Dutch railway architecture. One of his first works was Hengelo, which opened in 1899 to replace the small earlier existing building. Next came Baarle–Nassau (1904) on the Dutch-Belgian border, intended to be a customs inspection station but whose capacity was never fully utilized. Together with the government architect D.E.C. Knuttel, van Heukelom designed

FIGURE 58

The old station at Maastricht, shortly before demolition. Such an important location demanded a station as impressive as the one designed by van Heukelom that would open there in 1912. (Postcard, Collection NVBS)

Roosendaal, another customs station on the Belgian border, complete with engine sheds and signal cabins (1905). In 1912 all stations—Eindhoven, Geldrop, Heeze, Maarheeze, and Weert—along the new cutoff Eindhoven-Weert were van Heukelom's work, as was the grand building, part through station, part terminus, of Maastricht (1912). Besides these large stations, he designed many smaller buildings along the State Company's lines, and also the new headquarters of the State Railways at Utrecht—the third headquarters in a row—which looked like an enormous red brick tower of Babylon and today serves as the headquarters of Netherlands Railways.

The Great Railway Strikes of 1903

THE RAILWAY WORKERS

The first railway companies were generally considered to be good employers. Wages and working conditions were on a par with those of other companies, and most jobs were year-round, not seasonal. The combined number of railway company employees rose from 15,000 in 1889 to 21,000 in 1899 to 32,000 in 1909. The railways were among the first companies to set up benevolent societies and pension funds for their employees. A Holland Railway fund begun in 1843 paid at least part-wages in cases of sickness, and two years later, the company started a pension fund. Higher-up staff, including locomotive engineers and conductors, paid 3 percent of their salaries into the fund, the lower ranking staff 2 percent, and the company matched 67 percent of these contributions.

The Rhenish followed suit in 1864 with a support fund financed by the company that paid allowances to sick and disabled workers and their dependents, and a pension fund a couple of years later. The State Railways set up a pension fund for all permanent staff in 1874. Membership was mandatory and all had to pay in some percentage of their wages. The State Company also had a sickness benefit fund and made good its annual deficit, which averaged around 12,000 guilders ($5,000).

Although the railways in the nineteenth century were privately owned and operated, and, according to the liberal thinking of the day, the government should not meddle with their operations, it did step in now and then regarding

FIGURE 59

A State Railways employee
checks a signal bridge at night.
Twenty-four-hour railway
service meant irregular hours
for railway men.
(Photo Staatsspoorwegen,
Collection NVBS)

the working circumstances of employees. With the Railway Act as a foundation, the government in 1875 set limits on employee working hours, more for
safety reasons than out of compassion for the men on the road. But because the
Railway Supervisory Board had no system for monitoring working hours, railroads in large part ignored the regulation. In 1899, the government limited
working hours to a maximum of sixteen hours per day, and for certain categories such as signalmen to ten hours. Every employee should have twenty-six
days off every year, the government ruled, of which eight had to be Sundays.

But the railways proved more stubborn than politicians had expected and
regularly broke these working hour limits. Infringements were difficult to
spot and prove, and therefore almost impossible to punish. In addition, rail-

way directors, like many other employers, held a strong paternalistic attitude toward their workers: Workers were in a state of tutelage and should remain so, because the directors knew best what was good for them. Even with mandatory membership in the pension funds, for example, only the directors and middle cadres governed the monies, and no representative of the lower ranks was admitted to the boards. Trade unions were out of the question. Directors simply refused to talk with the unions as representatives of the workers. Membership in a union was cause for immediate discharge at some railway companies.

In the last quarter of the nineteenth century, wages gradually fell behind the slowly increasing cost of living. Although the Holland Company generally paid a bit better than the State Railways, there, too, wages were out of step with the cost of living. Most other industries had raised wages, but the family of a railway laborer could hardly get by on his wages alone, and often his wife had to work as a gatekeeper or at similar employment. Locomotive engineers complained that their wages depended too heavily on bonuses awarded for their economic use of coal, lubricating oil, and such, and for arriving on schedule. But the men on the footplate had no control over the weather, the mechanical condition of their engine, or the quality of the coal provided, making the

FIGURE 60
Members of the Recht en Plicht railway workers' union, Haarlem branch. The banner reads: For God, Duty, and Property. (Collection NVBS)

amount of their bonuses uncertain at best. All these circumstances made for an atmosphere of discord and discontent among the men at the end of the nineteenth century, something the directors failed to see or refused to acknowledge.

The level of organization among railway workers was relatively low. The oldest and most militant of the trade unions was the socialist Association of Railway Workers Steeds Voorwaarts (Forever Onward). In 1893, Steeds Voorwaarts had some 4,600 members, but its popularity declined as a result partly of internal strife, partly of a new union, and in 1897 it was dissolved. The new union was the Anti-Social-Democratic Association Recht en Plicht (Right and Duty), with some progressive Roman Catholic priests among its leaders. Dr. H.J.A.M. Schaepman, a member of Parliament, and A. Weyers were foremost among these. Recht en Plicht wanted consultation, not confrontation, but the results of their efforts were almost negligible.

Another older union was the Nederlandsche Vereeniging van Spoor–en Tramwegpersoneel (NV, Netherlands Association of Railway and Tramway Workers), which had begun in 1886 more as a social club, with membership open to all grades of staff, than as a trade union. Under its chairman, Jan Oudegeest, the NV gradually moved to the Social-Democratic Left and concentrated on looking after the material interests of its members; by that time most members from the higher or middle cadres had left.

At the Holland Railway, specialist brotherhoods had grown popular since 1896. Engine drivers had their Eendracht maakt Macht (Unity Is Strength), conductors their Ons Belang (Our Interest), crane drivers their Ons Aller Belang (The Interest of All of Us), and the track laborers their Verbetering door Vereeniging (Improvement Through Union). In 1901 these four united to form the Federatie van Spoorwegorganisaties (Federation of Railway Organizations), which claimed some 2,200 members, a redoubtable force.

THE FIRST RAILWAY STRIKE OF 1903

The first strike of railway employees erupted unexpectedly on January 30, 1903, out of solidarity with striking dock workers in Amsterdam. The dock workers had been on strike for some weeks in an attempt to force employers to hire union members only, the closed-shop system abhorred by most employers. In support, the railway workers refused to handle freight from the "infected" warehouses and shipping firms.

The directors of the railway affected first, the Holland, refused to give the workers a hearing or discuss the problems but simply suspended the strikers. The strike then quickly spread throughout Amsterdam and reached the State Railways too. Traffic to and from the capital came to a standstill, and the strike threatened to spread to other regions of the country. But the next day, the Holland Railway directors capitulated and accepted the demand of the unions to stop all switching for the "infected" warehouses. The strike had been completely spontaneous and unorganized, and wage demands had not even been put forward. Union leaders, as surprised by the strike as the railway directors, had no time to formulate demands. Nothing had really been

solved, but the self-confidence of the workers and their unions had increased enormously.

GOVERNMENT MEASURES AND THE SECOND STRIKE

The strike made a profound impression on the public and the government. That a few "rioters and dynamite men" had been able to stop railway traffic in the heart of Holland was something that should never be allowed to occur again. Discussing working conditions and hours was possible, maybe even with the trade unions, but a strike was unforgivable. The government, under Prime Minister Abraham Kuyper, had Parliament pass a series of laws meant to put an end to these outrages. The undisputed leader of the Anti-Revolutionary Party, a fairly right-wing Christian-Protestant party, Kuyper was feared and detested by his opponents. They called these measures "strangling laws," but Parliament passed them with little opposition. From now on, striking vital services such as railways and public utilities was forbidden under threat of heavy penalties.

A railway battalion in the Army Corps of Engineers was trained to run the most vital services in case of a future strike. But because even the most reactionary conservatives had to concede that something was wrong with the working conditions on the railways, a parliamentary commission of inquiry

FIGURE 61

During the great railway strike of 1903, impatient travelers wait at Amsterdam Central Station for trains that will not come.
(Collection NVBS)

would look into the problem. And to be prepared for every eventuality, the army called up some classes of recruits.

Opposition outside Parliament was strong and formed a Comité van Verweer (Committee of Resistance) to unite all groups. Several trade unions were represented, among them Oudegeest's NV. The Sociaal-Democratische Arbeiders Partij (SDAP, the Social-Democratic Workers Party), a moderate left-wing political party, also sent delegates. Against the advice of the SDAP, the committee called for a second railway strike the night of April 5, 1903. The militant anarchist and syndicalist elements in the committee strongly favored a strike, and the SDAP was overruled.

This time it was a political strike directed against the "strangling laws" and the other government countermeasures. But the strikers found the authorities well prepared. Stations, signal boxes, and other important railway property were immediately occupied by soldiers; the police and the military protected employees willing to work (chiefly Protestants and Roman Catholics and the higher ranks); and emergency schedules went into effect. Automobiles for the first time carried important mail, a harbinger of the future.

The strike disrupted traffic, especially around Amsterdam, again the center of the strike, but never stopped it completely. After two days, it became clear that the strike was not going well, but the left-wing anarchist elements on the strike committee nonetheless called for a general workers' strike all over the country. Outside Amsterdam, hardly anyone heeded this call, and on April 10 the committee had to end the strike.

The railways sacked strikers by the hundreds: Of the 13,500 workers at State Railways, 1,878 men had struck, and 1,035 were discharged. Of Holland Railway's total workforce of just over 9,100 men, 1,475 had participated in the strike, and 989 of them were fired. The strike leaders and those who had ignored the call to report for work until it was too late were discharged first. Kuyper pleaded in vain with the companies to take back at least half those sacked, but the directors were glad to be rid of the militant troublemakers. Well represented among the strike leaders were workers who had been in Transvaal with the Netherlands-South African Railway, and who had returned to railway service in the Netherlands after the Boer War. They were considered too independent, too used to fending for themselves in the wilds of Transvaal, and they did not adapt easily to the narrow confines of Dutch railway service, where initiative from below was not encouraged.

The railways found, however, that it was hard to replace the skilled workers among the discharged men—locomotive engineers and signalmen, for instance—and railway service suffered for a long time after the strike.

Internal dissension among the trade unions was one of the chief causes of the strike's failure. Moderate Social Democrats fought an internecine war with the dogmatic anarchists and syndicalists, and this lack of unity among the leaders affected the policies of the Comité van Verweer. The trade unions lost a large part of their membership.

Two new unions were formed after the strike. The Roman Catholic Saint Raphael founded in 1903 was, along with its Protestant counterpart, for a long time the only union more or less tolerated by the railway directors. It soon became the largest union. Its Protestant counterpart (a split along religious lines was unavoidable in the Netherlands of those years) was the Protestants Christelijke Bond van Spoor–en Tramwegpersoneel (PCB, Protestant-Christian Association of Railway and Tramway Workers), also founded in 1903 and also seen by the companies as somewhat respectable. Both St. Raphael and the PCB considered discussion and negotiation with the railway directors, not strikes, the way to reach their goal, the improvement of working conditions for railway workers. The "strangling laws" equated railway staff with civil servants, who also had no right to strike, and the old antagonism between private and government ownership and operation flared up again. Many viewed as incongruous the fact that workers for a private railway company were as strongly regulated by government as were public service workers. However, for the time being the opponents of public railway working carried the day.

THE INQUIRY OF 1903

The Parliamentary commission of inquiry was chaired by J. D. Veegens, a left-wing liberal ex-member of the Second Chamber, and later the minister of agriculture, industry, and commerce. Veegens went to work quickly and his report was clear: By and large the commission judged as wholly justified the complaints about long and irregular working hours, low wages, lack of representation on the boards of the pension funds, arbitrary dismissal, disciplinary penalties, and so on. Veegens set forth a long list of recommendations to rectify the more glaring complaints, and the government put his advice before the railway directors. But the directors, more inclined to look after the financial well-being of their companies than the welfare of their staff, reached no agreement with the government. Again, problems grew out of differences of opinion: Should the state work the railways, in which case the government could impose any regulations it wanted, or should the Dutch practice of mixing private company involvement in public services continue?

Not until 1905 did the directors of the railways agree to reduce working hours—always the sore point. Some wages were also raised. Only then were the legal status and the payment of railway staff materially improved and adequately regulated, although the problem of irregular working hours was never resolved. Two years later a new scheme for working hours came along, again with some increase in wages.

The growing influence of the state on the legal status of workers was part of a changing social policy practiced by the cabinets of these years. The Accident Law of 1901, the Building Ordinances of the same year, and the Invalidity Law of 1913 were links in a chain meant to improve the position of workers in general. Security in case of accidents at work, improved housing conditions, and a guaranteed income in case of permanent disability made life for workers safer and better.

The Glory Days of the Steam Locomotive

GENERAL TECHNICAL DEVELOPMENTS

Netherlands railways were quick to adopt new inventions from all over Europe, as we have seen, and technical journals such as the *Organ für die Fortschritte des Eisenbahnwesens* were widely read and eagerly scanned for possible improvements. Dutch mechanical engineers frequently participated in international conferences and published regularly in the *Organ* and elsewhere.

In the field of track structures—rails and ties—J. W. Post of the State Railways was an internationally acknowledged authority. His system of steel ties was published extensively and used in the Netherlands and in other countries as well. Another well-known engineer was E.C.W. van Dijk of the Central Railway. He experimented extensively with rail fastenings and in 1909 developed the system of cast steel chairs holding a heavy (46 kg/m) flat-bottom rail and fixed to the wooden ties not with the usual spikes but with screws. This track was an instant success, copied immediately by all Dutch railways. Here and there it is still in use by Netherlands Railways as NP 46 (Normal Profile, 46 kg/m) on wooden ties. In Germany it became known as the Holländisches System and was used by the German Reichsbahn after World War I.

The doubling of busy lines continued in this period. The Holland Railway rebuilt the whole Apeldoorn-Deventer-Almelo-Salzbergen line, which was partly a light railway, to main line standards with double track. The State Railways did the same with its line south to Maastricht and on the Zwolle-

FIGURE 62
Final inspection of the tracks
leading to the new bridge
across the North Sea Canal
near Velsen, 1905.
(Collection NVBS)

Groningen line in the North as far as Hoogeveen. The Central doubled
Utrecht-Amersfoort-Zwolle, except for the IJssel River Bridge near Zwolle,
and even the impecunious North Brabant–German managed to double its
Boxtel-Goch line. Most light railways, with their low traffic density, remained
single tracked.

The Holland Company also developed plans to quadruple the busiest
parts of its Old Line but in the end shrunk from the vast expenditures
involved. Here the company paid the price for its lack of foresight regarding
depreciation and investment in the future. In other countries, lines such as
Amsterdam-Haarlem and The Hague-Rotterdam would have been quadrupled
long before.

The railways built new bridges in this period, replacing old weak ones
and adding new ones required by canal widening or building. A high steel

FIGURE 63

Testing the new bridge over the Merwede Canal near Utrecht on the old Rhenish Railway line, October 23, 1891. The engines are Great Green Ones, 2-4-0s.
(Photo General State Archives, author's collection)

bridge that carried two single tracks and a roadway replaced the ancient wrought- and cast-iron swing bridge of the old Rhenish Railway across the IJssel River at Westervoort. The two low swing bridges across the North Sea Canal to Amsterdam at Velsen and De Hem (near Amsterdam) were replaced with enormous high swing bridges for double track, with electric motors that opened and closed the bridge in minutes. For a time these were the largest swing bridges in Europe. When the Merwede Canal was dug in the 1890s to better link Amsterdam with the Rhine River, two new railway bridges went up near Weesp (east of Amsterdam) and Utrecht. Steel was now the favored construction material, as its qualities had improved beyond all doubt.

ROLLING STOCK

Passenger carriages were still mostly four- or six-wheelers. For international traffic, six-wheelers were favored, although the French Nord Railway continued to use very long four-wheelers, which came as far as Amsterdam. Germany no longer allowed four-wheelers in fast international trains, so only six-wheelers ran there.

After 1888, heating with steam from the locomotive gradually replaced the smelly briquettes or soda acetate foot warmers. The first lavatories were added, in first and second class only, in 1890, in 1900 in third class. Gaslighting was universal until 1903, when the Holland Railway introduced electric lighting, first powered by batteries and later by axle-driven dynamos as well.

The addition in the late 1890s of corridor connections or corridor coaches, called D-coaches in Dutch (D for Doorgang), was a significant improvement. Almost all main line passenger stock was of the compartment type, without internal corridors. Only light railways used cars of other types. In most European countries, this so-called English compartment system was the rule; very few railways used the "American" system of cars with one big compartment and doors only at the ends. In 1893 and 1894, both the Holland and the State Railways put corridor coaches into service on four-wheel bogies, with bellows connections at the ends, converting the train into virtually one long unit. These coaches were preferred for international trains and regularly traveled as far as Italy, Romania, and Poland.

For domestic traffic, the State Railways built compartment coaches on bogies in 1893, followed by the Holland in 1901 and the Central in 1909. The six-wheeler, however, continued to dominate the Dutch railway scene for many years. All cars were still made of wood, with iron or steel underframes. Beijnes built almost all the Holland's cars, and other companies ordered from him as well, though competition from German and Belgian factories was severe.

All passenger stock wore the same rather somber paint: very dark green, with elaborate black, red, and white decorative lines in the upper classes, and much polished brass work. Only the State and Central Railways also had coaches with bodies of varnished teak. The Central distinguished itself by using big, sumptuous, and very comfortable stock on its regional lines around Utrecht. The company built the first of these, still of six-wheel configuration, in its own shops in 1898, and bogie coaches came shortly after. The public soon took a fancy to them; for many years the cars were a familiar sight at Utrecht. As was true for all light railways, they carried only second and third class.

Freight stock still had a Prussian look—wagons had to run on German and other European railways, so it made sense to adhere to the Prussian Normalien. To facilitate the use of each other's wagons and to settle intercompany debts for through operations, a Central Railway Clearing House and Wagon Checking Office was set up at Amsterdam in 1891, with the Holland, State, and Central Railways all participating. Every wagon got its own number, so after that year the companies could no longer duplicate each other's numbers, which triggered an extensive renumbering of freight stock.

German and Belgian works built a large share of the freight wagons, as Dutch import duties on finished products were low. Duties on half-products such as axles and wheels were much higher, however, so Dutch factories that had to import these items were at a disadvantage. After the turn of the century, these duties were lowered and finally completely abolished. Only then could the Dutch factories, notably Beijnes of Haarlem and Werkspoor of Amsterdam, take over most orders.

Like passenger stock, freight stock was wooden, on iron and later steel underframes. Shortly before 1914, the State Railways started experimenting with all-iron coal trucks, following the Prussian example. The Central in 1916 bought fifty all-iron coal wagons on bogies, which could carry thirty tons. Most Dutch freight stock was painted gray; insulated wagons that carried such commodities as butter, beer, meat, and fish were generally painted white. Owner's marks were clear and legible. The Holland Railway stenciled HOL-LAND in large capitals on the doors, while the State and Central Companies used NEDERLAND. The State added two red, white, and blue Dutch flags on each side, with the wagon number in one white field and the letters SS—for Staats Spoorwegen—in the other. The marks showed up at a distance as long as wagons stayed clean—usually not very long.

THE GLORY OF STEAM

In these years troubled by the reorganization of the railway network and by labor unrest, the most beautiful steam locomotives were built, in a mind-boggling array of types, sizes, and colors.

In 1890, the Holland Railway still had an almost uniform locomotive stock built by Borsig that looked very German indeed. The State Railways at the same time had an English—mostly Beyer, Peacock—look. The first big change came with the division of the Rhenish Railway's big new Rhine bogies between the State and Holland Companies. The engines were too long for either company's turntables, and since the State was not prepared to convert its many turntables, the company sold its Rhine bogies to the Holland, which had fewer turntables.

The Holland's locomotive superintendent after the departure of Middelberg to South Africa was J. A. Roessingh van Iterson, who came from the State Railways and was more used to British locomotives than to Middelberg's Ger-

FIGURE 64

Haagsma's masterpiece, the outside-framed 4-4-0 express engine, on the turntable of the 's-Hertogenbosch roundhouse, with two more in the background, circa 1925. (Collection NVBS)

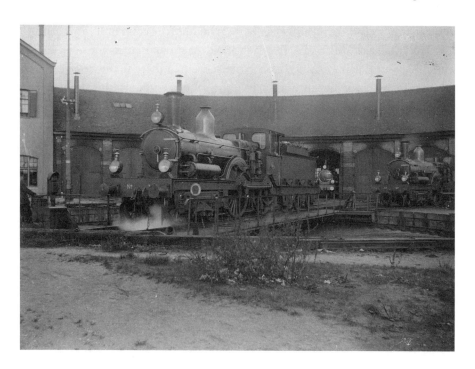

FIGURE 65

An *Atlantic* at the head of an international express, circa 1905. Haagsma's handsome engines proved disappointingly rough riders. (Collection Stichting Spoor-en Tramwegverzamelingen)

man fleet. From then on, Borsig delivered not a single locomotive to the Holland—all new engines were modifications of the successful Rhine bogie 4-4-0 express. Sharp, Stewart, later part of the North British Locomotive Company of Glasgow, supplied fifty more 4-4-os similar to the original Rhenish engines, and then Dutch industry took over.

Beginning in 1907 the Nederlandsche Fabriek van Werktuigen en Spoorwegmaterieel of Amsterdam built forty more of these 4-4-os, slightly bigger and heavier versions equipped with a superheater (later NS series 1900). The company was the successor to the old Paul van Vlissingen and Dudok van Heel Company and soon was generally known under its telegraph abbreviation, Werkspoor. From this successful type, tank engines were developed for regional railways and for suburban traffic. They came as 4-4-2 and 4-4-4 tank types, and 0-6-os for freight service, with boilers and other parts sized to those of the contemporary 4-4-os, which made maintenance cheaper and easier.

Most newer engines came equipped with the superheater invented by the German engineer Wilhelm Schmidt of Cassel. The last major invention to significantly improve the efficiency of the steam locomotive, the superheater meant impressively lower coal and water consumption, and railways all over the world adopted it. Schmidt's firm demanded high royalties, however, which prompted engineers to invent their own systems, but with little success. The Holland Railway stayed with Schmidt's equipment from the start.

At the prompting of Middelberg and other engineers, Amsterdam's Werkspoor factory (Werkspoor became the official name in 1929) began building steam locomotives again, for the first time in half a century. The Netherlands South African Railway Company needed hundreds of engines at short notice, and although German companies could and did build for Transvaal, Middelberg wanted a Dutch company to participate. The first engines from Werkspoor—fairly heavy narrow-gauge (1067 mm) 0-6-4 tanks—reached Pretoria just before the outbreak of the Boer War in 1899, but the British authorities canceled the remaining orders. The Holland Railway and later the State Railways and the railways in the Dutch East Indies stepped in to fill the gap. Werkspoor was to build scores of engines for the Indies, including enormous 2-12-2 tanks and 2-8-8-0 Mallets.

Stous Sloot was still in charge at the State Company in 1890, and construction of his well-tried and popular Big Greens continued until 1895. His successor, S. E. Haagsma, then designed an enlarged version, a 4-4-0 but still with double frames and inside cylinders, again an economical and popular engine (later NS series 1700). Beyer, Peacock supplied 125 of these units before 1905, when Werkspoor constructed another ten. Like their older 2-4-0 siblings, they were also used for freight trains, and the State Company consequently ordered no special freight engines.

Despite these new and more powerful engines, the heavy Flushing mail trains had to be double-headed with two of the 4-4-0s. Clearly, Haagsma needed something bigger, and he came up in 1900 with an Atlantic, with the newly popular 4-4-2 wheel arrangement (NS series 2000). These Dutch Atlantics, among the first of this type constructed in Europe, were unique in their arrangement, with inside cylinders and double frames. But what should have been Haagsma's masterpiece became a dismal failure. At the intended high speeds of 90 km/h and more, the Atlantics rode the track to pieces. All

FIGURE 66

No. 32, one of Beyer, Peacock's Blue Brabantians, North Brabant–German ten-wheelers, Utrecht, 1920. This low-angle shot accentuates the engine's clean lines and massive look. (Photo L. Derens, Collection NVBS)

FIGURE 67

No. 710, a State Railways 4-6-0, brings a train from Groningen into Utrecht Central, in the pooled Central—State Railways service, 1913. Designed jointly by Haagsma and Westendorp in 1910, the series was the State's response to the North Brabant–German's ten-wheeler. (Photo L. Derens, Collection NVBS)

the remedies tried were to no avail; they had to be taken off the mail trains and were then relegated to freight service.

After 1900, the express trains became heavier every year with the use of bogie stock. International trains, with sleeping and dining cars of the twelve-wheeler variety, were heavier still; the steam engines had trouble managing these loads and had to be used in pairs. It is remarkable that the poorest and smallest railway company, the North Brabant–German, was the first to introduce the 4-6-0 type, or ten-wheeler. Until then it had used its 2-4-0 engines, in pairs when necessary, to pull the Flushing mail trains, but in 1908 Beyer, Peacock delivered the first of a small series of impressive inside-cylinder 4-6-0 engines, very British looking, and finished in dark blue livery with black trim (later NS series 3500). These were successful in service too, and the State Company even borrowed one to test for its own trains.

The test results were so positive that Haagsma, with his assistant F. Westendorp, then designed his own 4-6-0, but with four cylinders instead of two and with greater power. Beyer, Peacock delivered the first of them (later NS series 3700) in 1910, and they soon proved their mettle in service. They ran as quietly as sewing machines, with no destructive hammer blows on the rails, thanks to their well-balanced four cylinders; despite their relatively high weight (seventy-two tons, engine only), they did not damage the track as had their Atlantic predecessors. Beyer, Peacock, along with Werkspoor and three German factories, built 120 of them by 1928.

Although after 1890 the State Railways had authority over the Central Railway—with ownership of the majority of its stock—Central's locomotive

FIGURE 68

Old and new locomotives
at the State Railways engine
sheds at Utrecht, circa 1914.
At left, one of the new 2-8-2
tanks intended for coal trains
in the South.
(Photo L. Derens,
Collection NVBS)

department proved remarkably independent. Its engines were mostly British-looking 4-4-0s for the faster trains, and 2-4-0, 4-4-0, and 4-4-4 tank engines, often rebuilt in its own Utrecht works, for the regional lines. When the Utrecht-Zwolle trains became too heavy for the available power, the Central's locomotive superintendent, J. W. Verloop, did not choose one of the two 4-6-0 types already on Dutch rails but ordered a completely different design from Maffei of Munich. The design was based on an existing Bavarian 4-6-0 compound engine, but Verloop opted for a simple four-cylinder style.

FIGURE 69

One of the first Zeppelins of
the Central Railway near its
Utrecht destination with a
train of twenty-three cars from
Groningen, 1910. The first car
is a typical Central fish-belly
bogie van, with the conductor
visible in his brake stand; the
second is a State Railways
bogie mail van. Six-wheelers
and bogie carriages make up
the rest of the train, which
has sections for Amsterdam,
The Hague, and Rotterdam.
(Photo L. Derens,
Collection NVBS)

Between 1910 and 1914, Maffei constructed eight of these seventy-ton engines (later NS series 3600), with a big streamlined cab and pointed smokebox door that soon earned them the nickname Zeppelins, after the contemporary airships of the German count of that name. They were finished in a handsome livery of golden ochre, with lots of copper and brass work. In service they played with their loads, and they have been timed with trains of twenty-three cars, 730 tons altogether. One negative element in the prototype was a kind of steam drier, designed by Verloop himself, in place of a regular superheater. Verloop hated to pay the high royalties to the Schmidt superheater works and thought that he could do better. Soon, however, all the engines were rebuilt with Schmidt equipment.

The Holland Railway lagged somewhat behind in the development of bigger engines. Its turntables, although adapted after 1890, had not been sufficiently lengthened to accommodate the long 4-6-0s, so W. Hupkes, successor to Roessingh van Iterson as locomotive superintendent, designed a heavy 4-4-0 (NS series 2100). Although less powerful than the State and Central machines, the engines were almost their equal in tractive effort and could run faster, so they were later much preferred for light, fast international trains. Their axle load was seventeen tons, high for the time, but owing to their inside cylinders, they ran quietly enough. Schwartzkopff of Berlin and Werkspoor of Amsterdam built thirty-five of them between 1913 and 1920.

—— EARLY ELECTRIFICATION ——————————

Early in the twentieth century, the United States and several European countries experimented with using electricity for traction instead of the relatively inefficient steam locomotive. The Prussians even ran a high-speed

FIGURE 70

An interurban of the Electric Railway Company on its way to Zandvoort beach, crossing the main line of the Holland Railway near Heemstede-Aerdenhout, south of Haarlem, circa 1910. This Amsterdam-Haarlem-Zandvoort line proved a strong competitor for the Holland Railway, which soon took it over. (Postcard, Collection NVBS)

FIGURE 71

The yards and shops of the South Holland Electric at Leidschendam, shortly after opening in 1908, with the generating station to the right. Extended and modernized, these are still among the main shops of Netherlands Railways. (Photo NS, Collection NVBS)

electric train on a line near Berlin that reached a record high of 210 km/h. In the United States, a new electric vehicle, the interurban tramway, gave steam railroads some keen competition over short distances. This fast and heavy electric streetcar became tremendously popular, and extensive interurban networks were created in some states, among them Ohio and Indiana. In the Netherlands, the Electrische Spoorweg Maatschappij (ESM, Electric Railway Company) put in a double-track line on the meter gauge between Amsterdam and Haarlem that along with its rolling stock and hardware looked very much like a U.S. interurban, probably because an American firm, White and Company, built it.

The ESM ran parallel to the Holland's Amsterdam-Haarlem main line, and the company recognized it as a strong competitor. Moreover, the Holland remembered the Holland Electric Railway, which had threatened to build a third Amsterdam-Haarlem line that was killed only in the nick of time by van Hasselt. So when in 1900 a new company was incorporated, van Hasselt paid attention. The company, the Zuid-Hollandsche Electrische Spoorwegmaatschappij (ZHESM, South Holland Electric Railway Company), planned to build an electric railway between Rotterdam (Hofplein), The Hague, and Scheveningen. Two engineers, N. J. Beversen and J. van Heurn, were the original incorporators, but they were supported discreetly by the State Railways, which saw a great opportunity to penetrate the heart of Holland Railway territory—a replay of the HESM affair. Van Hasselt moved quickly to buy a large block of ZHESM shares that had not yet been issued and so acquired a majority. Again, the State Railways had to withdraw and lick its wounds.

Originally the ZHESM line had been planned along the lines of an American interurban, with that country's common direct current of less than 1,000 volts and only moderate speeds. The Holland Railway, however, transformed it into a full-blown main line railway with speeds of 90 km/h, and electrified with alternating current of 10,000 volts, a system little tried at the time. The well-known German electrical engineering firm of Siemens and Halske signed

FIGURE 72

Interior of a South Holland Electric third-class car with seats of wooden slats, light and pleasant during the day and lit at night by electric lamps to a brightness unprecedented on the rails.
(Works photo J. J. Beijnes, Collection NVBS)

up to make the electrical equipment, including the power station at Leidschendam. Stork of Hengelo provided boilers and turbines for that station, and Beijnes of Haarlem built the rolling stock with a marked American exterior, with electric equipment provided by Siemens and Halske. Despite initial problems with the insulation of the overhead catenary, the line was a great success. Successful trial runs early in 1908 between Leidschendam and Pijnacker led to the line's opening in October.

The rails entered Rotterdam above street level, and at the request of the Rotterdam council a reinforced concrete viaduct of some two kilometers was erected for them to run on, the first large-scale use of the new construction material in the Netherlands. The pioneer here was A.C.C.G. van Hemert, whose company, incorporated for the purpose, built the viaduct. This company became the predecessor of one of today's largest Dutch contracting firms, the Hollandse Beton Groep (HBG).

SAFETY AND ACCIDENTS

The Holland and State Companies adopted the block system introduced by the Rhenish Railway, which allowed only one train at a time on any section of the line. Where the Rhenish, under its English signal superintendent Robert Wright, used English equipment, the Holland and State Railways chose German hard-

FIGURE 73
A State Railways Rotterdam-Gouda train at Nieuwerkerk, May 27, 1899. The drawbridge guard overslept and failed to close the bridge for the first train of the day. The engine jumped the gap, but the tender got stuck. No one was seriously hurt. Despite the large number of drawbridges in the Netherlands, this kind of accident was rare. (Collection NVBS)

ware from Siemens and Halske. A Dutch firm, the Alkmaarsche IJzergieterij (Alkmaar Iron Foundry), copied the Siemens and Halske equipment and produced it for the Holland and State on a large scale. It allowed interlocked points and signals, protected by the block system, to be set from one central point. Later the same firm produced much simplified equipment for lines that did not use the block system.

Distant signals, to indicate far in advance the position of the next home signal (which gives an absolute stop or proceed order), first tried in 1877, soon came into universal use. All signals were semaphores or revolving disks. At night a red light meant stop, green meant caution, and white was all clear. In 1934, yellow replaced green for caution, and green replaced white for all clear—the proliferation of white lights around stations and in built-up areas was causing confusion. (England had made the same change from white to green back in 1893.) Stations and signal boxes had communicated by telephone since 1885, and stations along the line later adopted that system.

These improved safety measures could not prevent every accident, however. Human errors, faulty brakes, failing equipment, and fog and bad weather could still mean disaster. Fog caused the worst railway accident of the nineteenth century. In November 1899, one State Railways train rammed another from behind near Capelle aan de IJssel, between Rotterdam and Gouda. The driver had not seen a signal at danger (a signal that shows a red light and/or a horizontal arm, both requiring an absolute stop) and failed to notice the red taillights of the other train, standing before a signal at danger, until it was too late. The last coach of the standing train was reduced to matchwood, and eight passengers were killed.

To prevent accidents of this kind, railways experimented with equipment that would warn the foot-plate crews of signals at danger. Between 1909 and 1915 the State Company on the Gouda–The Hague line tried out the system used by the English Great Western Railway, which gave an audible warning in the cab of the signal readings along the line. It worked quite well, as indeed it did in England, but because the necessary batteries were no longer available in the Netherlands during the First World War, it could not be maintained. Between Leiden and Woerden, the State Company tried out the system invented by a Dutch engineer, van Braam. It not only gave an audible warning in the cab when passing a signal at danger, but also operated the automatic air brake. This system too worked, but mechanical defects prevented its general introduction elsewhere.

The first years of the twentieth century saw a number of alarming derailments, some of which were never adequately explained. Bad or too light track, lack of maintenance, greater train weights, and higher speeds all combined to cause some of these derailments. Near Almelo, a Holland Railway train derailed at high speed in 1907, with two passengers killed. The derailment of a State Railways train in 1913 between Hooghalen and Beilen, south of Assen (Drente), killed five passengers, among them the son of a cabinet minister. The discussion about its possible causes resulted in a long and acrimonious correspondence between the company and the Railway Supervisory Board.

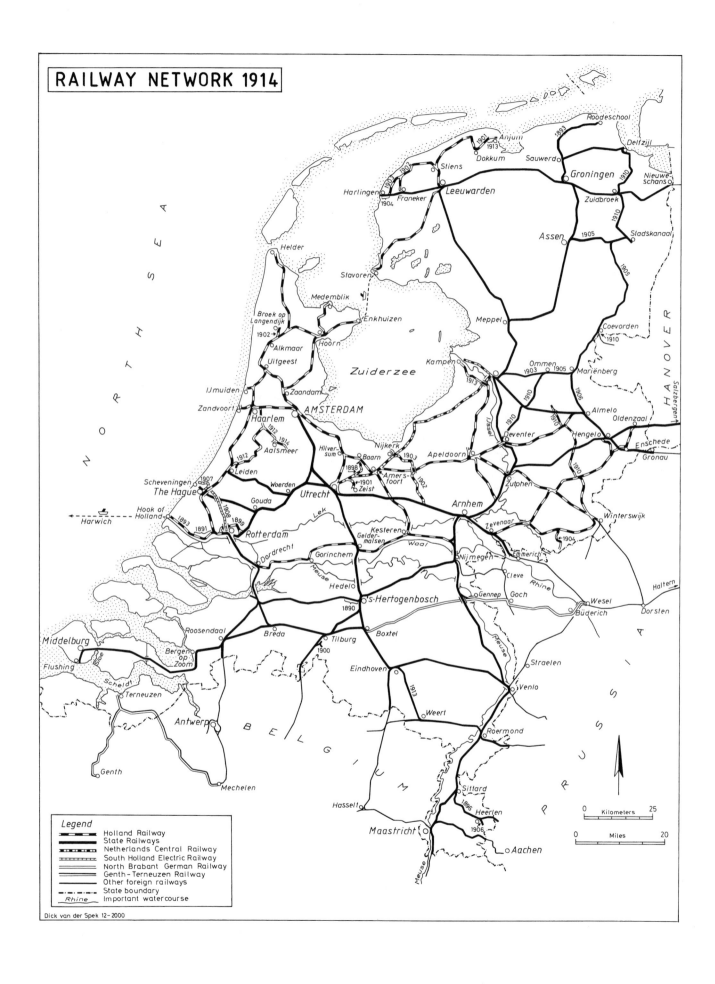

RAILWAY NETWORK 1914

Legend

- Holland Railway
- State Railways
- Netherlands Central Railway
- South Holland Electric Railway
- North Brabant German Railway
- Genth-Terneuzen Railway
- Other foreign railways
- State boundary
- *Rhine* — Important watercourse

Dick van der Spek 12-2000

NORTH SEA

Roodeschool
Delfzijl
Anjum
1901
1913
Dokkum
Sauwerd
Groningen
Nieuwe-schans
Stiens
Leeuwarden
Harlingen
Franeker
1904
Zuidbroek
1910
Stadskanaal
Assen
1905
1905
Coevorden
1910
Helder
Stavoren
Meppel
Ommen
1903
1905
Mariënberg
Medemblik
1910
1906
Almelo
Oldenzaal
Broek op Langendijk
Enkhuizen
Kampen
1913
1910
Alkmaar
Hoorn
Zuiderzee
1910
Deventer
Hengelo
Enschede
Uitgeest
Gronau
IJmuiden
Zaandam
Nijkerk
Apeldoorn
1910
Zandvoort
AMSTERDAM
Hilversum
Baarn
1903
Zutphen
Haarlem
1912
1914
Aalsmeer
1898
Amers-foort
1902
Winterswijk
1912
Zeist
1901
Leiden
Scheveningen
1907
Woerden
Utrecht
Arnhem
The Hague
Gouda
Zevenaar
1904
Hook of Holland
1908
1899
Kesteren
Emmerich
Harwich
1893
1891
Rotterdam
Gelder-malsen
Nijmegen
Cleve
Dordrecht
Gorinchem
Waal
Goch
Haltern
Hedel
's-Hertogenbosch
Gennep
Wesel
1890
Büderich
Dorsten
Middelburg
Breda
Tilburg
Boxtel
Flushing
Bergen op Zoom
1900
Eindhoven
Straelen
Scheldt
Weert
Venlo
1913
Terneuzen
Antwerp
Roermond
Genth
Sittard
Mechelen
1896
Heerlen
Hasselt
1906
Maastricht
Aachen

HANOVER

Salzbergen

BELGIUM

Lek
Meuse
IJssel
Rhine
Meuse

0 Kilometers 25
0 Miles 20

One result of these accidents was that the minister of the Waterstaat was authorized to institute an inquiry commission whenever necessary to probe the causes of a railway accident. He first used these powers in 1917, when a train derailed near Schalkwijk, south of Utrecht. Queen Wilhelmina was onboard, traveling in one of her own carriages, and her presence partly caused the great outcry raised. It was found that the excessive heat of that day had pushed the track out of gauge. Fortunately, only some passengers were lightly injured, and the queen was unharmed.

An accident near Weesp in 1918 caused multiple deaths. A train was just entering the bridge over the Merwede Canal when the high earthen dam leading up to the bridge suddenly collapsed. The engine was caught in the girders of the bridge, but the train fell down the high embankment, killing forty-one passengers and injuring as many more. This would remain the worst railway accident in the Netherlands for the next forty-five years. It was found that the embankment had become completely waterlogged by heavy rains, which made it unstable; the vibrations of the moving train caused it to collapse. Nobody was to blame here, as the embankment's dangerous condition was not visible from the outside. The Delft Polytechnic School afterward developed techniques to inspect soil and earthworks to prevent this kind of accident.

ROYALTY AND RAILWAYS

King William I, that enthusiastic promoter of railways, abdicated before he could travel on many trains. His son William II, while still crown prince, made a railway journey in September 1839, a week after the opening of the Amsterdam–Haarlem line. Special horse cars were ordered for the royal stables, and when the king traveled himself, he used the elegant director's carriage of the Holland Railway. In 1848 the first royal carriage was put into service, a sumptuous but uncomfortable looking six-wheeler, finished in dark blue livery with gilded silver ornaments.

King William II died in 1849, and his eldest son ascended the throne as William III. As the railway network of the Netherlands slowly grew, the king used the railway more and more. His favorite palace was Het Loo, near Apeldoorn, and trains were the chief mode of travel between Apeldoorn and The Hague. Both the Holland and the Rhenish Railways had special saloon carriages built for royal use, mostly six-wheelers, but four-wheelers for the royal suite. In 1873, King William III had his own saloon built by Gastell of Mainz, which he often used for his frequent foreign journeys. Although built according to the standards of the Verein, the saloon was considered too wide for the narrow tunnels of the French Est Company, so on his many trips to the south of Switzerland, the king had to detour through Germany instead of taking the more direct route through Alsace-Lorraine. Another saloon ordered by the king had an open balcony at one end, from which he could greet his assembled subjects.

King William III died in 1890. His only daughter, Wilhelmina, born in 1880, succeeded to the throne under the regency of her mother, Queen Emma,

FIGURE 74

The old royal train at Goes, on the Flushing line, on a rainy August 25, 1894. *At right,* young Queen Wilhelmina, then almost fourteen years old, and her mother, Queen-Regent Emma, stand on a carriage platform. Royal trains were always double-headed.
(Photo S. R. Elzinga, Royal Archives, The Hague)

until 1898. By then the old royal saloons and carriages, worn and uncomfortable, needed replacements. The Holland and State Railways put aside their ongoing war and together presented the young queen with a splendid royal train of four bogie carriages, complete with all modern amenities and comforts. Beijnes built the four cars, which were delivered in 1903. Three years later, a fifth car was added to provide more room for servants on longer journeys. Queen Mother Emma had a carriage of her own, presented by the Central Railway in 1900, which looked like the Central's light railway stock with its characteristic varnished teak exterior; the interior was much more elegant, of course. The Queen Mother used it regularly on her travels to her relatives in Waldeck-Pyrmont.

All coaches of the royal train were heavily damaged or destroyed during the Second World War. After 1945, the Netherlands Railways remodeled some existing saloons and first-class coaches into a new royal train, with a generator car built from a German Reichsbahn bogie van found in the country after the war. Queen Juliana and her husband, Prince Bernhard, used this train frequently for official visits to foreign countries. Since 1983, Queen Beatrix has had one modern saloon coach, which she uses only occasionally.

War and the Move to Public Ownership

GOVERNMENT AND RAILWAYS

The outbreak of war in 1914 ended forever the enmity between the Holland and the State Companies. On July 31, 1914, the government requisitioned all railways in the country, and the next day they began carrying military traffic. Plans for this emergency had been made long before, when the international horizon darkened. In three days, without serious delays or mishaps, the railways transported the Dutch field army to the southern and eastern frontiers— 170,000 men, 6,600 horses, hundreds of light and heavy guns, ammunition, vehicles of all kinds, and whatever else the army needed.

Although civilian traffic was resumed shortly after, not until May 1916 would trains run on their prewar schedules. Staff problems were severe, as many railway men had been called to arms.

In the First World War the Netherlands managed to avoid armed conflict and remained strictly neutral, but the conflict soon made itself felt. The German armies invading Belgium passed just outside the Dutch borders south of Maastricht. The closing of all borders disrupted international traffic completely; it was later resumed on a limited scale as military operations permitted. Belgian refugees streamed into the country by the hundred thousands to escape the horrors of war; they had to be transported, housed, and fed. Foreign combatants who crossed the border accidentally or on purpose to escape enemy prison camps had to be interned and transported to inland camps.

For all this extra traffic, the railways presented a hefty bill to the government—too hefty, according to government officials, and it would take about a year for the parties to reach agreement. As long as the railways remained requisitioned by the government, the Holland and the State Companies obtained a guaranteed dividend of 4 percent, and the Central one of 2.19 percent; the North Brabant–German, which had never paid any dividends, was guaranteed its fixed costs. This arrangement, meant to be temporary, would remain in force until January 1, 1920.

A railway's most pressing problem was the shortage of coal. Coal for the steam locomotives was chiefly imported from Germany, with Belgium and England providing a smaller share. The production of the domestic mines in Limburg was still small. Although the mines there were fully operative during the war, their coal was considered less suitable for steam locomotives. Germany continued to export coal, but in smaller quantities and at much higher prices. Moreover, the German government demanded all sorts of equivalents in the form of deliveries of foodstuffs, which in turn caused problems with England and the other Allies. And last, German coal for the Netherlands could be transported only in Dutch coal trucks, as the Germans needed all their wagons for their own military and civilian traffic. A severe shortage of freight trucks was the result, necessitating more government regulations, which provided that henceforth some freight could be carried only by boat.

Rationing of ever more products in short supply caused other problems, and some materials, such as rails, spare parts for locomotives, lubricating oil, and wheels and axles for cars, could be bought from the usual suppliers in Germany, England, or Belgium at greatly inflated prices—or not at all. It was clear that the former competitive conditions no longer held.

FIGURE 75

During the mobilization of the Dutch army in August 1914, many locomotives were brought into safety behind the so-called Holland Waterlinie, the flooded defense line east of Utrecht. These twelve State Railways machines stand on the connecting line near Breukelen, west of Utrecht, among them a new ten-wheeler.
(Photo L. Derens, author's collection)

COOPERATION

FIGURE 76

At the end of the first World War, these automobiles brought the German emperor William II, an exile, and his party to the platform of the border station at Eijsden, in the far south of Limburg, where William waited for permission to enter the Netherlands on November 10, 1918. On the far track is the imperial train in camouflage colors that arrived safely the next day; William had not used it because of rumors of sabotage by Belgian railway workers.
(Collection NVBS)

Not the government, but the Holland and State Companies themselves toward the end of 1916 took the initiative to move toward cooperation. They came forward with a plan to integrate the two railways under one central management. The legal entities—the limited companies as incorporated—were to remain separate, each with its own share capital and bonded debt. All rolling stock, stores, staff and employees, services, and so on were to be integrated completely. They would divide profits and losses according to the share capital of each. It was not a complete merger, but outwardly it looked like one. The move surprised the government and Parliament, who after some objection were forced by the exceptional circumstances to agree.

On November 25, 1916, the agreements were signed, and they came into force January 1, 1917. The new combination called itself Nederlandsche Spoorwegen (NS, Netherlands Railways). A directorate of three managed the new company: J. A. Kretschmar van Veen of the State Railways, and W. F. van der Wijck and J. A. Kalff, both of the Holland. Seniority here favored the Holland Railway, although the State Company was the larger of the two.

The legal corporate seat of NS became Utrecht, where G. W. van Heukelom's huge office building was opened in 1920. The Holland Railway left its old headquarters in Amsterdam, opposite the Central Station, and moved to Utrecht.

With the impending union of the big two, something had to be done about the Central Railway. Even with more than 50 percent of its shares in the hands of the State Company, the Central had maintained its own corporate existence, with its own shareholders, staff, and rolling stock. On January 1, 1917, the day the Holland and State Companies came together, the Central and State Companies signed a document along the same lines.

Two years later, on May 1, 1919, all operations and staff of the Central were officially transferred to the State Company, and the Central continued to exist on paper only. This ambivalent situation ended only on January 1, 1934, when the government bought the Central's outstanding stock and real estate, including all railway lines. The claim of the city of Kampen, dating back to the early years of the line, that all trains must run through it was bought off. The corporate existence of the Central Railway was over.

The North Brabant–German Railway had always been the black sheep of the Amsterdam Stock Exchange. Its shares had never paid a dividend and were accordingly quoted at minimum prices there. The railway had paid the interest on its bonded debt irregularly and converted the rest into new deferred debts. Shortly before 1914, revenues from the company's international long-distance traffic were rising at last, but the operating ratio had climbed too, partly because of the construction of double track. In 1913, the railway sought a rapprochement with its arch enemy, the State Company. The resulting working agreement would take effect on January 1, 1914: The North Brabant–German remained an independent company and continued to work its lines, but the State Company held the purse strings.

The outbreak of war in 1914 abruptly ended all rosy visions of growing traffic and revenues. Flushing-Berlin through traffic was terminated at once, and local traffic in the sparsely populated Brabant Peel region had never amounted to anything. In 1919, the company reached a new agreement with the State Railways: All possessions of the North Brabant–German went to the State Company, which would run all trains. The Flushing mail, the flagship of the old company, never returned to this route.

Irate bondholders who had not received interest payments over the past thirty-five years petitioned for bankruptcy proceedings against the North Brabant. The Netherlands government then bought the Dutch section of the line, and the new government of the Weimar Republic bought the German section. From the proceeds of this sale, holders of first-mortgage bonds obtained 34 percent of the nominal value of their bonds in cash, while second-mortgage bond holders received 12.5 percent. In 1925, the North Brabant–German Railway could finally be liquidated and laid to rest.

MORE GOVERNMENT INFLUENCE

When the requisitioning of the railways by the government ended on January 1, 1920, new arrangements between public and private interests had to be worked out. After lengthy negotiations, an agreement was reached, and Parliament put its seal upon it in 1921. The most important provisions were:

1. A new emission of shares of both Holland and State Companies would give the government a clear stock majority of both companies. The government would appoint the majority of directors and board members.
2. The right accorded to the Holland and State Companies to unilaterally cancel the 1890 agreements was abolished.
3. The remaining private shareholders were guaranteed dividends of 5 percent annually.
4. The two remaining companies would work all new railways to be constructed by the government.

This agreement instituted a new mixed form of railway ownership and working—public working of the railways under the name of a limited company, as ex-minister C. Lely aptly defined it.

Meanwhile, revenues lagged far behind operating expenses, and the government had to make good the losses. Not until 1924 was the first small profit generated; financial results then got better and better for some time. Passenger traffic and coal traffic from Germany and from the State mines in Limburg

FIGURE 77
A peaceful scene at Enkhuizen in the 1920s. The train from Amsterdam has just arrived behind a 4-6-4 tank engine of the former State Railways, and passengers are walking to the steamer waiting to take them to the other shore of the Zuiderzee at Stavoren. (Photo NS, Collection NVBS)

both grew spectacularly. After the short-lived but serious recession of 1921, the economy firmed up again, and traffic grew accordingly.

Apart from the economic upswing, the financial improvements resulted from internal measures of Netherlands Railways itself. A wage reduction of 8.5 percent in 1923, disguised as an improved pension plan, brought some relief, and a true wage cut of 10 percent in 1924 did even more to improve the results of the company. Trade unions had great difficulty swallowing these measures, of course, but saw their necessity. Simplifying a number of departments, integrating formerly separate organizations, and mechanizing office work also improved the financial situation. Level crossings on less busy roads were no longer guarded, which meant a considerable saving in wages.

DEFINITIVE AGREEMENT WITH THE GOVERNMENT

During these years of reorganization, the pressing problem of the lack of depreciation and reservations had not been touched upon at all. A committee set up for the purpose in 1927 found an astounding shortage in this field, 229 million guilders, and although current finances looked good, there was no reserve for hard times. The government accepted the findings of the committee and offered to pay 5.5 million guilders annually into the reserve funds, not enough but something. Everyone assumed that the present wave of prosperity would continue, making the railways less dependent on outright government subsidies, an assumption that ended with the worldwide crisis of 1929.

Public-private railway ownership had some drawbacks. The government had to make good all deficits, yet it was not free to run the railways as it wanted. A better arrangement between the government and private shareholders was needed. After 1929, however, the government had more pressing problems, such as the fast-growing unemployment, and railway management remained at a stalemate. In 1931 some relief came from reducing the dividend guarantee to private shareholders from 5 to 4 percent, with the option to exchange the shares for bonds, also bearing 4 percent, plus a small bonus. More than forty million guilders' worth of shares was exchanged this way.

In 1936 a new law came before Parliament to settle the railway problem once and for all; it passed on May 26, 1937, without much opposition. A new limited company was incorporated, NV Nederlandsche Spoorwegen (NS, Netherlands Railways Ltd.); both Holland and State Railway Companies were dissolved; the total share capital of the new NS was reduced to ten million guilders, with all shares but two in the hands of the goverment; the government took over part of the debts of the companies, 290 million guilders, and converted them into Netherlands state bonds bearing 3 percent; payment of interest on these bonds was to be made by the new NS company. On January 1, 1938, the Nederlandsche Spoorwegen started with a clean slate.

This gradual move toward more influence by the government on vital branches of industry was in line with the general political-economic thinking of the day. The liberal thinking of the nineteenth century had left virtually all economic activity in the hands of private parties. The less the government did in these fields, the better. Measures taken by successive governments after 1900 to improve the working and living circumstances of workers have been noted in a previous chapter. The liberal parties in Parliament lost power and frequently quarreled among themselves, and the later mixed cabinets of Christian democrats and liberals took a different line on government influence. The world crisis of 1929 and its aftermath, which hit the country hard, also contributed to this gradual change of economic thinking in government circles.

The government mines, which thrived during the war, were government owned out of necessity at first but were later considered a public good and remained in public hands. The government also sponsored a complex of blast furnaces and iron and steel foundries erected near the mouth of the North Sea Canal at IJmuiden shortly after the war to make the Netherlands more self-sufficient. Government takeovers of gas, water, and electric companies had begun in the later nineteenth century, so that virtually all power stations and gas companies at the end of the First World War were either municipally or provincially owned. In this process of (semi-) nationalizing public utilities and vital industries, the new organization of the railway system had been a logical step.

THE 1917 ORGANIZATION AT WORK

The new company had to be thoroughly reorganized, of course. Two widely different company cultures had somehow to be married into one new organization, a prospect that found little support among older workers and staff. Generally, seniority decided who was appointed to executive positions. I. Franco, locomotive superintendent of the State Company, became the new man in this position with NS, while his younger colleague from the Holland Railway, W. Hupkes, was made responsible for the reorganization and integration of the several railway works and repair shops in the country.

After Franco left the service in 1928, Hupkes succeeded him as chief but left the construction of new steam locomotives in the hands of his assistant P. Labrijn, a former State Railways man. Labrijn's early training and influence gave a distinctive State Railways look to all new locomotives built for Netherlands Railways.

The Permanent Way Department was split in two: New construction was headed by G. W. van Heukelom of the State Company, and operations and maintenance had H. P. Maas Geesteranus, a Holland company man, as its chief, assisted by E.C.W. van Dijk of the Central. Signaling fell under operations and maintenance, so the new signaling system became strongly Holland Railway in outlook, to the great disappointment of L.H.N. Dufour, former chief of signaling of the State Railways. Dufour considered his own system the best and had said so many times in books and articles in the technical press. In all departments and branches, the feeling of competition was more or less the same, which led to a lot of grumbling and complaining. It would be several years before the new uniform system worked smoothly. The depressed

FIGURE 78
On the footplate somewhere in the country. On double track, trains keep to the right with the signals on the right-hand side as well. (Photo NS, Collection NVBS)

economic situation of the early years after the war was to pose a severe test for the viability of the new company.

A positive point was the uniform numbering of all rolling stock, begun in 1921 with the steam locomotives, more than half of which came from the State Railways. Passenger cars were renumbered in the same year. Of the total of 3,360 cars, the State Company brought in 1,614, the Holland 1,581, the Central 124, and the North Brabant–German 41. Of the total stock, four-wheelers, six-wheelers, and bogie stock each comprised one-third. In 1924, the freight stock was finally renumbered. Of some 30,000 cars, about two-thirds came from the State Railways, reflecting the role freight traffic had played in the company. Of all these cars, mostly four-wheeled, only about 20 percent had a continuous brake that would make them suitable for passenger trains. Others with a continuous airline but no brake of their own could be run in slower passenger trains. Most freight trucks, however, had no brake at all.

THE NEW ORGANIZATION IN PRACTICE

Despite the 1917 agreements, the financial situation of the railways in the Netherlands had grown worse during the war. Coal shortages and rising prices for everything including food that in turn led to higher wages and special bonuses for the staff drove up working expenses to unprecedented levels.

The operating ratio, already high at 70 in 1913, rose to over 92 in 1917, and to an unheard of high of 99.40 in 1921. Some unremunerative train services were abolished, rates were raised, and some classes of freight were no longer carried, all to no avail.

The armistice of 1918 brought no immediate relief. The political chaos in Germany prevented a resumption of the coal traffic at prewar levels, and international traffic, both passenger and freight, came back much more slowly than expected. On top of these ills came the integration of all locomotive services of the Holland and State Companies, which happened much too fast. State Railways engines got Holland crews who had no experience with them, and vice versa. Many of the steam locomotives were sensitive beasts, needing a lot of attention and skillful handling to work properly. Repair shops and sheds were allocated locomotives for which no spare parts or tools were available.

On State Company engines, the driver had always stood on the left side of the foot plate, because on State lines, even with right-hand running on double track, the signals stood on the left side of the rails. Dufour had always maintained that this improved the visibility of the signals in bad weather. On the Holland, however, signals had always been on the right-hand side of the tracks, with the driver on the right side of the cab. Drivers were now ordered to run engines they did not know, sometimes on lines they had never traveled before, with signals in unexpected places, seriously jeopardizing safety.

FIGURE 79

The freight shed at Utrecht in the late 1920s, with horse drays and primitive motor trucks both in evidence. (Photo NS, Collection NVBS)

Supplies of coal were too small or of inferior quality, making it difficult to fire engines properly. Consequently, locomotives went dead on the road with their trains, which could disrupt traffic for hours. The situation grew worse and worse, until the government was urged to set up a special commission of inquiry to look into the causes. When this commission reported in 1921, however, the outlook was much brighter, as the railways themselves had managed to put their house in order.

The inquiry made it abundantly clear that in the past not nearly enough had been invested in improving infrastructure. Stations were too small, yards too cramped, shunting facilities too few, and works and repair shops ill-equipped and too sparse. Staff was not numerous enough for the services demanded, and more double track should have been laid. These conditions went back to the days immediately after 1890, when ferocious competition had forced the companies to maintain money-losing train services. They simply had not enough money left to put aside for future improvements. The negotiations between the government and railways after 1917 had attended to this lack of reserves and to depreciation, and it was indeed remedied to some degree in 1937, as has been noted.

An incident in 1926 brought this lack of maintenance to the fore in a most horrible way. An express hauled by a steam locomotive derailed at speed near De Vink (Leiden). Two passengers—a well-known theatrical couple—and two railway men were killed, and a number of others injured. An official commission of inquiry concluded that the track, which had been too hastily renewed after the recent electrification of the line, had not yet settled enough to accommodate heavy, fast trains. As soon as the track had been relaid, it had been unwisely assumed that it was fit for all traffic at all speeds.

Meeting Competition from the Road

NEW MODES OF TRANSPORTATION

The Netherlands waterways had traditionally posed stiff competition to the railways in terms carrying freight, especially bulk goods such as ores, coal, stone, and—later—oil. A number of factors have given the waterways an added edge: the ongoing straightening and deepening of the major rivers; the opening of the Merwede Canal in the 1890s from Amsterdam to the Rhine; and the faster steamboats, and steam tugs hauling long rakes of barges, that replaced sailing ships.

Toward the end of the century, an ever larger share of the international freight traffic from the ports of Amsterdam and Rotterdam inland went by water, although in absolute figures the freight tonnage of the railways was still growing. In 1920, for instance, domestic and international freight traffic on the water was about double that carried by rail, 33.7 million tons against 16.7 million. Ten years later, the tonnage on the railways had increased by almost half, to 22 million tons, but the volume carried by water had nearly tripled, to 94 million tons. By 1938 the gap was still greater, 91.5 to 14.6 million tons.

When the Juliana Canal in Limburg and the Twente Canal opened in the late 1920s and early 1930s, the railways suffered, for the lucrative coal traffic from the Limburg mines to Holland and the Twente industrial area shifted from rail to water. Here is clear proof of a muddled government transportation

FIGURE 80

Loading cherries at Tiel, the center of the fruit-growing region of the Betuwe, in the early 1930s.
(Photo NS, Collection NVBS)

FIGURE 81

State Mine Maurits, 1952. Although the canals made heavy inroads into the coal traffic by rail, the mines in Limburg remained important customers for NS into the 1950s.
(Photo NS, Collection NVBS)

policy. The government built the canals with tax money, and they could be used free of charge; the resulting loss to the railways had to be made good by that same government. The ratio of revenue from passenger and freight traffic was still about 50:50 in 1928, but by 1938 the ratio reached 65:35, a trend that continued until receipts from passenger traffic made up more than 90 percent of all revenues, almost a return to the early days of the Holland Railway.

If the water was a perennial competitor to be reckoned with in the freight sector, a new mode of transportation challenged the monopoly of the railway

FIGURE 82

Cattle continued to travel by rail in the interbellum, so Utrecht's cattle dock was a busy place in 1935. (Photo NS, Collection NVBS)

for its passengers: the road. Bicycles presented the first serious road competition: Their numbers grew from some thousands before 1914, mostly used for sports, to some four million shortly before 1940, used chiefly for short-distance transportation and commuting. Local tramways were hardest hit, but the railways felt the impact too in suburban traffic.

The automobile, until 1914 a rich man's toy, still presented no threat in 1920, but by 1930, with 68,000 automobiles and 44,000 motor buses and trucks on the roads, the situation had changed fundamentally. Freight carried by road amounted to 33 million tons in 1930, and eight years later 63 million tons, far outstripping the rails. While no dependable figures exist for bus passengers, the bus, not bound to fixed routes or schedules, took a large number of customers from the rails, especially for short and middle distances. Who would not prefer a comfortable bus with soft suspension and padded seats that picked you up or put you down just around the corner, over a long walk or bike ride to a railway station and an old-fashioned smoky steam train with hard wooden seats, six in a row in third class? The automobile, rubber, and gasoline lobbies never tired of expounding on the advantages of their products.

NETHERLAND RAILWAYS' REACTION

The railways first reacted to road travel as a competitor with disbelief. How could the railways, with a near monopoly for a century, be made superfluous overnight by a passing fad? But soon it dawned upon the railway leaders that

FIGURE 83

The Rotterdam Lloyd Rapide
boarding passengers at
Rotterdam (Delftsche Poort),
1929, headed by a fast 4-4-0
of Holland Railway origins.
The two major shipping lines
to the Dutch East Indies,
the Netherland Line from
Amsterdam and the Rotterdam
Lloyd, shortened the long
journey by operating fast
connecting trains to Marseilles
or Genoa, thereby avoiding
the sea voyage around
Gibraltar and through the
stormy Bay of Biscay.
(Photo J. Quanjer,
Collection NVBS)

something had to be done, and quickly. The trade journal *Spoor- en Tramwegen*
(Rail- and Tramways) founded in 1928 was a first step toward closer cooperation between tramway and railway companies, who just over a decade ago
had been sworn enemies. The new journal became the voice of the rail lobby
and the technical journal for all concerned, under the vigorous and competent
direction of its editor-in-chief, S. A. Reitsma, whose previous journalistic and
railway experience came in the propaganda department of the State Railways
on the island of Java, in the Dutch East Indies.

The journal was only the first salvo in the rails' war against the road. It
seemed natural enough for the railway executives to turn to the government
for support. The government made good the losses incurred by the railways,
and some regulation of the motor bus, then still unhindered by government
measures, might help. In 1926, the government called for a system of licenses
for any bus running to a published schedule along an established, fixed route.
The provincial authorities were to issue these licenses, which proved to be a
flaw in the new regulation, as some provinces were most liberal, while others
adhered to stricter standards. For more than a decade these differences
remained, until in 1937 the national government began issuing the licenses
itself. Beyond this somewhat half-hearted regulation, the mostly Christian
Democratic-Liberal cabinets of the day did not want to go. There was no
money to make fundamental changes, and politicians were preoccupied with
combating the effects of the worldwide economic crisis, which hit the Netherlands hard after 1930. (The strict adherence to the gold standard caused more

stagnation than was necessary, but the gold standard had become almost an article of faith and not until 1937 did the nation finally abandon it, the last Western European country to do so. Although the shift gave the economy a boost, it did not materially reduce unemployment.)

With no coherent national transportation policy, the government's measures were mostly stopgaps. The Verkeersfonds (Traffic Fund) established in 1934 did not alter the distorted relations between the several modes of transportation. Although in 1937 all buses, including those for pleasure outings, along with taxis and rental cars, were required to take out licenses, "wild" buses continued to defy the law. These unlicensed buses followed their more or less established routes and schedules until 1939, when the authorities cracked down on them after many complaints from the railways and the regular motor bus companies. A 1933 proposal to license trucks did not get the necessary support in Parliament and was dropped.

Apart from prodding an unwilling government into action, another way to fight the competition was to buy it up. This idea was not new, as the railways, especially the Holland, had since the 1880s practiced an intensive policy of buying competing tramways and regional railways. In North and South Holland most regional tramways had been absorbed by the Holland Company, which in 1919 had taken over the best of them all, the electric interurban ESM, with its double-track Amsterdam-Haarlem-Zandvoort main line. All these tramways were grouped together in the Noord-Zuid-Hollandsche Tramweg Maatschappij (NZH, North and South Holland Tramway Company), which operated an extensive network of tram and bus services from The Hague in the South to Alkmaar in the North, including the local services in the cities of Leiden and Haarlem. Elsewhere, south of The Hague, the Holland held a stock majority in the Westlandsche Stoomtram Maatschappij (WSM, Westland Steam Tramway Company), which operated a network of standard-gauge tramways in that area. In contrast to the NZH, passenger traffic was never very important in this region of glass greenhouses, whose vegetables and fruit made for busy rail traffic—chiefly for export to Germany—in main line freight trucks. This traffic was to continue well into the 1960s, thanks to the fortunate choice of the standard gauge back in the 1880s.

The Central Railway had acquired—at the request of its parent company, the State Railways—a majority of the stock of the Nederlandsche Tramweg Maatschappij (NTM, Netherlands Tramway Company) with its extensive network of tramways in the northern provinces. Here too, standard-gauge tracks carried freight traffic well into the 1960s, with the last remnant closed only in the 1980s. All these tramways passed into the possession of the Netherlands Railways in 1938.

Beyond the mergers in the regional tramway market in the 1920s, large bus companies bought up or subsumed a number of small bus operations. Some of these never operated more than one line, not financially viable in the long run. The government looked favorably upon this concentration, as it made the crazy patchwork of services and licenses a bit easier to survey. Netherlands Railways also remained active in this field, as for instance when

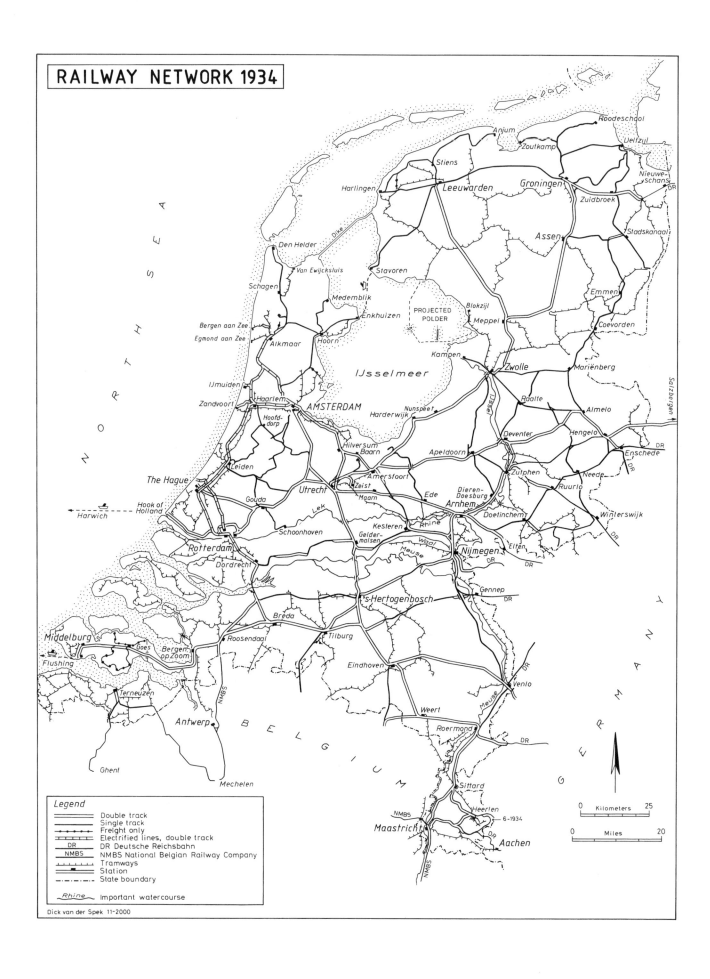

RAILWAY NETWORK 1934

North Sea

Roodeschool
Anjum
Zoutkamp
Ueltzijl
Stiens
Harlingen
Leeuwarden
Groningen
Nieuwe-schans
Zuidbroek
Assen
Stadskanaal
Den Helder
Van Ewijcksluis
Stavoren
Emmen
Schagen
Medemblik
Blokzijl
Coevorden
Enkhuizen
PROJECTED POLDER
Meppel
Bergen aan Zee
Hoorn
Kampen
Egmond aan Zee
Alkmaar
Zwolle
Mariënberg
IJsselmeer
IJmuiden
Raalte
Almelo
Haarlem
Harderwijk
Nunspeet
Zandvoort
Hoofd-dorp
Hilversum
Deventer
Hengelo
Leiden
Baarn
Apeldoorn
Enschede
The Hague
Amersfoort
Zutphen
Neede
Utrecht
Zeist
Ede
Dieren-Doesburg
Ruurlo
Gouda
Maarn
Arnhem
Hook of Holland
Lek
Doetinchem
Winterswijk
Harwich
Schoonhoven
Kesteren
Rhine
Geldermalsen
Waal
Elten
Rotterdam
Meuse
Nijmegen
Dordrecht
Gennep
's-Hertogenbosch
Middelburg
Breda
Goes
Bergen op Zoom
Roosendaal
Tilburg
Flushing
Eindhoven
Venlo
Terneuzen
Weert
Antwerp
Roermond
BELGIUM
Meuse
GERMANY
Ghent
Sittard
Mechelen
Heerlen
6-1934
NMBS
Maastricht
Aachen

Salzbergen
DR

Legend
	Double track
	Single track
	Freight only
	Electrified lines, double track
DR	DR Deutsche Reichsbahn
NMBS	NMBS National Belgian Railway Company
	Tramways
	Station
	State boundary
Rhine	Important watercourse

0 Kilometers 25

0 Miles 20

Dick van der Spek 11-2000

it acquired the Gooische Stoomtram, which had given up most of its tramway lines and now operated a network of bus lines in the suburbs east of Amsterdam. During World War II, this process of merger and acquisition went on, until around 1980 very few smaller companies remained outside the holdings of Netherlands Railways.

ATO AND VAN GEND EN LOOS

To battle the enemy with its own weapons, Netherlands Railways in 1927 founded its own road transportation company, the ATO, Algemeene Transport Onderneming (General Transportation Company). Intended to be both a passenger and freight carrier, the ATO arrived on the scene too late to obtain the licenses required for the better motor bus lines, already scooped up by others, and had to content itself with a few less remunerative lines in outlying districts. The ATO was much more successful in the freight business, especially after taking over the drayage services at railway stations in 1928. These services, involving some five hundred horse drays and motor trucks, had been provided until then by the old firm of Van Gend and Loos, which had operated stagecoach and horse dray services all over the country since the 1820s. When Netherlands Railways refused to renew its contracts with Van Gend and Loos for the drayage business, the owners of the venerable firm sold out to the railway company.

ATO and Van Gend and Loos were combined, and in the 1930s the door-to-door service of Netherlands Railways and ATO–Van Gend and Loos

FIGURE 84
A five-ton closed container being transferred from a railway truck to a highway trailer constructed by the DAF factory of Eindhoven, circa 1935.
(Photo NS, Collection NVBS)

became a very successful side of the business. The service could deliver not only a closed container of dry goods to one's front door, but also a load of coal in an open container straight from the mines in Limburg.

Netherlands Railways also negotiated contracts with some of the still independent tramway companies, such as the Geldersche Tramwegen (GTW, Guelders Tramway Company). This company was an amalgamation of the many independent steam tramways in Gelderland province, all operating on the 750 mm gauge. Despite this very narrow gauge, the GTW had modernized its services with sleek and relatively fast motor trams, and had also opened its own motor bus lines. Netherlands Railways contracted with GTW to carry less-than-carload general merchandise and parcels from the railway stations into the wilds of Gelderland, where the steam tram or motor bus reached the smallest townships and communities, a through service that benefited the public and both contracting parties.

—— NETHERLANDS RAILWAYS' INTERNAL CHANGES ——

Aside from asking the government to make good the deficits, Netherlands Railways itself worked at reducing its losses, first by cutting back on operating expenses. The company closed unremunerative stops, downgraded stations to unstaffed stops, removed guards from level crossings in minor roads, and stepped up the mechanization of its offices and workshops begun in the early 1920s. All these measures reduced the numbers of railway staff. Between 1918 and 1921, the total staff of Netherlands Railways had grown from 39,000 to 51,000, chiefly as the result of problems caused by the rash implementation of the 1917 agreements. Now the process was reversed. In 1936 the total number of staff was down to 32,000, and in 1939 to 29,000. Wages were cut some 30 percent in the 1930s, in line with general practices at the time everywhere in the country.

Another way to cut operating expenses was to close branch lines where passenger traffic had dropped to unprecedented lows, including a number of the lines opened after 1918. Most of these later lines were planned before 1914 in a transportation world very different from that of the postwar years, and unwisely the government had pushed through their construction to open up the countryside. (Apparently no one in a responsible position doubted the wisdom of this construction or foresaw that these lines would never pay their way. Road construction or improvement would have been a better and cheaper alternative in most cases.) In the far North, a Winsum–Zoutkamp line had been opened in 1922, followed by Stadskanaal–Ter Apel–Rijksgrens two years later, and Groningen–Slochteren–Delfzijl in 1929. In Limburg in the South the beautiful but clearly superfluous Schaesberg–Simpelveld—aptly nicknamed the Million Guilder Line—was opened as late as 1934, and in Zeeland, on the island of South Beveland, a tramway built to main line standards was opened in 1927. Last but not least, certainly not in regard to cost, was Gouda–Alphen aan de Rijn, opened in 1934. Here the old joke about railway building in the Netherlands proved true: It takes five engineers to build a rail-

FIGURE 85
A signalman pulling his levers.
Despite all the labor-saving
machinery introduced, the
railway remained a labor-
intensive operation.
(Photo NS, Collection NVBS)

way in Holland, four to buy sand as cheaply as possible, and the fifth to build
the line. Gouda–Alphen ran through one of the lowest parts of South Holland,
mostly soggy marshes or drained lakes, requiring immense quantities of sand
to make a stable roadbed. Ironically, this line is the only one of these post-1918
railways that still exists, now electrified, although still single track. All the
others have been closed down, most before 1940 and some after barely a
decade of troubled existence, wiping out capital investments in a way not
practiced by other European countries until after 1945.

While these post-1918 lines presented a financial problem and drained the
resources of Netherlands Railways, the pre-1914 lines worked by Netherlands
Railways were an even greater nuisance. In their eagerness to be first, both

Holland and State Railways had signed working contracts with the owning companies such as the GOLS and the Willem III. Most of these contracts contained clauses about a fixed rental sum and a percentage of receipts. When receipts dropped below the fixed rental sum, as often happened in the 1930s, working these lines became a liability to the now unified Netherlands Railways. The only viable way to terminate these contracts was compulsory purchase of the lines in question by the government, which could then relieve Netherlands Railways of the obligation to work the line.

In 1935, the government thus bought up and closed the Noord-Friesche Locaal, some lines in North Holland, and parts of the old NOLS in Drente and Overijssel, altogether some 350 km. Most of the lines of the GOLS in Gelderland, owned by Netherlands Railways for some time, were now closed. In most cases, only unprofitable passenger traffic was ended, and the lines remained open for an occasional freight train. This process of compulsory purchase and termination of passenger traffic went on unabated until 1940 and was resumed after the war. Around 1950 the government pruned the Netherlands Railways network of all unremunerative branches and regional lines, the first of the European countries to make such a move. The resulting

FIGURE 86

Boy Scouts at Bennebroek-Vogelenzang, south of Haarlem, for the 1937 World Jamboree. Thousands of scouts from all over the world came to the little village, where temporary platforms accommodated the many extra trains required. (Collection NVBS)

loss in total receipts was more than offset by the decline in operating expenses, always the intended goal.

FREIGHT TRAFFIC

As was true all over the world, the less-than-carload freight showed the greatest losses of all goods traffic. It needed a lot of manhandling and transshipment from one car to another, and despite the well-coordinated ATO–Van Gend and Loos door-to-door services, Netherlands Railways saw this traffic as an expensive nuisance. The motor van was much more suitable for this kind of traffic, and although in the 1930s most of this business shifted to private truck operators, Netherlands Railways continued this service until 1984.

Carload freight remained very profitable between the wars. Wagons of coal were delivered all over the country at small stations and still smaller stops, where the local coal merchant got supplies for his customers. Other mass goods such as fertilizer, ores, and grain were also still carried by rail, and although this traffic was not losing money, Netherlands Railways tried to improve efficiency and introduce cost-cutting measures here too. It took two approaches, the grouping system and the so-called locomotor, a light motor locomotive.

FIGURE 87
Netherlands Railways No. 7124 (ex–State Railways) at Stiens on the North Frisian Local, June 27, 1934. Closure of the line for passengers was less than a year away.
(Photo L. J. Biezeveld, Collection NVBS)

FIGURE 88

Netherlands Railways diesel-electric locomotor No. 246 (Werkspoor-Amsterdam, 1935), of the second, heavier series, after the Second World War. The controls that enable the driver to operate the machine from the foot boards during switching maneuvers are clearly visible.
(Photo NS, Collection NVBS)

Under the grouping system, the country was split up into about thirty groups, each with one main freight station and a number of smaller stations, stops, and industrial spurs. At the main group station, cars coming in from the smaller stations were marshaled into trains, and vice versa, which involved a lot of switching. Between the large group stations, trains ran by steam and mainly at night, which generally meant picking up a car at the shipper's loading dock and delivering it to the stop closest to the addressee within twenty-four hours.

Locomotors were responsible for local shunting and transfer to the branch lines and industrial spurs. A steam engine, large or small, needed a two-man crew and could not be shut off easily between duties. A locomotor was a light four-wheel vehicle with a gasoline engine, mechanical transmission, and a gearbox with a manual shift; when it was not needed, the engine was simply shut down. A simple layout of all handles and levers made it possible for shunters to drive the machines instead of more skilled and higher-paid locomotive engineers, circumventing the railway laws, which did not contain the word "locomotor."

After some experimenting beginning in 1927, a first series of fifty locomotors was built between 1930 and 1932, soon followed by heavier machines with improved diesel engines and electrical transmissions. Hundreds have been built since, and many are still in use for switching and light maintenance work. The staff loved them, fondly nicknaming them "sik," or pony.

Netherlands Railways also modernized its freight stock, replacing the old stiff friction bearings with roller bearings. With the introduction of the continuous brake for freight trains, the maximum speed could be raised to 90 km/h. Just before the Second World War, the company introduced welded-steel coal trucks that could carry twenty tons.

For the ATO–Van Gend and Loos door-to-door service, the company ordered light (three-ton) containers. A special freight truck could carry three of them and transfer them to a custom-built road trailer at stations, where they became a familiar sight as they were driven to homes and businesses. Bulk coal and oil were also shipped in this way.

NEW BUILDINGS AND STATIONS

The development of the mining industry in Limburg required new infrastructure to handle the long coal trains. A big engine shed had already been constructed at Heerlen, in the heart of the coal area, and between 1914 and 1921, a large gravity switching yard was laid out at Susteren, where the coal trains came together before going on to different destinations. G. W. van Heukelom designed a large complex of water towers, engine sheds, workshops, and

FIGURE 89

The level crossing at Amsterdam Linnaeusstraat, circa 1935, shortly before the tracks were raised. Only pedestrians and cyclists could use the overhead bridge; motorists had to wait. (Photo NS, Collection NVBS)

FIGURE 90

Amsterdam Weesperzijde, circa 1935. Before the tracks were raised, long lines of cars waited for a train to pass, including, here, a Mercedes-Benz limousine, *right*.
(Photo NS, Collection NVBS)

company housing, all built in rapid succession. Elsewhere, new construction, especially engine sheds, generally replaced buildings that had become too small or dilapidated.

Amsterdam Central Station acquired a second overall roof beside the existing one in 1923. New station buildings of advanced design were built to the plans of H.G.J. Schelling, Netherlands Railways architect, at Sittard (1923) and Naarden-Bussum (1924). Schelling also designed a small country station building of pleasing lines for Putten, north of Amersfoort (1929), on the old Central line. For the Gouda-Alphen line he designed station buildings cum freight sheds, all opened in 1936.

Extensive new works were out of the question during the Depression years, but in Amsterdam all lines to the east and southeast were raised above street level, the Weesperpoort Station of the old Rhenish Railway was vacated and demolished, and a new loop connecting with the Central Station ended the terminus nuisance. Street traffic had grown so much that the frequent closures of level crossings on the old lines had become almost unbearable, and new raised tracks were laid out for higher speeds as well. New stations had to be constructed, Amsterdam-Amstel replacing the old Weesperpoort, and Amsterdam-Muiderpoort, in the fork of the lines to Utrecht and Amersfoort, replacing an earlier station there. The Amstel Station, designed by Schelling, became a showpiece of efficient modern railway architecture, with lots of glass and a layout that made it easy for travelers to find their way about. Built too far from the city, it has only recently come into its own with the opening of office towers and industrial parks close by. Most of the works around

Amsterdam were finished just before the outbreak of war in May 1940, and the few remaining pieces were opened for service in 1942.

Another big project was the raising of all railway lines radiating from Utrecht, again because the many level crossings interfered with road traffic. Utrecht Central Station, dating back to the years of the Rhenish Railway, was adapted to the exigencies of the times from designs by S. van Ravesteyn, one of the new generation of architects of Netherlands Railways. It opened in 1938 but burned to the ground that same year. Although van Ravesteyn then constructed a new building of outstanding modern design instead of again adapting the old structure, he kept the old iron overall roofs over the tracks, some of which remain today.

One new line never got past the planning stage. When the thirty-kilometer dike between North Holland and Friesland closed off the old South Sea from the North Sea in 1932, it converted that body of water into a large freshwater lake. A double-track railway line had been planned for the top of the dike, next to the roadway, but it never materialized and the space was later used for a four-lane freeway instead. New bridges were constructed in this period in Zeeland, on the Flushing line, near Vlake, where the low swing bridge was

FIGURE 91
Utrecht Uit en In, the original entry to the short-lived separate station of the State Railways, circa 1936, before the tracks were raised here, with the first administration building of the State Company in the background.
(Photo NS, Collection NVBS)

FIGURE 92

Utrecht Central Station, 1935. Additions spread out from the original Rhenish Railway station in the center. After a fire on December 17, 1938, Netherlands Railways architect S. van Ravesteyn designed a new glass and steel facade to hide the old structure. (Photo NS, Collection NVBS)

replaced with a higher bascule, or drawbridge, and near Zwolle across the IJssel, where a double-track girder bridge replaced the single-track bridge dating back to the 1860s, with its restrictive load limit.

The signaling system did not change much, apart from the substitution of green for white lights as the all-clear. Much more dependable and brighter gas and electric lights replaced the old oil lamps, giving a clearer signal at night. The automatic block system, based on an American plan, came into use here and there, with semaphore signals of American pattern. Experiments were also carried out with color light signals in places where the common semaphore was not possible, for instance on long bridges. In 1939, between Voorschoten and The Hague, a system of color daylight signals was set up, combined with the automatic block, again with American equipment, making the signalmen superfluous. Only after 1945 would the automatic block be introduced on a nationwide scale.

STAFF AND TRADE UNIONS

After the disastrous second strike of 1903, the membership of the Nederlandsche Vereeniging had declined dramatically, while that of the two new confessional unions, St. Raphael and the Protestantsch-Christelijke Bond, had grown. But the NV had made a comeback in 1916 and soon was the largest union again. Although strikes were now out of the question, its leadership was willing to go far to reach its goals, higher wages and better working conditions. The two Christian unions, more moderate in their actions, had the same goals. All three had close links with political parties in Parliament, Social Democrat, Roman Catholic, and Protestant.

In 1917 a new union arose, the Neutraal Verbond van Spoorwegpersoneel (NVS, Neutral Association of Railway Personnel), that wanted to remain free of party politics. After internal dissension, the NVS became the Neutrale Bond van Spoorwegpersoneel (Neutral Union of Railway Personnel), which was quite successful in its first years but by 1921 was forced to merge with some smaller unions into a Centrale Bond van Spoor- en Tramwegpersoneel (Central Union of Rail- and Tramway Personnel). All these unions represented chiefly the blue-collar workers, not the white-collar staff in the railway offices, who felt somewhat underrepresented. They set up a separate union in 1917, the Bond van Ambtenaren in dienst van de NS (BANS, Union of Officers in the Service of Netherlands Railways).

Although all the unions shared the same goals, they disagreed on how to reach them. A lot of bickering went on among them, and shifting alliances

FIGURE 93

A color daylight signal on the experimental layout between The Hague and Voorschoten, 1939. The Hague (Hollandse Spoor) station is barely visible in the background. (Photo NS, Collection NVBS)

weakened their position. They nevertheless worked out a new rulebook for working hours and breaks, together with higher wages, with Netherlands Railways in 1921. But the economic situation after the crisis of 1929 put an end to the new rules. The unions resisted the longer hours and lower wages imposed during the 1930s, but in the end they had to acquiesce. Railway workers were not the only ones to suffer wage cuts in those days.

After long and tedious negotiations, a Personeelraad (Personnel Council) was instituted in 1936, a central representative council of the whole railway staff, on which all existing unions were represented. Only the BANS opposed the council, as its members, the middle- and upper-level officers, saw their interests as very different from those of the rank-and-file. Negotiations between the Personeelraad and the directors of Netherlands Railways generally went well, although in wage-cut negotiations the unions could do no more than try to restrict the damage.

—— NEW DIRECTORS OF NETHERLANDS RAILWAYS ——

Toward the end of 1937, when the incorporation of Netherlands Railways was well on its way, director E.C.W. van Dijk died. The sole remaining director, H. van Manen, wanted to retire, opening the way for the government to cut through the established hierarchies and outdated ways of thinking and to infuse new blood into the company. The government viewed the internal candidate of Netherlands Railways, W. Hupkes, the chief mechanical officer, as too much a member of the old elite and unfit for the rejuvenating work ahead. Hupkes was passed over in favor of J. Goudriaan, professor of business economics at Rotterdam and Delft Universities, and also one of the directors of the Philips electronic company. Hupkes became second-in-command, responsible for motive power and permanent way and buildings, and a third director, W.F.H. van Rijckevorsel, was made responsible for traffic matters.

Goudriaan did indeed introduce a number of innovations, but his changes sometimes came too thick and too fast, and his relationship with the staff, with his fellow directors, and with the minister of Waterstaat suffered. Yet, this triumvirate was destined to lead the company through the German attack on the Netherlands in 1940 and during the first year of the war.

Technical Innovation Between the Wars

ELECTRIFICATION

The popularity of electric traction was spreading worldwide, and indeed the Rotterdam–The Hague–Scheveningen electric line had run successfully since 1908. No wonder the Netherlands Railways saw electricity as a solution for lines choked with traffic. (An alternative would have been the quadrupling of some lines, but this would have involved extensive destruction of property through the cities and would have been ruinously expensive.) A Netherlands Railways internal commission in 1919 advised electrification of part of the network, beginning with the Old Line, Amsterdam–Haarlem–Leiden–The Hague–Rotterdam, as it was at maximum capacity. The commission proposed a 15,000-volt alternating-current system, in operation in several European countries since the early days, but added a rider: Because of the war, the commission had no opportunity to examine more modern direct-current systems.

About this time, the government was questioning the desirability of the railways themselves generating electricity, as had been done at the Leidschendam power station since 1908 because no adequate generating station existed. But several large municipal or provincial power stations were now in operation, and the national government envisaged a countrywide network of high-tension electric lines connecting the larger of these power stations. Although this idea of a national grid did not make it through Parliament, a new joint government–Netherlands Railways commission was ordered to examine two issues—the best system for electrifying the railways, and the best way to generate electric power. Chairing the commission was the first director of the South Holland Electric, L. M. Barnet Lyon. After an exhaustive study of railway electrification in France, England, Germany, Switzerland, Sweden, and the United States, in 1922 he came up with his recommendations.

The most important recommendation for the railways was the use of 1,500 volts direct current (DC), a voltage low enough that work could proceed on the catenary from insulated ladder carts with the current switched on. Electric motors and switch gear had been developed to fit the narrow confines of the trucks of the multiple-unit electric trains that were planned. The drawback of a relatively heavy catenary with frequent substations was taken in stride, because the Dutch network was a fairly short one.

Discarded was the English system of 750 volts DC with a third rail, as used by the Southern Railway, judged problematic because of the low voltage and the third rail, which would be a nuisance and a considerable danger in stations, yards, and at the many level crossings. Also rejected was the Chicago, Milwaukee and St. Paul's 3,000-volt DC system used in the mountains of Montana and Washington. Although eminently suitable in most respects, 3,000 volts would not permit ongoing work on the catenary. (Shortly after the Dutch decision, the French Orléans Railway Company also opted for the 1,500-volt DC system, largely on the same grounds. Most of the French network was

FIGURE 94

An electric motor train at Voorschoten on The Hague–Leiden, the first stretch of the large electrification program of the 1920s. The train is in the original green and cream livery. The two contact wires in this experimental system were unusually far apart.
(Author's collection)

FIGURE 95

A long train of motor cars and trailers in Amsterdam Central Station in the more sober green livery that replaced the green and cream. The third car is a Wagon-Lits Company dining carriage, which ran in certain Amsterdam-Rotterdam trains between 1928 and 1934, after they were equipped with the necessary m.u. cables. (Photo NS, Collection NVBS)

electrified with this system until the high-voltage AC system was installed in the remaining non-electrified regions in the 1960s.)

The joint commission further advised that Netherlands Railways buy the necessary electricity from existing power stations and close down its own generating plant. Both the government and Netherlands Railways accepted the commission's recommendations, and it was decided to start a trial electrification of a stretch of the Old Line between Leiden and The Hague. American, German, English, and Dutch factories supplied the necessary rolling stock, electric motors, switch gear, and substation equipment. In 1924 electric service between Leiden and The Hague got under way, and its success was immediate and complete. Three years later the whole Amsterdam-Rotterdam line was electrified, plus Haarlem-IJmuiden. The pioneer Rotterdam-Scheveningen line was converted in 1926 to the 1,500-volt DC system. By 1938 the electric network reached as far as Alkmaar, Arnhem, Eindhoven, and Dordrecht, covering about five hundred kilometers of the busiest lines.

The electrification was both a technical and financial success. Traffic increased, while operating expenses dropped spectacularly. One motorman could operate trains of twelve or more cars, with two or three conductors on duty in the train. Unlike the later experience of other countries, the Dutch trade unions never required a fireman on diesel or electric trains and engines, which meant an important saving in wages. A dead man's handle provided enough safety in case of the sudden sickness of the motorman. Energy costs also decreased with the use of cheap electricity instead of expensive coal. And the more efficient electric motors made better use of the power than the inefficient steam locomotive, which wasted fuel.

The psychological effect on travelers was another significant factor in this success. At last the railways had managed to replace their image as an old-fashioned, outdated business with a new image—fast, clean, and frequent. A fixed schedule put in place in 1934 meant a train every thirty minutes or every hour at the same time all through the day. Only freight and international trains were still hauled by steam locomotives. In 1939, a joint study with Belgian Railways considered the viability of electrifying the Amsterdam-Antwerp-Brussels line. Technical problems could be solved, although the

FIGURE 96

Erecting the portals for the catenary on the Schiedam–Hook of Holland line in the early 1930s. This overhead system was more elegant and markedly different from the 1924 plan.
(Photo NS, Collection NVBS)

FIGURE 97

Rotterdam Delftsche Poort station in the 1930s, electric railroading at its best. From here, electric lines stretched in every direction.
(Photo NS, Collection NVBS)

FIGURE 98

The famous Etoile du Nord Amsterdam-Paris luxury train approaching The Hague from the north, circa 1935. International trains were still steam-hauled under the wires. *To the left,* the electrified tracks of the old Hofplein line from Rotterdam run to The Hague.
(Photo NS, author's collection)

Belgians used 3,000 volts DC, but erecting catenary over the Dordrecht-Roosendaal-Antwerp stretch would cost too much. War prevented further elaboration of the plans, but the electric locomotives envisaged for this service were built after the war as NS series 1000. The electric Amsterdam-Brussels through service opened in 1957, with Dutch multiple-unit trains instead of electric locomotives.

—— INTERNAL COMBUSTION TRACTION ——

Electrification was viable only on the lines with the heaviest traffic because of the high cost of infrastructure and equipment. Outside the western and central parts of the country, went the received wisdom, electrification would never pay for itself. But on less busy lines it might still be advantageous to replace the labor-intensive steam locomotive. Hupkes, responsible for internal-combustion traction, was thinking of light motorcars with gasoline engines, such as some tramways used. In 1923 the first three big bogie motorcars, built in Germany, entered service. They had two gasoline engines each, with a mechanical transmission through a hand-operated gearbox. They resembled the American doodlebugs of a somewhat later period, but with less conspicuous radiators on the roofs.

FIGURE 99

Two "doodlebugs" at the engine shed, Gouda, 1937. *Left*, a 1929 four-wheeler; *right*, a much larger 1924 bogie car.
(Photo L. J. Biezeveld, Collection NVBS)

FIGURE 100

One of the first diesel-electric trains on a test run at The Hague (State Railways), 1934. The contrast with the ancient square compartment cars on the adjoining track is striking. (Photo NS, author's collection)

The success of these three cars encouraged Hupkes to order ten more the next year, now from Werkspoor and Beijnes, but still with German gasoline engines and gearboxes. They saw service on the NOLS and Zwolle–Apeldoorn lines and were well liked by both passengers and staff. Seven more bogie motorcars, still with gasoline engines but of different construction, were ordered in 1929 for the new Groningen-Slochteren-Delfzijl line.

The tramways on the island of South Beveland in Zeeland, opened in 1927, needed something smaller, as only light traffic was expected. A four-wheeled motorcar was designed, with mechanical transmission, but for the first time with diesel engines of Danish and German origin. These engines were troublesome and broke down frequently, and in 1934 they were replaced with new diesel engines from the domestic supplier Thomassen in De Steeg, Gelderland. Six very similar motorcars, again with gasoline engines, followed in 1929, but these too later got Thomassen diesel engines.

All this motorized rolling stock proved eminently suited for the subordinate role Hupkes had in mind, but they would not do for fast trains over longer distances. Streamlined, articulated trains with diesel engines were just being introduced in other countries. In Germany the Fliegende Hamburger two-unit diesel-electric trains had run successfully since 1933, and in America the Union Pacific and the Chicago, Burlington, and Quincy Railroads had led the way with their M-10000 and Zephyr trains, both introduced in 1934.

FIGURE 101

Out on the line a sleek three-unit diesel-electric train speeds along in the later dark green livery.
(Photo NS, Collection NVBS)

Hupkes, apparently inspired by the German train, now designed a three-unit streamlined articulated diesel-engined train with electrical transmission. Werkspoor, Beijnes, and Allan built forty of them in 1934, with diesel engines from Maybach of Germany and Ganz of Hungary, the latter constructed under license by Stork of Hengelo. Electrical equipment came from Heemaf-Hengelo or Smit-Slikkerveer. The steel and aluminum car bodies were electrically welded, using new techniques invented by Hupkes in collaboration with the builders. Automatic couplers were used, and coupling of train sets was a matter of simply driving them slowly together—and all electrical and air connections were made. Maximum speed was 140 km/h, but in ordinary service 125 km/h sufficed. Steam trains did not go much faster than 100 km/h at the time, so the diesel meant a big improvement in travel time. The German two-car train carried only first- and second-class passengers at extra fare, while the Dutch trains entered ordinary service and had second- and third-class compartments, 160 seats altogether, with a level of comfort that set the standard until the 1950s. In one bold stroke, Hupkes had pushed Netherlands Railways to the forefront of railway technology.

The diesel's sleek light-gray and silver exterior impressed both the engineering world and the general public. Raymond Loewy, a well-known U.S. industrial designer, praised the Dutch train in his 1937 book *The Locomotive: Its Esthetics:* "Three cheers for this. In the writer's opinion it is the best looking Diesel-electric unit-train built so far. Its aerodynamics are nearly perfect; the front end treatment and the flush side windows are most attractive and efficient. Paint scheme good. This is a perfect example of what good taste and restraint can produce." Diesel became the rage in the Netherlands and stood for modern, clean, efficient, and other superlative qualities. Advertisements for vacuum cleaners, detergents, and school textbooks all took advantage of the diesel name.

But the sudden introduction of forty trains of untried design created problems. The Maybach engines especially proved troublesome, and as a result many trains had to be withdrawn temporarily for repairs and changes. Their fast schedules were ably taken over by steam locomotives with three-coach trains. Only the very best locomotives available were used for these services, for which the term Steam Diesel was coined. When the Diesels took over again, schedules on the central lines were speeded up considerably, and after Eindhoven and Arnhem had been brought under the wires, the Diesels reached Maastricht and Groningen too. Fully electric articulated trains of two-, three-, and four-car configuration, with the same streamlined exterior and level of comfort, were introduced as well, and the general image of Netherlands Railways improved considerably.

The top of the line were twenty fast—160 km/h—five-car articulated diesel-electric trains of 1940, meant for long distances and even international services. Their fuel tanks were large enough for service far into Germany or Belgium and back without refueling, but the war put an end to such grandiose plans.

For steam trains, all-steel corridor coaches were also built, no longer with five seats in a row in third class, but with well-padded seats two-by-two along a central corridor, or four in a row with a side corridor.

NEW STEAM LOCOMOTIVES

All these new modes of propulsion did not entirely replace the old faithful steam locomotive. Freight and international trains were still steam-hauled, and a lot of the regional trains still ran behind steam. Shortly after 1917 a beginning was made with the scrapping of old and obsolete engines, small series, or engines with troublesome defects such as a propensity to overheat their bearings or crack their frames. Most of the Borsig fleet of the old Holland Railway disappeared under the torch. The imposing Blue Brabantians of the North Brabant–German were first downgraded to freight service and then scrapped because of cracked frames, and a host of other, smaller engines went to the junkyards.

This slow process of scrapping combined with the growing traffic to create a need for modern, fast steam locomotives. Franco was officially responsible for all traction, but he was more interested in the electrification projects and left the building of new steam engines to his assistant P. Labrijn. When Hupkes succeeded Franco as chief mechanical officer in 1928, this situation did not change.

For the heavier expresses, the old 700 series of the State Railways (NS series 3700) were still good enough, so more of these were constructed until

FIGURE 102

The Amsterdam-Basel luxury train, *Rheingold*, at the border station of Zevenaar, headed by a big 4-6-0 of the 3900 series, June 10, 1938.
(Photo NS, Collection NVBS)

1921, with an order for five more in 1928. After the maximum axle loading on most main lines was raised from sixteen to eighteen tons, a heavier engine became possible, still a four-cylinder simple 4-6-0, but weighing eighty-four instead of seventy-two tons, with eight-wheel tenders. These engines of the 3900 class were strong and fast but burned a great deal of coal. For the fast outer suburban services around Amsterdam, Labrijn constructed ten 4-6-4 tank engines, again with four cylinders, which made them very quiet runners.

For freight traffic, some big 2-8-0 engines were built, but with only two outside cylinders. They were unpopular, as they shook the roadbed and the engine crew nearly to pieces. More successful were Labrijn's large—127 tons—4-8-4 tank engines, series 6300, for the heavy Limburg coal traffic. For a time the heaviest tank engines in Europe, they proved as suitable for slow coal drags as for faster passenger trains. Like all new Dutch engines, they were heavy coal users. Between 1930 and 1931, twenty-two of these mammoth machines were delivered, the last steam locomotives built for Netherlands Railways to its own specifications.

In the 1930s it had become clear to all the top Netherlands Railways people that steam would be phased out soon, and it was decided that the 6300 class was to be the last steam design for Netherlands Railways. If the Second World War had not intervened, diesel-electric locomotives for freight and switching work would have taken over in the early 1940s. Werkspoor had a number of suitable designs on the drawing boards, but war interfered with all these optimistic plans.

All newer Dutch steam engines were solidly built machines, well suited for their purpose but with little to distinguish them. They incorporated modern techniques, such as bar frames and one-piece cast-steel cylinder blocks, even the four-cylinder engines. All were superheated, of course, but mechanical stokers were not yet deemed necessary. However, Labrijn seems to have been unaware of the revolutionary ideas of André Chapelon—streamlining all internal steam passages and improving the exhaust system of steam engines, for much greater power and efficiency—although railways in the Dutch East Indies were following Chapelon's precepts closely at the time, with marked success. Several classes of older steam engines of the State Railways of Java were reconstructed with spectacular results.

In the years after 1918, during the coal shortages, Franco experimented with cheap coal dust as fuel. The coal from the Limburg mines was less suitable as locomotive fuel than the imported German coal, but when ground to powder it was usable. A large coal-dust bunker, with a grinding mill, was built near Amsterdam-Weesperpoort station, and some locomotives of the 3700 class were equipped with special burners in the firebox and bunkers on the tender. The system worked after a fashion, but most of the fuel blew out of the smokestack unburned, blanketing the train with black dust. As the worst shortages were over by then, the experiment was terminated in 1921.

During the streamlining rage of the 1930s, Netherlands Railways gave some of its steam locomotives a fashionable, modern, streamlined look. In England and Germany, new high-speed streamlined locomotives were attracting a lot of attention, and people were wondering why Netherlands Railways did not try something similar. With record-breaking speeds out of the question over the short distances in the Netherlands, there was no need for such new engines. Instead, in 1936, six of the faithful 3700 series were equipped

FIGURE 103

An international train to Germany in the 1930s, headed by a 3900. The fourth car in the train is a dining car of the Mitropa, the German counterpart of the French/Belgian Wagons-Lits Company. (Photo NS, Collection NVBS)

FIGURE 104

NS 4-6-0 engine No. 3804 in streamlined guise. As no streamlined train was ever built, the effect of the streamlined engine alone was minimal.
(Photo W. J. Haarman, Collection NVBS)

with a streamlined hood—an upturned bathtub, critics called it. These Pot-vissen (Sperm Whales) looked heavy and solid, and as the necessary streamlined train was never built, they were not notably more efficient than the unstreamlined locomotives. Moreover, maintenance was a nuisance, as the inside motion and other internal parts were hard to reach with oil can and wrench, and during the war the hood was quietly removed.

War and Destruction

The German attack on the Netherlands in the early morning of May 10, 1940, came as an almost complete surprise. People had hoped for a repetition of 1914–1918, when the country had managed to stay out of the armed conflict. The Netherlands army had been mobilized since Germany had invaded Poland in August 1939, but nobody, including railway officials, had believed that an attack on a strictly neutral country would really come. All hostilities had passed outside the borders of the country in 1914, so why not this time? was the general opinion.

Yet some preparations had been made. Military authorities expected the great river bridges to be the first strategic target of a possible attack, so all bridges had been mined and small concrete bunkers had been built on nearby riverbanks to repel attackers. And indeed, at the approach of the Germans in the early morning of May 10, the Netherlands military blew up all bridges but one across the IJssel and Maas Rivers, some not until enemy soldiers were crossing them. The only remaining bridge, which fell undamaged into German hands, was the Meuse Bridge at Gennep, on the old North Brabant–German line. An enemy armored train crossed there but was derailed soon after. Most bridges in the rest of the country also were destroyed in time, although the Moerdijk Bridge was occupied by German paratroopers before its defenders had time to blow it up. Elsewhere, only the inland bridges at Culemborg, Dordrecht, and Rotterdam survived more or less undamaged. All over the

FIGURE 105

Rotterdam Delftsche Poort Station with an electric train with 1924 equipment. The postmark on the reverse of this postcard reads: Vacation in a Peaceful Homeland, Rotterdam, May 9, 1940. The next day the German armies invaded the country, and four days later the station went up in flames. (Collection NVBS)

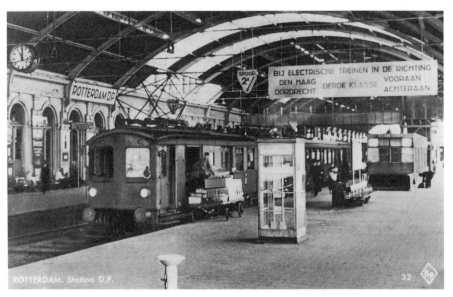

FIGURE 106

The Rhine bridge at Rhenen, provisionally repaired with parts from other bridges after it was destroyed during the heavy fighting in the area in 1940. The Germans blew up the repaired bridge during their retreat in 1945, and it was never rebuilt. (Photo NS, Collection NVBS)

country, the retreating Dutch army also blew up smaller bridges and viaducts to slow the German march.

The engine sheds at Zwolle were set on fire by the defenders, and some other buildings were destroyed here and there. During the heavy fighting at the Grebbeberg line near Rhenen (east of Utrecht), one of the main Dutch lines of defense, a lot of property—including railway structures—was destroyed. The unprecedented bombardment of Rotterdam from the air on May 14 caused by far the most damage. The railway stations at Delftsche Poort, Beurs, Maas, and Hofplein all went up in flames, and the iron viaduct through the heart of the city was distorted by the heat of the fires and explosions. Some trains and coaches were destroyed in Rotterdam, but most rolling stock elsewhere was unharmed.

ROTTERDAM BEURS STATION

RESUMPTION OF RAILWAY SERVICE

After the Netherlands army surrendered, the relatively light damage to the railways was soon repaired, apart from the great river bridges and the lines through Rotterdam and the stations in that city. But people had to adjust to the new situation, to decide how to meet the invader and its military and civil authorities. Queen Wilhelmina and the cabinet had sought refuge in London to continue the struggle from there, and the civilian power in the Netherlands had been placed in the hands of the secretary-generals, the highest-ranking civil servants, who stood just below the cabinet ministers. They were supervised by German officers and civilians, but during the early years of the occupation the Germans left a lot to the Dutch authorities. Netherlands Railways came under the Dutch secretary-general of Waterstaat, D.G.W. Spitzen, and the directors managed to establish a good relationship with him. But in 1943 Spitzen was sacked by the Germans and replaced with a member of the Dutch Nazi party, the Nationaal Socialistische Beweging (NSB), the National Socialist Movement, which meant a lot of trouble for Netherlands Railways.

For the time being, the directorate of Netherlands Railways wanted to cooperate with the German authorities as fully as possible to make sure the trains kept running, a priority for the Dutch population. In an order to the staff on May 20, 1940, Netherlands Railways outlined this policy. That Netherlands Railways also had to take charge of German military Wehrmacht transports was taken in stride. Resistance was still almost unknown.

Goudriaan, president of Netherlands Railways, was arrested by the Germans in October 1940 on a charge that had nothing to do with railway matters,

FIGURE 107

The Rotterdam Beurs Station, burnt out after the bombing of the city on May 14, 1940. Although the viaduct through the city was damaged, it was soon reopened for traffic. The station was not rebuilt until after the war. (Postcard, Collection NVBS)

FIGURE 108

Train SF7 (Amiens-Kiel) with German soldiers on furlough at Herfte-Veldhoek, August 6, 1942. Long-distance trains chiefly carried German military traffic. The front lamps of the engine have been shielded to make the train less visible to Allied airmen at night. (Photo A. D. de Pater, Collection NVBS)

and after his liberation some time later he was discharged because of his general anti-German attitude. Hupkes, no less anti-German but possibly more cautious than Goudriaan, was put in charge as deputy-president and would guide the company through its most difficult period. His policy was to cooperate with the Germans, keep the business in his own hands as far as possible, and keep the German and Dutch Nazis away from the company as much as was prudent. Apparently loyal to the Nazis to a certain extent, he was left in charge, but maintaining his policies demanded a kind of balancing act. Too much cooperation would become collaboration with the enemy, while too much obstruction could mean a German takeover and loss of independence. Close contacts with the Personeelraad, consisting of the later dissolved pre-war unions, were of the utmost importance to Hupkes, to ensure company-wide support.

By stressing the indispensability of railway workers, Hupkes managed to avoid the drafting of his people in Germany into war industries work. The influence of new Nazi trade unions remained minimal because the Personeelraad stood loyally behind him. And when German demands became too severe, Hupkes made the matter a question of confidence, and the Germans backed down. They needed Hupkes and did not want to lose him.

This apparent cooperation with the enemy had its darker side too, of course. Not only did the railways take care of German military transportation, but they carried Dutch prisoners of war to Germany and transported Dutch Jews to the Westerbork Concentration Camp in Drente and from there into

Germany. Understandably, many were unhappy with this situation, but Hupkes maintained that refusing these transports would trigger a complete German takeover. The Germans would be entirely capable of carrying out these services themselves, with collaborators if possible but if need be with German staff, and the Dutch population would be deprived of railway service. The dilemma was impossible to resolve, but Hupkes thought that his policy served the national interest best.

RAILWAY SERVICE DURING THE WAR

After the rubble of May had been cleared away, railway service resumed, as far as was possible. The prewar schedules were followed—although much slowed down and thinned out—but soon crisis management was necessary, The occupying forces rationed diesel oil and gasoline almost immediately, and most internal combustion trains, as well as motor buses, had to be set aside. Steam took over again.

As private automobiles were requisitioned or could not be refueled because of rationing, people had to resort to the train. Where Netherlands Railways had carried 95 million passengers in 1940, the company had to cope with a flood of 232 million in 1943—with less serviceable cars and locomotives available and under trying circumstances. The blackout at night, to offer Allied aircraft no visible targets, made it hard for the staff to observe signals and other trains, which jeopardized safety. Allied attacks on railway targets became more frequent. Station, yard, and bridge bombings were commonplace, and shooting at trains on the open road became an almost daily occurrence. Although most Allied pilots gave ample warning before an all-out

FIGURE 109

Netherlands Railways No. 3713, Zwolle, May 13, 1944. A concrete shelter on the tender gave some protection against air attacks; cab roofs and sides were sometimes reinforced with thick steel plates. (Photo A. D. de Pater, Collection NVBS)

attack, so that a train could stop and passengers run for cover, many railway employees were killed on duty. Adding concrete shelters to the tender and armor plating the cab offered some protection, but never enough.

The railway shops, choked with damaged engines and cars, also had to repair German stock. Dutch drivers and engines had to run trains far into Germany to make German personnel available for service on the eastern front. Steel rail and copper for the catenary had to be sold to the Wehrmacht for war purposes, and to cover these losses some less frequented lines had to be lifted. Despite the hardships, railway service continued through these dark times, until the general strike was called.

THE RAILWAY STRIKE OF 1944

All through the war years Hupkes had dismissed the idea of a strike as a strategy for resisting the Germans. He would endorse only a general strike ordered by the Netherlands government in London. During earlier, spontaneous strikes, such as the February 1941 strike against the deportation of Jewish Netherlanders, the railways continued to operate. An alternative, sabotage to the fixed plant or rolling stock, was deemed too dangerous, as such actions were bound to injure innocent persons. Hupkes did recognize, however, the need for some kind of organization in case of a general railway strike, and consequently toward the end of 1943 he approached one of the many resistance groups in the country, the Orde Dienst (OD), Organization for Order. A fairly conservative group, the OD was chiefly interested in filling the anticipated power vacuum created by the inevitable defeat of the Germans. Together with the OD, Hupkes and a few trusted employees prepared for a general strike, but as they did not envision such a strike lasting long, they made no decisions about practical things such as the payment of wages to the strikers.

When the Allied offensive toward Arnhem began, Hupkes received on September 17, 1944, the coded radio message from London that was to set the strike in motion: "The children of Versteeg [Hupkes' code name] should go to bed." Railway workers all over the country observed the strike, and in a few days the whole railway network was shut down, apart from a few places up north in Groningen. Staff and employees went underground. Furious at the unexpected strike, the Germans were forced to operate the necessary military trains with their own personnel. They rode chiefly at night, as the Allied air force was master of the air and made any movement during daylight hours suicidal.

Optimistic expectations for a strike of short duration were shattered when the Allied offensive bogged down before reaching Arnhem. The western part of the country would endure one more long winter of darkness and hunger. Out of revenge, the Germans forbade all transport of food and fuel by water or road to the cities in the West, and when they finally agreed to open the waterways to such transports, winter made all travel by water impossible. The result was widespread hunger.

FIGURE 110

The bombed-out shell of Nijmegen Station, 1945. Train service was soon resumed in temporary sheds inside the ruins. (Photo NS, Collection NVBS)

Despite the lack of organization, improvisation made possible the payment of full wages to the strikers. Millions of guilders were smuggled out of De Nederlandsche Bank, the national bank, under the noses of the bank's German caretakers and their Dutch henchmen, and distributed by volunteers all over the country. One volunteer would later become director-general of Netherlands Railways, F. Q. den Hollander, who made his rounds by bike or on foot with hundreds of thousands of guilders in his pockets. The strikers even received their usual Christmas bonus!

The railway strike had originally been ordered to support the Allied offensive, but it is doubtful if it contributed much toward that goal or to a quick end to the war. On the other hand, its psychological effect was considerable. It was seen as a victory for the Dutch spirit of resistance and a slap in the face of the hated German army.

LIBERATION OF THE SOUTH

Despite the failure of the drive to Arnhem, the part of the Netherlands south of the great rivers had been liberated in 1944. British, Canadian, and U.S. military engineers had repaired the most useful lines and bridges for their own transportation needs. Civilian traffic was allowed only when a line was no longer necessary for military purposes. Antwerp, on the Scheldt River, became the major supply port for the Allies after the Dutch island of Walcheren was taken, opening the Scheldt to seagoing ships. The Antwerp-Roosendaal-Nijmegen railway became the lifeline for the British troops near Arnhem, while the Americans rode their trains by way of Maastricht and Heerlen toward the front in Germany. Both armies brought their own locomotives, rolling stock, and personnel and generally used the American dispatching system, whereby one central officer regulated all traffic on the line by telephone. Signals and other safety devices were out of order or simply not used.

— THE WAR DAMAGE —

While life in the South slowly resumed its normal ways, the North, and especially the densely populated western part of the country, endured a last miserable winter. The railway strike had put the railway system in German hands for seven months. When the German armies finally surrendered on May 5, 1945, the railways took stock of the situation. An appalling picture presented itself. Destruction of the railways was nearly complete. Besides damage caused by military operations, the Germans had wantonly destroyed every-

FIGURE III

Railway yard at Arnhem, with only the running lines on the left so far restored. The retreating Germans deliberately destroyed this and other railway yards. (Photo NS, Collection NVBS)

thing they could lay hands on, whether of military importance or not, including museum pieces of rolling stock. All major bridges except the Culemborg Bridge were destroyed again, this time more thoroughly than in 1940. The Germans blew up not only the steel spans, but also some of the piers, which made repairs much more difficult and time consuming.

Of the prewar network of 3,149 km of lines, some 913 km had been lifted for the rails and other ironwork and had disappeared over the eastern border. The Haarlem-Zandvoort and The Hague–Scheveningen lines and the extensive marshaling yards at Amsterdam-Watergraafsmeer and Rotterdam-IJsselmonde were completely gone, while on many lines one track had been lifted. Catenary had been destroyed almost everywhere, the copper used for war purposes. Stores of rail, ties, and copper wire had been stolen, and the complete inventory of the Haarlem and Amersfoort shops had been transported eastward. The Tilburg shops were simply gutted, leaving only the empty shells of the buildings.

Of all major stations, apart from the Rotterdam stations bombed in 1940, Arnhem, Nijmegen, 's-Hertogenbosch, Hengelo, and Flushing were also destroyed, while many others were severely damaged. Shops, engine sheds,

FIGURE 112

After Germany's surrender on May 5, 1945. The interior of a streamlined electric train vandalized by the Germans. (Photo NS, Collection NVBS)

freight houses, signal cabins, and telephone exchanges were destroyed, damaged, or looted.

The rolling stock presented a particularly sorry picture. Of 866 steam locomotives in service in September 1944, only 144 were usable in May 1945; the rest were either stolen or damaged. All 137 streamlined full-electric and all 57 diesel-electric multiple-unit trains were out of order or missing. All of the 298 motor and trailer coaches of the 1924 electric stock were gone or out of order. Of the coaches for steam trains, only some 10 percent were usable, and almost all 29,000 freight wagons were either missing or damaged and out of order.

Balanced against these staggering losses were some acquisitions. The German armies had left behind some 5,000 wagons, mostly of German origin, but also Belgian, French, and others. About 300 German passenger cars were found in the Netherlands, most in usable condition, and of some 130 German steam locomotives found, about 40 could be repaired sufficiently to serve as makeshift units.

Patrols under military orders were sent out all over Europe to scour the continent for missing locomotives and rolling stock, as far as Poland and Czechoslovakia. The Iron Curtain, which came down in 1947, soon ended these forays outside the Western occupation zones, and some stock was never found. As recently as 1965, the Deutsche Reichsbahn in the German Democratic Republic placed in service an electric multiple-unit train rebuilt from a stolen Dutch streamliner.

Financing the rebuilding presented a problem for an impoverished country. Not only were the railways in bad shape, but the whole infrastructure had suffered enormous damage from the war and wanton destruction by the

FIGURE 113

Long lines of damaged steam locomotives in the yards of the largely unused border station at Baarle-Nassau, 1947. Most of these engines had to be scrapped; only a few could be restored to working order. (Photo L. J. Biezeveld, Collection NVBS)

FIGURE 114
Netherlands Railways
locomotor No. 247 recovered
from Czechoslovakia, Haarlem,
1947. CSD is the mark of the
Czechoslovakian Railways.
The large tank at the rear is a
generator of wood gas, which
replaced diesel fuel, unavailable
during the war years.
(Photo NS, Collection NVBS)

Germans. Total damage to the railways alone came to about 700 million guilders, which included the services performed for the Germans that had never been paid for. The Netherlands government, however, decided not to make reimbursement for those services to the enemy and was prepared to compensate only for direct war damage and destruction, a sum of 373 million guilders. A great help in this respect was the 1947 U.S. Marshall Plan, meant to repair the war damage in Europe. Wisely, the Netherlands government used these U.S. dollars mostly for rebuilding infrastructure, and the railways got a large share of them. Locomotives, rolling stock, signaling systems, and new shop equipment could be bought with hard dollars. Without the Marshall Plan's help, the rebuilding of the railway system could never have proceeded so quickly.

CHAPTER

14

The Railways Resurrected

— PROBLEMS AT THE TOP —

Before the repairing and rebuilding of the railways could get under way, a decision had to be made about who would run Netherlands Railways after the war. Hupkes was only deputy director-general. Goudriaan, discharged by the Germans, had crossed the front lines in September 1944 from his home in the occupied North and was now living in Eindhoven. He was the first of the prewar triumvirate to be liberated and wanted to return to his position as director-general. On October 2, 1944, he had resumed his duties, confirmed in his position by the minister of Waterstaat in London, J. W. Albarda. When the rest of the country was liberated, Goudriaan came north to railway headquarters at Utrecht, where Hupkes and Van Rijckevorsel refused to cooperate with him. The new minister of Waterstaat, T. P. Tromp, back in The Hague, whose main priority was to avoid a quarrel among the top Netherlands Railways executives, asked Goudriaan to request a formal dismissal, which was granted with honors. But Goudriaan felt snubbed, and subsequently he would put in a book his view of the conflict and the way he was shoved aside.

Hupkes, although past retirement age, was formally appointed director-general for one more year to oversee the first phase of the reconstruction. The way he had led the company through the war years met with criticism from several sides in 1945, but he was cleared of all blame by an official Netherlands Railways purge commission. The government supported him when it

was found that his direction during the war years had been largely beneficial
and honest. An honorary degree at the Technical University of Delft in 1946
was another proof of the general appreciation of his conduct and of his personal integrity and leadership qualities.

But Hupkes was past sixty-five, and a successor had to be found immediately. The choice fell upon F. Q. den Hollander, who was appointed director
and deputy director-general on March 1, 1946; on January 1, 1947, he succeeded Hupkes formally as director-general. Den Hollander had no previous

connection with Netherlands Railways, but he did have a railway background. He had started his career with the State Railways on the island of Java in the Dutch East Indies, and back home in the 1930s he had been director of the State Armament and Munitions Works at Hembrug, near Amsterdam, until dismissed by the Germans. In 1945, after the liberation, he was for a short period director-general of transportation at the Ministry of Waterstaat at The Hague. Then he moved to Utrecht to lead the rebuilding of Netherlands Railways.

THE RECONSTRUCTION

After these delicate matters had been settled to everyone's satisfaction but Goudriaan's, the work of reconstruction could begin. The first priority was to open the lines to supply the hungry and freezing population of the West. In 1945, the bridges at Deventer, Arnhem, Nijmegen, and Buggenum (near Roermond) were provisionally repaired, making coal traffic from Limburg to Holland possible again, albeit along a roundabout route by way of Nijmegen, Culemborg, and Utrecht. The bridges at Hedel and Zaltbommel had sustained so much damage that repairs took longer. For the rebuilding, use was made of German spare bridges or bridge parts left behind, and Allied Bailey army

FIGURE 117

Rebuilding the piers of the Zaltbommel Bridge, 1947. Salvaged and reconditioned parts are stacked for reuse. (Photo NS, Collection NVBS)

FIGURE 118
Cleaning one of the leased
Swedish passenger coaches,
1947.
(Photo NS, Collection NVBS)

bridges. With great foresight, the Netherlands government in London had purchased the old Waterloo Bridge across the Thames, when that structure was renewed, for use after the war, so more parts were available.

In 1946 the bridges at Zwolle, Zutphen, Dordrecht, and Moerdijk were repaired, and the last three, Zaltbommel, Hedel, and Baanhoek (between Sliedrecht and Papendrecht, east of Dordrecht) followed in 1947. Only the bridge at Rhenen, on the Amersfoort-Kesteren line, was never rebuilt, as the line itself had become superfluous. A road bridge was later constructed on the old piers. Most bridges were repaired provisionally, generally with just a single track, and they presented a strange picture, with a hodgepodge of temporary piers and short and long spans. Many years would pass before all of them were double track and without speed limits again. The Hedel Bridge was doubled only in the 1960s, while the Baanhoek Bridge remains single track to this day.

The Netherlands Railways bought, borrowed, and rented passenger coaches from the Swiss, Swedish, and Danish railways, and everything movable, German or Dutch, was put in service. Cattle trucks and passenger cars without interiors, with rough wooden benches, with refurbished prewar seats, or with old sofas or chairs, were better than nothing, and as long as the trains were running again, the traveling public did not complain. Passenger traffic tripled from 56 million in 1945 to 174 million the next year.

Because many lines could not be used as a result of destroyed bridges or other obstacles, Netherlands Railways obtained allied army trucks as emergency buses, equipped with wooden benches and steps at the back. Soon real buses replaced them, English Crossleys and other makes, some 1,600 altogether. After 1948, when most railway lines were up and running, the buses were passed along to the subsidiary regional bus companies.

Repairs, temporary or permanent, went fast: At the end of 1945 some 1,400 km of railways was in use again, and one year later more than 3,000 km were usable out of the 3,174 that existed just before the 1944 strike. Re-electrification took longer, although a first stretch, Amsterdam-Haarlem-Overveen, was in use by August 1945. Shortages of copper, transformers, and switch gear caused delays, and only in 1948 was the prewar electric network in service again. The electrification of Amsterdam-Amersfoort, begun before the war,

FIGURE 119

The war-damaged Zutphen Station building, August 24, 1946. British army trucks were pressed into service as improvised motor buses while the railway tracks were under repair.
(Photo L. J. Biezeveld, Collection NVBS)

FIGURE 120

The coffee man at Utrecht Station, 1949. Station stops were long enough for these men to serve drinks and sweets to at least part of the train, with the customers hanging out of the windows to be served.
(Photo NS, Collection NVBS)

had to be stopped when the German authorities did not release the necessary copper wires. The line finally opened under wires in August 1946.

Train speeds were slow at first, as strict speed limits were enforced in many places. In 1946, the 217-kilometer journey from Amsterdam to Maastricht took almost seven hours because of roundabout routes and single tracks. One year later the trip took four and one-half hours, and two years later, just over three hours. Electrification reached Maastricht in the South in 1949.

Hupkes' goal had been train speeds of 160 km/h, and heavier rails had been laid on some lines for this purpose. However, the electric locomotives to be used proved unsuitable for this kind of fast service. The idea for these electric locomotives dated back to 1939, when a full-electric Amsterdam-Brussels service had been suggested. The locomotives (NS series 1000), patterned after Swiss prototypes and delivered after the war, were unsteady at speeds of more than 100 km/h.

Den Hollander had different goals—not high speeds on some lines but a regular, rigid timetable for every line, with speeds of 130 km/h maximum and 120 km/h in ordinary service. For these speeds, the existing rail of 46 kg/m was sufficient (NP 46 in Netherlands Railways parlance). Considering the relatively short distances in the country, high speeds did not reduce overall traveling time by much, and frequent service with good connections was deemed more important by Den Hollander.

Another of Den Hollander's ideas was the introduction of electric locomotives for the long-distance expresses. These engines could also haul freight trains at night, a combination that was technically possible, as the passenger trains did not have to go much faster than 130 km/h, while the freight trains since the introduction of continuous brakes generally ran at 100 km/h.

The fast rebuilding of the railway network caught the public fancy, and Netherlands Railways made skillful use of this positive reaction by introducing regular weekly radio broadcasts under the title "de spoorwegen spreken" (Hear the Railways Talking). The chief of the traffic department, P. T. Posthumus Meyjes, who made the broadcasts, managed to find some interesting news every week—a new station opened, a bridge repaired, a new service instituted, a new locomotive built—that made these programs very popular.

—— STEAM LOCOMOTIVES ——

Both Hupkes and Den Hollander had discarded the steam locomotive before 1940 in favor of electric or diesel-electric traction. The exigencies of the times, however, made them return to the faithful old iron horse, if only as a stopgap. During the war it had been clear that steam would be needed to run the trains for some time, and accordingly the Netherlands government in exile in 1943 had ordered from the Swedish manufacturer Nydquist and Holm fifteen 4-6-0 passenger engines (NS series 4000) plus thirty-five 0-8-0 freight engines (NS series 4700), to be delivered after the end of hostilities. They were based on Swedish designs dating back to 1927, but they came with modern details such as roller bearings and electric lights. Their life span was short, and the last went to the junkyard in 1956, not so much because of inherent defects, but because Netherlands Railways had discarded steam altogether.

Apart from the German engines left behind, which were sent back to Germany in 1947, other war locomotives entered service with Netherlands Railways. The English War Department's Austerity engines, 2-8-0s and 2-10-0s, had seen service in Europe after D-Day and had also run in large numbers on Dutch rails during their war careers. They were built according to the most modern principles, simply but efficiently equipped, and were found most suitable for the Dutch railway network. Their light axle load permitted them to go almost anywhere, and accordingly Netherlands Railways rented and bought hundreds of them (NS series 4300 and 5000). After some slight adaptations to Dutch circumstances they performed well, and they lasted until the very end of steam in the Netherlands. One of them, NS 5085, named *Longmoor* after the English military railway camp, was the thousandth War Department locomotive and has been preserved at the Utrecht railway museum. Together with these big war babies, called "jeeps" by the Dutch, the government took over some smaller 0-6-0 tanks from the English War Department for Netherlands Railways switching work (NS series 8800) and the state mines.

FIGURE 121

One of the British ex–War Department "Jeeps," Utrecht, 1945. The old WD number 77234 is still legible underneath the new Netherlands Railways number 4416. (Photo NS, Collection NVBS)

Toward the end of the war, the Netherlands government in London had bought twenty engines in Switzerland that had become superfluous there with the ongoing electrification. Five 2-6-0s, eight 2-6-0 tanks, and seven light 0-6-0 tanks came north, and when the Swiss also offered twenty-two 4-6-0 passenger locomotives for sale, the government bought them too, in October 1945. All of these ancient engines were in good condition, although some were more than fifty years old. Most were compound engines, which made them awkward for the Dutch drivers who were not used to this kind of complication. They had relatively short lives with Netherlands Railways, with the last retired in 1952. No new steam locomotives of Dutch design were built after the war.

ELECTRIFICATION

Hupkes and Den Hollander knew that large-scale electrification was the only way for the railways to keep a fair share of the country's transportation business. Den Hollander envisaged the rebuilding of the prewar electric network by 1948, which he then wanted to expand. All double-track lines and even a few single-track, less frequented lines were to be electrified, sometimes when revenues hardly warranted the capital investment. For instance, Leiden–Woerden, single track and at the time not a well-used line, could not remain a diesel-electric island in a total electric environment, so it was electrified.

In 1947, Netherlands Railways published a new electrification plan that embraced all main lines and some regional lines as well. Work went ahead quickly, and by 1949 Utrecht–Eindhoven–Maastricht and Heerlen were electric. One year later, Dordrecht–Roosendaal, Eindhoven, and Leiden–Woerden followed. Early in 1951 electrification reached Apeldoorn, and later that same year Enschede and Oldenzaal. Amersfoort–Zwolle joined the network in 1952, and some months later Groningen and Leeuwarden. The last line of the 1947 plan, Arnhem–Zutphen–Zwolle, was finished in 1953. Altogether 1,343 km of the busiest lines were now electrified out of a total of 3,186 km; over this electric network ran some 65 percent of all traffic. One old electric line was closed, the Hague–Wassenaar–Scheveningen, part of the pioneer electric line of 1908, never very remunerative after 1914. (Today such a line would never have been closed and lifted but instead converted into some light rail scheme.)

The total investment in new equipment and infrastructure between 1945 and 1952 came to one billion guilders, of which about one-third went to rolling stock, one-third to infrastructure and signaling, and the rest to buildings, office equipment, and miscellaneous purposes. The capital came from the war indemnity, depreciation (467 million), and new share capital (290 million), all procured by the government as sole shareholder.

Later extensions of the electric network were Eindhoven–Venlo and Gouda–Alphen aan den Rijn (single track) in 1956, Roosendaal–Flushing, Roosendaal–Breda, and Roosendaal–Esschen (Belgium) and Tilburg–'s-Hertogenbosch–Nijmegen in 1957. The last electrification, in 1958, the year of Den Hollander's retirement as president-director, was Alkmaar–Den Helder. By then, out of 3,227 km of railway lines, slightly more than half, 1,624 km, had been brought under the wires.

ELECTRIC ROLLING STOCK

A series of new multiple-unit streamlined electric trains ordered in 1940—twenty-five five-car sets and fifteen two-car trains—were delivered in 1942 by Beijnes and Werkspoor despite wartime conditions. The design of the bogies was not very successful, and the trains rode badly, especially after electric rail brakes had to be added to cope with the 160 km/h speeds planned.

After liberation, seventy-nine two-car and sixty-five four-car articulated trains were built to a new design by the Dutch firms of Werkspoor, Beijnes, and Allan. Unfortunately, their riding characteristics were almost as bad as those of their 1940 predecessors, but the trains had to be used despite their drawbacks. A real improvement in riding quality did not come until the 1954 trains, nicknamed the "dogs' noses." New ideas in vehicle dynamics, the use of coil and air springs combined with hydraulic dampers instead of the former heavy leaf springs, made for a velvety ride much appreciated by the traveling public. Of this type, sixty-eight two-car and seventy-three four-car trains were built. All electric streamlined trains, old or new, could be coupled indiscriminately by means of the automatic Scharfenberg couplers, which made all electric and pneumatic connections just by driving two trains slowly together.

Until now, Netherlands Railways had no electric locomotives, although they had been planned for the abortive prewar Amsterdam-Brussels service, as discussed earlier. The first electric locomotive in the Netherlands was an engine borrowed from the London and North Eastern Railway, a machine

FIGURE 122

A train of 1946 electric articulated units near Hazerswoude on the Leiden–Utrecht line, 1952. (Photo NS, Collection NVBS)

built in 1941 for the Manchester-Sheffield line, which was to be electrified with 1,500 volts DC. Owing to wartime shortages, the catenary had not been strung, and the locomotive could not be used. The LNER was happy to loan it to Netherlands Railways in 1947, where it mainly pulled passenger trains, as it was equipped with a steam boiler for train-heating purposes. It was nick-named Tommy, the popular name for British soldiers after 1945. In 1952, it returned to England for service on its home line.

As Tommy proved successful in service, Netherlands Railways decided to rent electric locomotives from the French National Railways, SNCF. Six French double-bogie (Bo-Bo) electric engines of a type popular type in France were rented for passenger trains between 1949 and 1951. It was a good way to acquaint the Netherlands Railways staff with French design and technology, as the currency restrictions of the time made the purchase of locomotives in France mandatory. The later NS series 1100 was a straight derivative of the rented machines.

The first electric locomotives owned by Netherlands Railways were the ten machines ordered in 1942 in Switzerland. As the engines could not be

FIGURE 123

One of the unfortunate Swiss-Dutch electric locomotives of the 1000 series with the Rheinpfeil international train into Germany, nearing Oisterwijk, 1952.
(Photo NS, Collection NVBS)

FIGURE 124

A French double-bogie electric locomotive of the 1100 class in turquoise green livery, leaving Amsterdam Central with a train of postwar stock in the same color, 1953.
(Photo NS, Collection NVBS)

FIGURE 125

A freight train with a 1300 Co-Co electric engine at the head, in solid dark blue livery, leaving the new Moerdijk Bridge, 1961.
(Photo NS, Collection NVBS)

delivered then, design alterations were made to fit them for the 160 km/h speeds Hupkes had in mind. The first three came straight from Switzerland after the war, and the rest were built by Werkspoor under Swiss licenses. They had a 1-Do-1 wheel arrangement but rode badly at high speeds and had to be used chiefly for freight trains.

The next sixty electric locomotives, NS series 1100, came from the French manufacturer Alsthom, Belfort between 1948 and 1955. Based on a double-bogie current and a highly successful French machine, they did good service in the Netherlands as well, although their riding qualities left something to be desired at higher speeds. From the same works came sixteen six-axle (Co-Co) machines (series 1300) between 1952 and 1956, again based on a French machine then in wide use by the SNCF. One of these SNCF machines, specially geared, reached a speed of 331 km/h in France, a world record. It could have gone faster, but the overhead wires started to melt, putting an end to the experiment. The Dutch engines, geared for no more than 140 km/h, were strong haulers and gave good service. Practically new, No. 1303 was destroyed in an accident in 1953, so no more than fifteen were ever in service at one time.

Almost simultaneously with the French machines, twenty-five American locomotives entered service, NS series 1200. They were of a Baldwin, Philadelphia, design based on the current American practice. Similar engines were running on the New York, New Haven, and Hartford and on other U.S. railroads. Werkspoor, Amsterdam, built the locomotives under license, but the six-wheeled bogies and other parts came from the United States, paid for with Marshall Plan dollars. Heemaf, Hengelo built the electrical equipment under license from Westinghouse. These 1200s were most successful, popular with

FIGURE 126

No. 1203, an American engine
of the 1200 class, with some
1100s behind, at the shed at
Maastricht, 1953.
(Photo W.R.G. van den Broek,
Collection NVBS)

the staff, and equally at home with freight or passenger trains. Some of them
are still in use with one of the new companies competing with Netherlands
Railways on some international freight services.

With this fleet of electric locomotives, Netherlands Railways ran all international and freight trains and some long-distance passenger trains until 1970,
while the multiple units took care of the rest of the services. Apart from the
1000s, which started out in green livery, all electric engines were painted a
striking turquoise green, patterned, it was said, after a favorite dress of Mrs.
Den Hollander. In service, the livery proved to soil easily, and after some
years a dark blue color was introduced instead.

DIESEL-ELECTRIC TRACTION

Den Hollander had declared the steam locomotive obsolete on non-electrified
lines. In its place, refurbished prewar diesel-electric three-car trains, demoted
from main line service by the ongoing electrification, were to provide the service. Of the forty prewar diesel-electrics, thirty could be reconditioned with
new Werkspoor diesel engines. The rest had to be scrapped. The eighteen fast
five-car units of 1940 had done little service owing to the war, and the Germans had used the engine units for their demagnetizing apparatus for ships.
Most came back with serious damage, and only twelve could be rebuilt with

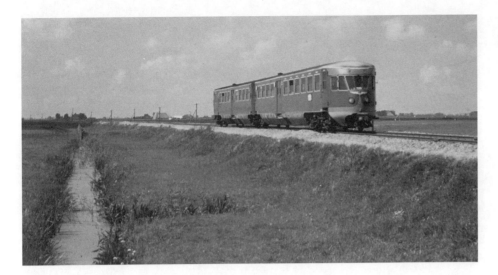

FIGURE 127

A two-car Blue Angel in the vastness of Friesland near Oudega, 1958.
(Photo J.G.C. van de Meene, Collection NVBS)

new Werkspoor diesels. But their great days were over, and they spent the rest of their lives in subordinate service.

It was clear from the outset that this prewar stock could not last long and would have to be replaced soon. Moreover, five-car and even three-car units were too large for many of the intended regional services, so the new diesel-electric trains for these lines were designed as two-car and single units. Allan of Rotterdam built forty-six two-car and thirty single motorcars between 1952 and 1955. Nicknamed Blue Angels because of the wings on their fronts and their light blue color, they became a familiar sight all over the country on regional lines. Re-engined and rebuilt, some of them are still in service.

FIGURE 128

NS 2009, one of the ex–U.S. Army diesel-electric locomotives, shunting freight trucks at Broek op Langendijk wharf, a center of vegetable traffic, 1958. The next year this machine would be withdrawn and scrapped.
(Photo J. C. de Jongh, Collection NVBS)

FIGURE 129

NS 2470 shunting at Valkenswaard, on the old Liège-Limburg line, 1958. The station building dates from the 1860s.
(Photo J.G.C. van de Meene, Collection NVBS)

FIGURE 130

NS 4734, a postwar Swedish locomotive, at the head of a short freight, December 30, 1957, near Meerssen in Limburg, one of the last strongholds of steam.
(Photo J.G.C. van de Meene, Collection NVBS)

In freight service, it took somewhat longer to phase out steam. In 1946, Netherlands Railways bought nineteen used diesel-electric double-bogie Bo-Bo engines from U.S. Army surplus stores (NS series 2000). In service, they proved troublesome, and new diesel prime movers of Dutch manufacture cured the problems only partially. The whole series was scrapped in 1958. Diesel-electric traction, however, would remain.

Quite a few of the small prewar diesel-electric engines, the locomotors, survived the war, but to replace those lost, Werkspoor built forty-eight more between 1949 and 1951. Heavier, six-wheel switchers bought from the British army worked so well that Netherlands Railways bought a hundred more new from English manufacturers.

For road service over longer distances, 150 heavy double-bogie Bo-Bo diesel-electric engines were purchased between 1955 and 1958. These Netherlands Railways Nos. 2201–2350 were of U.S. design, built under license by Allan of Rotterdam and Schneider of Le Creusot (France). Heemaf, Hengelo provided the electric equipment, and Stork, Hengelo, and Schneider constructed the U.S. diesel engines under license. Four of them working in a multiple unit could haul heavy ore and coal trains, with only one motorman at the controls.

FIGURE 131

A train of chiefly ex–Central Railway stock, with a 4-4-0 tank at the head, at Mijdrecht, south of Amsterdam, 1950—the light railway at its best. The line and the rolling stock would soon be gone.
(Photo NS, Collection NVBS)

The series 2301–2430, of French design and French construction, was a somewhat lighter double-bogie Bo-Bo engine built by Alsthom of Belfort between 1954 and 1957. Like the 2200s, these machines could be seen all over the country, and all had long lives. Here, too, currency restrictions played a significant role.

After all these foreign, U.S., English, and French engines, a purely Dutch design saw service in 1953. Designed and constructed by Werkspoor, the six 2600s, the heaviest and most powerful diesel-electric machines, proved troublesome in service. With their high, steep fronts, they were nicknamed Beelen after the high, bald forehead of the prime minister, L.J.M. Beel. Soon demoted to secondary service, they all were gone by 1958.

Post-War Development to 1958

CHAPTER

15

After the war, railway infrastructure in need of repair went far beyond bridges. As new station buildings replaced those damaged or destroyed, the opportunity was often taken to raise the level of the rails through cities, which generally necessitated even more new station buildings. Leiden was one of the first to get a new high line through the city, with a new station, which made several busy level crossings superfluous. Eindhoven, Tilburg, and Delft followed, although Delft's charming nineteenth-century station building remained in service.

The situation in Rotterdam required special attention. Not only had all the destroyed stations to be replaced, but the nuisance associated with two main line stations was also to be remedied if possible. The line from Utrecht/Gouda that still ended in the terminus of Rotterdam-Maas was now relaid on a new route west of Nieuwerkerk and directly linked to the existing belt line. In place of the old Delftsche Poort Station, a big new Central Station went up, the terminus for all lines. Only the pioneer electric line from The Hague by way of Pijnacker still ended in the Hofplein Station, for which a new simple building was constructed. Many trains on this line ran straight through to the Central Station, however, by way of a connecting link just north of the old belt line.

In Drente, a new line was laid to the oil fields of Nieuw Schoonebeek, where oil had been found in large enough quantities for profitable exploitation. Daily oil trains ran from there to an area west of Rotterdam where many

FIGURE 132

Old and new at Delft.
The old line along the canal
(the old city moat) at street
level, with a train of prewar
electric stock, 1956. In 1966,
the new high-level line is
finished and the canal filled in,
but the windmill, standing on
part of the old city ramparts,
is still there. The turreted
station is to the left of the
tracks in the far distance.
(Old photo J. C. de Jongh,
new photo NS,
both Collection NVBS)

oil companies had built refineries and chemical works, making this locale one
of the oil capitals of Europe. Not only oil companies located there, but other
port facilities as well opened on the deep water of new North Sea inlets—coal
and ore terminals and, much later, container facilities. The existing Rotterdam
harbor railway was extended westward again and again to link all this new
industry with the European railway network. In Amsterdam, a similar move
westward, away from the old port installations of the last century, also
occurred, bringing new railway construction in its wake.

FIGURE 133

Laying prefabricated track
with concrete ties on the
Eindhoven-Venlo line near
Helmond, 1955.
(Photo NS, Collection NVBS)

In some areas, it was necessary to strengthen the roadbed to accommodate higher axle loading and higher speeds. Between Gouda and Oudewater, the old Rhenish line engineered by Joseph Locke in the 1850s had to be completely rebuilt, as it tended to sink into the marshy subsoil. Other lines too required substantial strengthening, and to have curves flattened, switches straightened, and bridges reinforced. The planned quadrupling of the busiest lines, however, was postponed again because of the enormous expense involved; it would come only in the 1980s and 1990s.

The track structure itself, the combination of steel rails and wooden ties, had changed little since Van Dijk's successful introduction of his chaired track on the Central Railway before 1914. Only after 1945 was there experimentation with concrete ties to replace the expensive and fast-deteriorating wooden sleepers. A system was developed that consisted of concrete blocks in a zigzag configuration, linked by steel tubes, on which the rails of the new international UIC 54 standard were clasped. This became standard for most main lines in the country. Later, concrete ties of a more traditional kind were developed in Europe, and they found favor in the Netherlands as well.

Although less-frequented lines had been closed before 1940, closings accelerated after war's end. Many lines in the North and East, where passengers had always been rare, were now given over to regional bus companies. Mass motorization was expected to eat further into railway revenues, and in many cases buses could offer a better alternative to trains, as railway stations were sometimes too far from the centers of population. Among the many lines closed were those in the Haarlemmermeer, so fiercely contested in the 1890s, and parts of the old NOLS, Apeldoorn–Zwolle, Lage Zwaluwe–'s-Hertogenbosch. Generally, the tracks were left in place, as freight, especially coal, continued to be run on them. Limburg coal, for industrial and domestic use, remained one of the staples of railway traffic.

With these closings came some new acquisitions. In 1948, the Belgian government nationalized the remaining private (Belgian) company in Zeeland Flanders, Malines–Terneuzen, and Netherlands Railways took over the working of the Dutch part of the line. Although passenger traffic soon ended, the line continued to carry freight to the heavy industries around Terneuzen. As this line has no physical connection with the rest of the Netherlands Railways network, locomotives have to be brought over by way of Belgian rails to this day.

—— VOLUME OF TRAFFIC ——————————————————

The railway network expanded gradually after 1945 to its longest—3,347 km—in 1948 and then declined slowly to 3,227 km in 1958; 1,624 km of this

FIGURE 134

An oil train from the newly developed fields in Drente on its way to the refineries of Rotterdam, here still behind steam power, Hardenberg, 1948. The tank car is an ex–U.S. Army car. (Photo L. J. Biezeveld, Collection NVBS)

FIGURE 135

Beetles by train—German flat cars (ex–U.S. Army) carrying Volkswagens, Amersfoort, 1952. Located near Amersfoort, the Dutch importer of Volkswagen got his cars from the Wolfsburg factory by train (and he still does). (Photo NS, Collection NVBS)

was electrified. The total number of seats available for passengers in steam, electric, or diesel-electric trains declined from 202,000 in 1930 to 150,000 in 1940. After a wartime low in 1945, the number rose to 102,000 in 1950, then declined to only 97,000 in 1954, after which an all-time low it grew to 117,000 in 1958, an increase that continues. The intermediate second class, little used before 1940, was abolished in 1956, and the former third class became second.

The number of passengers grew much faster than the number of seats, a sure sign of improved efficiency. In 1940 the number had stood at 95 million, which mushroomed to 232 million because of wartime conditions in 1943, reached a more stable 158 million in 1950, and increased to 187 million in 1958. This trend also continues. Higher mobility, general population growth, roads choked with traffic, and a high number of commuters have all contributed to this increase in railway travel.

Freight traffic came back strongly after a 1945 low of 5.3 million tons; by 1947 it reached 16.1 million. Of this total, only 3.1 million had been international freight, but when the German economy started to gear up again, international traffic jumped to 8.3 of a total of 23.6 million tons in 1958. Ten years later, the international side of the business had left the domestic side far behind. The closing of many small yards and stops after the coal traffic dwindled to almost nothing caused the decline at home. The discovery of the enormous natural gas field in Groningen, and the almost total conversion from coal to gas as fuel for both industrial and domestic purposes, resulted in the closure of the Limburg coal mines in the 1970s, robbing the railways of one of their traditional shippers. The number of freight wagons declined to some 23,000 in 1958, but the construction of large wagons for specialized purposes resulted in a small growth of the total capacity available, from 450,000 to more than 500,000 tons in the same period. Grain, oil, automobiles, steel coils, and containers all got their own special large-capacity cars, generally on bogies and equipped with continuous brakes for higher speeds.

── INTERNATIONAL COOPERATION ──

Den Hollander had always advocated international cooperation in railway matters. Only by working together with other railway companies would it be possible to effectively combat the road and air competition, on the increase every year. The nineteenth-century international agencies such as the Verein, discussed earlier, had always been strongly German influenced, and after 1918 this seemed inappropriate. In 1922, the Union Internationale des Chemins de Fer (UIC, International Railway Union) was founded, acting on a French initiative.

FIGURE 136

One of the fast Swiss-Dutch TEE luxury trains at Amsterdam Central, shortly after their 1957 introduction. (Photo NS, Collection NVBS)

After 1945, the trend toward closer international cooperation became stronger in Europe, and at Den Hollander's suggestion, the Office de Recherches et d'Etudes (ORE, Railway Research and Study Office) was founded and headquartered in Utrecht. Within ORE, member railways (including most of the railways of Western and Southern Europe) exchanged experiences and practices and shared the results of new developments.

Another outcome of international cooperation, more visible to the ordinary traveler, was officially called the Groupement Trains Express Européens of 1957, and popularly called TEE. This again was Den Hollander's idea; he envisaged fast and luxurious through trains between the most important European cities on schedules that could compete with the airplane, and without tedious custom formalities at borders. His concept found favor with other railways and with the traveling public, and soon a network of fast TEE-trains covered Western and Southern Europe.

For these services, Netherlands Railways, together with the Swiss Federal Railways (SBB), acquired five diesel-electric train sets. The motorcars were built by Werkspoor, while the rest of the trains—three trailers each—were Swiss-made, a nice example of international cooperation in itself. They went into service Amsterdam-Paris (until 1964, when they were superseded by full-electric trains) and Amsterdam-Zürich and proved quite popular. The French, German, Italian, and later the Belgian railways each had their own diesel-electric and later full-electric trains built, but the colors of the exterior—red and cream—and the standard of comfort was the same everywhere.

SIGNALING

After the war, Netherlands Railways needed to decide what to do with the still serviceable but technically obsolete semaphore signaling system. Limited visibility on electrified lines because of the catenary masts along the tracks was a major source of complaints, and the existing semaphores could not indicate speeds allowed, only stop or go. This lack of posted speed limits was of major importance in International Railway Union circles, as well. Moreover, the old system with its many signal boxes was labor intensive. Color light signals could obviate most if not all of these drawbacks.

Netherlands Railways therefore in 1946 opted for a system of color light signals of the three-level kind, using current U.S. technology. Three lamps each were mounted in three round targets on one signal mast. Every lamp could show three colors plus white light, and in combination they could indicate exactly what speed the motorman was to hold and what to expect with the next signals. These signals were operated from one central point for a number of lines, making the many smaller signal boxes superfluous. The automatic block system came in at the same time, by which the trains themselves worked the signals, with the signal operator only supervising the running of the trains from a distance. By means of this new system, the capacity of the existing lines could be enlarged substantially, which pushed the problem of quadrupling further into the future.

FIGURE 137

The railway yards at Dordrecht, far inland, after the great flood of February 1953, the Netherlands' worst natural disaster of the twentieth century. Close to two thousand people drowned, and the damage was enormous. (Photo NS, Collection NVBS)

In day-to-day practice, however, the signals caused confusion and even led to occasional accidents, as was the case near Oldebroek (between Amersfoort and Zwolle) in 1955. In adverse weather, there was too small a distinction between green-white-green (meaning that the next signal would show yellow, lower speed) and green-white-white (the next signal would show all-clear, high speed). In 1955 a new system was adopted to replace the 1946 system—one target and generally only one color, green, yellow, or red, with, where necessary, a speed indicator in lighted figures underneath. This System 1955, as it was called, together with the automatic block system, was gradually introduced all over the network. In 1965, a system of automatic train control was added on the more frequented lines. Nevertheless, only in the 1990s could the last semaphore be dismantled.

The many level crossings had always been a nuisance, and the explosive growth of road traffic had only aggravated the problem. In the 1920s and 1930s, Netherlands Railways had abolished the manual guarding of many crossings as an economy measure. In 1936, the railways had tried out an automatic blinking light with success and after 1945 extended this system on a large scale for crossings in smaller roads without much traffic.

FIGURE 138

Color light three-aspect signal of the 1946 system, between Amersfoort and Zwolle near Nunspeet, 1952.
(Photo NS, Collection NVBS)

For busier roads, a new system with automatic half barriers was introduced in 1952 and later used widely, after some adaptations and improvements, but even then only together with programs of public education in the affected neighborhoods.

The best solution to these problems, removing all level crossings, was too costly. Only close cooperation with local and provincial authorities could accomplish this, as Netherlands Railways was not prepared to bear all the costs of building viaducts or tunnels. However, as most local government bodies were all too glad to get rid of the irritating and dangerous level crossings, they willingly bore part of the expense involved in constructing these safer crossings.

FIGURE 139

Two- and three-aspect color light signals of the 1955 system, near Amsterdam, 1971. The lighted figure 6 denotes a speed limit of 60 km/h. Both tracks are equipped for two directions to make the railway more flexible in emergencies.
(Photo J. A. Maassen, Collection NVBS)

CHAPTER

16

Last Years of the Twentieth Century

When Den Hollander retired officially as president-director of Netherlands Railways on January 1, 1958, he could look back on a railway company that had taken on new life in a highly modernized shape. In many respects, Netherlands Railways had become a leader in railway practice. On January 7, 1958, while British Railways was still designing and building new steam locomotives, and in other European countries steam still reigned supreme on many lines, Netherlands Railways enshrined its last steam engine in the Utrecht Railway Museum. The Dutch were the first in Europe to abolish steam completely. Two years earlier the last wooden-bodied passenger coach had been shunted onto the riptrack. In such varied arenas as signaling and office automation, Netherlands Railways presented an utterly modern image. Leaner and smaller than ever, the company could point to growing traffic figures every year, with an increasing number of frequent trains and a good safety record.

International cooperation also grew in a Europe that was becoming ever closer, less politically than economically. International freight traffic continued to grow, and the universal introduction of the container only speeded up this trend. The Rotterdam harbor line was extended farther westward, even into areas recently won from the sea, where large bulk freight and container terminals were constructed on deep water. Doubling the line became necessary, and in the near future it will be electrified as well. Electrification was also extended into Germany, where the line from Oldenzaal to Hanover was brought under wire as far as Bentheim on the Dutch 1,500-volt DC system. There an engine change takes place, because the connecting German electrification is 25,000-volt AC. The same has happened with the old Rhenish Railway line, where Emmerich became the system-changing station. In the Southeast the reverse was true, and German electric locomotives hauled the trains into Venlo, where Netherlands Railways took over.

NETHERLANDS RAILWAYS
IN THE 1960s AND 1970s

Despite these positive elements, some doubted the need for a modern railway system at all. Mass motorization seemed to provide a better answer, and even in government circles road construction was often deemed more important than railway building. A fairly comprehensive system of motorways begun just before 1940 was laid out during these years, and owning an automobile seemed to be everyone's goal. At railway headquarters at Utrecht a certain ossification appeared to set in, and Netherlands Railways did not market its product adequately. The vigorous elan under Den Hollander gave way to a certain smugness, and the management seemed oblivious to the winds of change. The financial results of Netherlands Railways also showed a downturn; government again had to make good the losses.

"THE RAILWAY TOWARD 1975"

In 1969 Netherlands Railways presented its plan for the immediate future, "Spoor naar 75" (the Railway Toward 1975). Its most important points were the need for more stations in new suburbs; new lines—to be financed by the government; and better separation of regional and long-distance traffic. Express trains running every thirty minutes or every hour at speeds of 130 or even 140 km/h between some forty of the bigger stations were to be supplemented by more frequent but slower regional trains providing service to all stations. Integration with existing local and regional motor bus, streetcar, and underground systems was also seen as a certain way to win back lost traffic.

At first, the railways thought carrying out this plan would require only a small investment in the existing infrastructure, but more trains meant more lines and more equipment as well. The government did approve of the general plan and showed itself willing to take on the construction of new lines, as recommended in "Spoor naar 75." Mass motorization seemed to have reached its limits, as cities could no longer provide parking for the growing numbers of cars, which choked the streets during rush hours. The exhaust fumes of the thousands of vehicles on the road threatened to poison everything around, raising environmental questions.

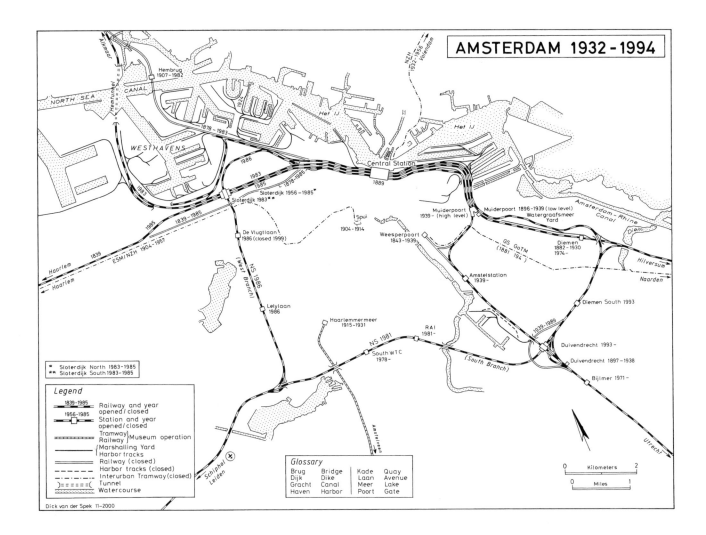

Legend

1839-1985	Railway and year opened / closed
1956-1985	Station and year opened / closed
	Tramway/ Railway} Museum operation
	Marshalling Yard
	Harbor tracks
	Railway (closed)
	Harbor tracks (closed)
	Interurban Tramway (closed)
	Tunnel
	Watercourse

* Sloterdijk North 1983-1985
** Sloterdijk South 1983-1985

Dick van der Spek 11-2000

Glossary

Brug	Bridge	Kade	Quay
Dijk	Dike	Laan	Avenue
Gracht	Canal	Meer	Lake
Haven	Harbor	Poort	Gate

— NEW CONSTRUCTION —

The first new line built was the Zoetermeer-line, a long loop branching off from the old Hofplein electric line, through Zoetermeer, the new suburb east of The Hague. Since its opening in 1977 it has carried large numbers of commuters, but no freight at all. A more spectacular direct line between Amsterdam and Leiden opened in stages between 1978 and 1981, laid out for speeds of 160 km/h. It passed through tunnels directly under the main terminal of Schiphol/Amsterdam Airport and became such a success that the Schiphol-Amsterdam section is being quadrupled and the underground airport station greatly enlarged.

Schiphol became not only a very busy airline terminal but also the focus of all kinds of commercial development; the underground railway station grew to the third largest in the country—after Amsterdam and Utrecht—in number of passengers.

The earthworks for a new belt line around Amsterdam were partly constructed in the 1930s as relief work for the mass of unemployed. Connecting with the Schiphol line, the belt line was finally opened some forty years later, making it possible to bypass the crowded Central Station in that city.

Another line, begun in 1982, ran out into the newly reclaimed land northeast of Amsterdam in the former South Sea or IJsselmeer, as it is called now. New towns such as Almere and Lelystad, partly intended to house the overflow of Amsterdam, had sprung up there and needed quick and easy communication with the old land. The line, built with no level crossings and the most modern technology, presently ends at Lelystad, but its continuation to Groningen or Zwolle (or both) is under discussion.

The quadrupling of lines planned in the 1890s began in the 1980s. Leiden–The Hague–Delft was quadrupled, Utrecht-Amersfoort in part, and the Schiphol line in part, while the lines westward out of Amsterdam were converted into a six-track stretch. Overpasses at many busy junctions prevent conflicting movements and eliminate a potential cause of accidents. The approaches at the west side of Utrecht Central were completely altered to allow simultaneous departures of trains to Amsterdam and Rotterdam/The Hague. A deep four-track tunnel under the river replaced the old double-track viaduct through Rotterdam, with its vulnerable lift bridge, that withstood the ravages of war.

The integration of railway and regional tramway and underground systems envisaged in "Spoor naar 75" never took place. The long-discussed takeover of both Zoetermeer and Hofplein lines by a new Randstadrail system, which would also embrace Rotterdam's underground and streetcar networks plus the streetcar system of The Hague/Delft, was postponed to the twenty-first century.

NEW STATION ARCHITECTURE

Between roughly 1960 and 1980 the country's financial straits dictated a cheap standard design for most new stations—a modular building, uninspiring inside and out, that provided only the bare necessities for the traveler. A cheap way of building something more attractive was to combine railway station and supermarket, post office, or office building. The Hague Central (1975), which replaced the old inadequate Rhenish/State Railways terminus of the 1870s, is a good example. The twelve-story office block looks a bit forbidding, but the lofty station hall behind it is light and pleasant, and best of all, over the twelve stub tracks of the railway terminal a covered bus and streetcar platform was built, an example of the integration of public transport under one roof that exists nowhere else in the country. Less successful from an architectural point of view was the renewal of Utrecht Central (1974), which was completely overshadowed by the surrounding urban shopping mall and fair buildings. A later addition in 1989 provided a light and airy station hall over the tracks, but from the street the station is still hardly recognizable as such.

The lean years ended by the early 1980s, and under the general direction of architect C. Douma a large number of new stations went up, some to replace outdated ones, some on new locations along existing lines, and many on the new lines of the period. One of the most spectacular is Amsterdam-Sloterdijk (1986) by H.C.H. Reijnders. At this award-winning bilevel station,

FIGURE 140

The Hague Central Station under construction, 1974. The concrete platform over the tracks will become the bus station; from the roof of the parking garage at the right, the streetcar lines will cross in front of the office block, under the roof with the glass pyramids. The Rhenish Railway station of the 1870s is still in use (the overall roof, and the low buildings shown *left* of the new deck). Today, the old buildings to the *left* are gone, and a hotel/shopping complex and the General State Archives occupy the empty spaces on the *right*. (Photo NS, Collection NVBS)

the lines to Haarlem and Alkmaar are at street level, and the Schiphol line crosses at right angles through the station hall on an upper level in an enormous glass tube. Almere Central (1987) by P.A.M. Kilsdonk, on the new line to Lelystad, is another example of the trend toward light and open big-city stations, a style that culminated in Leiden Central (1996), again by Reijnders, and 's-Hertogenbosch (1998), by R.M.J.A. Steenhuis, which replaced Van Ravesteyn's postwar edifice. At 's-Hertogenbosch, the nineteenth-century iron platform awnings and overall roofs have been meticulously restored and integrated into the new building. Many smaller buildings of pleasing outline and with more than adequate amenities have gone up in the past years, too many to mention here.

Financing these large-scale renewals and extensions was generally a matter for the government, part of the large infrastructure activities on canals, roads, river tunnels, and other public works. No private funding was asked for or needed until very recently. The 1994 decision to privatize Netherlands Railways may well alter the picture fundamentally.

208   RAILWAYS IN THE NETHERLANDS

NEW ROLLING STOCK

All these new lines and the growing traffic required new trains in large numbers. Werkspoor of Amsterdam/Utrecht at first still built these, generally to Netherlands Railways designs. In 1964 came a new design of an electric four-car multiple-unit train from Werkspoor, with a much higher acceleration and top speed than those of the earlier trains. Accordingly, they could not be coupled with the existing stock. These 31 four-car trains were followed by 245 similar two-car units, again from Werkspoor, and when Werkspoor closed its railway division in 1972, from Talbot in neighboring Aachen.

The new suburban lines such as that to Zoetermeer called for a new design. Netherlands Railways and Talbot in 1975 came up with a two-car electric unit called Sprinter because of its high acceleration. Talbot built ninety-five of these trains, subsequently also in a three-car configuration. Designed for mass movement over relatively short distances with frequent stops, they looked fairly spartan, and the two-car units had no first-class compartments. In the later three-car units, first class and toilets were added, although on some suburban lines, first class was officially abolished.

Beginning in 1977, Talbot built a new and very comfortable train developed for long distances, again in the multiple-unit configuration, with three- and four-car trains. The unmotorized middle cars of these trains were also

FIGURE 141

A push-pull, double-decker Amsterdam-Haarlem train in the futuristic bilevel Amsterdam-Sloterdijk Station, 1986. An Amsterdam-Schiphol-Leiden train is visible in the glass tube on the upper level, part of the belt line around Amsterdam.
(Photo NS, Collection NVBS)

FIGURE 142

The light and airy Zaandam Station, north of Amsterdam, that opened in 1983. A Sprinter class train is at the platform. (Collection NVBS)

ordered separately in large numbers for locomotive haulage. Alsthom of Belfort, France, delivered fifty-eight Bo-Bo electric locomotives (NS series 1600) for these trains and for freight work as well, as the older series were getting near retirement age. Alsthom constructed eighty-one more of these beginning in 1990, of a slightly improved design (NS series 1700). The old faithful of the series, 1100, 1200, and 1300, were then rapidly scrapped, although some of the American 1200s have received new life hauling the freight trains of one of Netherlands Railways' new competitors.

When traffic continued to grow through the 1980s, the old dilemma cropped up again—how to expand the service? Longer trains would not fit existing platforms and already crowded tracks could accommodate no more trains. In 1991, Netherlands Railways introduced 258 double-deck coaches in several series—a style that had been tried before in other countries but had never caught on. Electric locomotives of the series 1600 and 1700, equipped with automatic couplers for the purpose, would haul the carriages push-pull fashion. A seven-car double-decker just a few meters longer than two ordinary four-car units seats 932 compared to the 544 of the older train. The trains were a success, and the Swiss copied the design almost to the last bolt.

Netherlands Railways has been replacing the electric locomotives with a new kind of hybrid locomotive, with seats on the upper deck and all the electrical gear on the lower, riding on three four-wheel bogies and with all axles powered, giving the same acceleration as a 1600 locomotive. Four-car multiple-unit trains in the double-deck configuration have also been built for longer distances. The hourly Benelux service from Amsterdam to Brussels was upgraded with new stock of Dutch design, hauled push-pull fashion by a Belgian electric locomotive equipped for 1,500 and 3,000 volts DC. To mark this international collaboration, the trains and engines were finished in a combination of Dutch yellow and Belgian red.

On the regional non-electrified lines, the old Blue Angels were still going strong, many rebuilt with new diesel engines and other equipment and

FIGURE 143

The Leiden Central Station, opened in 1996, surrounded by a typical Dutch phenomenon, a sea of bicycles. (Photo J. Muijs, Collection NVBS)

FIGURE 144

One of the yellow two-car
diesel-hydraulic units for
lightly loaded regional trains,
at Groningen in 1996.
(Photo J. Muijs,
Collection NVBS)

repainted yellow, the new house style. The railway phased out the prewar streamlined diesel-electric trains, replacing them with new three-car units built by Werkspoor between 1960 and 1963. Since 1990, these have been supplemented by fifty-three two-car diesel-hydraulic trains built by Düwag-Krefeld and Talbot-Aachen. For lines with less traffic, the railway introduced a German-designed diesel-hydraulic train in 1981, built by Düwag as one- and two-car units.

SIGNALING AND SAFETY

The conversion from the 1946 signaling system to the new one in 1955 went on, and the old semaphore signals gradually disappeared; the last came down in 1991. Important stations and junctions got new Entrance-Exit (NX) systems, in which only two buttons set all points and signals governing the run of a train. After 1960, a lot of the smaller local signal boxes were concentrated in large centralized traffic control towers, until only some ten or twelve of these controlled the whole network early in the twenty-first century.

Despite a fairly high standard of safety after 1945, accidents still occurred. Defects in the trains and in the signaling equipment along with human error were the most frequent causes. Human error caused the worst crash on Dutch rails, when two trains collided almost head-on on January 8, 1962, near

Harmelen, east of Woerden. A train Rotterdam-Woerden-Amsterdam was moving through the junction at slow speed to run toward Amsterdam, when it was rammed at almost full speed by a heavy train from Utrecht. The driver of the Utrecht train had missed a yellow and a red signal and had applied his brakes only at the last moment. Both drivers and ninety-two passengers died, and fifty-two were injured.

After the Harmelen disaster, the discussion about automatic train control again grew intense, and in 1964 the decision was made to install such a system on the busiest stretches. The friendly relationship between Netherlands Railways and the General Railway Signal (GRS) Company that had existed since 1924 may have influenced the choice of the U.S. system, as developed by the GRS together with Netherlands Railways. Compared to German and Swiss systems on the market, it turned out to be more expensive and more difficult to install. On the plus side, the Philips electronic company and the old established foundry at Alkmaar, with a long tradition of constructing signal equipment, were licensed to build the necessary parts. After some experimenting, the GRS system worked adequately, and by 1992 it was installed on most of the network and rolling stock. Out on the road, the driver had to acknowledge the indication of the signals, audible warnings sounded in the cab, and an automatic full brake was applied if a driver failed to obey a red light. Since 1996 Netherlands Railways has been slowly introducing an advanced version of the same system.

——PRIVATIZATION AND SPLITTING UP——

In accordance with recommendations from the European Commission, the decision was made in 1993 to split Netherlands Railways into two general units, infrastructure and operations. The government would remain responsible for the existing infrastructure and future extensions and improvements, while the actual running of trains was entrusted to Netherlands Railways for the time being, with the possibility that others could enter this market also.

FIGURE 145

A caterpillar—a blue-and-yellow double-decker three-car train—on the old Rhine bridge near Arnhem, 1997. These three- and four-car units are the Netherlands Railways' newest rolling stock.
(Photo J. Muijs, Collection NVBS)

FIGURE 146

In some long-distance trains, special bicycle cars, converted from old baggage cars, are being run in summer to accommodate the large number of vacationers who want to bring their bikes with them.
(Photo NS, Collection NVBS)

Netherlands Railways itself then split up into business units, one for passenger traffic, one for cargo, one for stations, one for other real estate, and so on, all under the umbrella of a general holding company. It was envisaged that this company would be privatized in time, but it remains to be seen if this will ever come about. All business units are supposed to be profitable without government subsidies, although investment in new infrastructure will largely be paid for by the state.

For the ordinary traveler these changes, in force since January 1, 1994, have meant little until now, but in the future they may become more visible. For instance, Netherlands Railways-Cargo, the freight department, has recently merged with its German counterpart DB-Cargo, to become a stronger player in this highly competitive market. Other players have entered the rail market, especially in the freight sector, where several new companies have contracted to haul containers from the port of Rotterdam into Germany.

THE OUTLOOK SINCE 1995

In 1995, on a total network of 2,739 km, Netherlands Railways transported 305 million passengers between 372 stations and stops, and just under 21 million tons of freight, most of which was international. For this traffic, the company had a fleet of electric and diesel-electric multiple-unit trains and locomotive-hauled stock in service—altogether 196,000 seats, 526 locomotives, both electric and diesel-electric, and 3,237 freight trucks. To move, maintain, and administer all this, just over 29,000 men and women sufficed, a reasonably small number compared to that in other European countries. In the near future, a staff of 23,000 should be adequate to take care of the growing traffic.

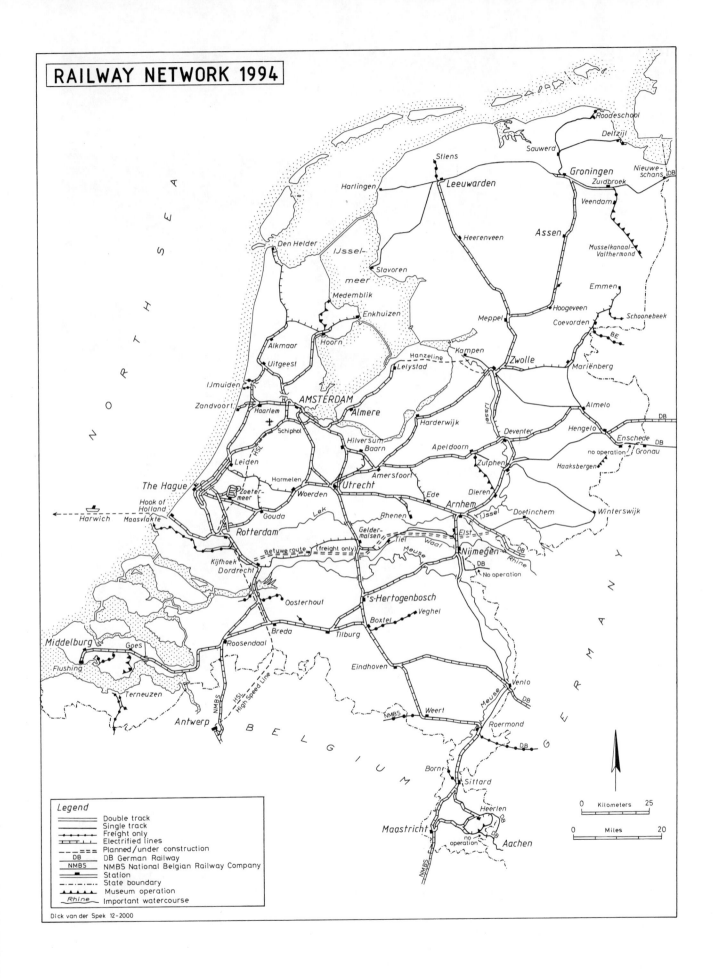

RAILWAY NETWORK 1994

Roodeschool
Delfzijl
Sauwerd
Groningen
Nieuwe-
schans · DB
Zuidbroek
Stiens
Leeuwarden
Harlingen
Veendam
Heerenveen
Assen
Den Helder
IJssel-
Stavoren
meer
Musselkanaal-
Valthermond
Medemblik
Emmen
Enkhuizen
Hoogeveen
Meppel
Schoonebeek
Hoorn
Coevorden
Alkmaar
Kampen
BE
Uitgeest
Hanzeline
Zwolle
Mariënberg
IJmuiden
Lelystad
Zandvoort
Almelo
DB
Haarlem
AMSTERDAM
IJssel
Deventer
Hengelo
Enschede
Schiphol
Almere
Harderwijk
Zutphen
DB
Hilversum
Apeldoorn
no operation
Gronau
Leiden
HSL
Baarn
Haaksbergen
Zoeter-
Harmelen
Amersfoort
Zutphen
The Hague
meer
Woerden
Utrecht
Ede
Arnhem
Dieren
Hook of
Gouda
Rhenen
Winterswijk
Holland
Lek
IJssel
Doetinchem
Harwich
Maasvlakte
Rotterdam
Geldermalsen
Elst
Betuweroute (freight only)
Tiel
Waal
Nijmegen
DB
Kijfhoek
Meuse
Rhine
DB
Dordrecht
No operation
Oosterhout
s-Hertogenbosch
Veghel
Boxtel
Middelburg
Goes
Breda
Tilburg
Roosendaal
Eindhoven
Flushing
Venlo
DB
Terneuzen
HSL High Speed Line
Weert
Meuse
Antwerp
NMBS
Roermond
BELGIUM
DB
Born
GERMANY
Sittard
Heerlen
DB
Maastricht
no
DB
operation
Aachen
NMBS

NORTH SEA

Legend
════	Double track
────	Single track
••••	Freight only
┼┼┼┼	Electrified lines
────	Planned/under construction
DB	DB German Railway
NMBS	NMBS National Belgian Railway Company
■	Station
─·─·─	State boundary
^^^^	Museum operation
Rhine	Important watercourse

Dick van der Spek 12-2000

0 Kilometers 25

0 Miles 20

FIGURE 147

Even with the most advanced technical equipment, a railway still relies on a dedicated and highly qualified staff.
(Photo NS, Collection NVBS)

Financial results of the passenger side of the business have improved, rising from a small profit of 8 million guilders in 1995 to 214 million in 1998. The latest developments in the railway sphere are the extension of the French and German high-speed lines into the Netherlands. Although Netherlands Railways already owns part of the French-Belgian-Dutch fleet of high-speed Thalys trains now running between Amsterdam and Paris, these sleek monsters may not go faster than 160 km/h on Dutch soil until the planned high-speed line is finished—the Amsterdam-Brussels leg is presently under construction. Several German ICE-trains are also on order by Netherlands Railways for the intended Amsterdam-Cologne-Frankfurt high-speed service, but the line itself remains in the planning stages. It is also uncertain whether these high-speed lines will be electrified with the existing Dutch 1,500-volt DC system, or with the German/French 25,000-volt AC system. Discussion is ongoing over the question of whether the whole electrified network should be changed over to 25,000 volts, a move with far-reaching consequences.

Environmental aspects and private interests—the not-in-my-backyard syndrome—figure largely in construction of new lines, high speed or not. A beginning has been made, however, with an all new double-track freight line from Rotterdam eastward into Germany and beyond, to move the thousands of containers brought to Rotterdam for German or other European destinations off the crowded roads.

Passenger traffic is confidently expected to grow in the coming years, as the road network during rush hours—despite the building of more roads—is more crowded than ever and public rail transportation seems to be the best way to keep traffic fluid.

Some regional lines have recently been shoved off onto local authorities, which will run the trains in close connection with existing motor bus services in the same area. Netherlands Railways generally participates in these new ventures, and provincial and municipal subsidies are clearly needed to cover working expenses on these often unprofitable but socially indispensable lines. It is still too early to judge the success of these measures.

Whether other experiments with direct competition with Netherlands Railways for passenger traffic on some main lines will result in improved services remains in question as well. It is doubtful if a second company will be able to run its trains on lines where Netherlands Railways already provides a frequent and convenient service, but it might be useful to prod a practical monopolist, as Netherlands Railways was until now, into giving even better and more punctual service to the public. Matters of safety also play a role here, as developments in England have shown all too clearly. The most recent news is that the only real competitor up till now, a Dutch-French company, gave up its service between Amsterdam and Haarlem for lack of revenues.

It is still not quite clear how much freedom the government will grant the privatized Netherlands Railways. In matters of fares, schedules, and such, the minister still will want the last word, and no doubt other instances may occur where private and public interests will clash. A provider of important public services such as Netherlands Railways will never be allowed to operate only for profit. Here the lessons of the past should make interesting and even profitable reading for politicians as well as railway directors.

BIBLIOGRAPHIC ESSAY

For my book *De IJzeren Weg in een Land vol Water. Beknopte geschiedenis van de spoorwegen in Nederland, 1834–1958* (*The Iron Road in a Land of Water: Concise History of Railways in the Netherlands, 1834–1958*)(Amsterdam: De Bataafsche Leeuw, 1998), of which the present volume is a much reworked, adapted, and extended version, my main sources were the printed annual reports of the railway companies, those of the Railway Supervisory Board, and the literature detailed here. The archives of Netherlands Railways were not available at the time, while those of its predecessors were scattered and disorganized.

ARCHIVES AND RECORDS

Students of the history of the railways in the Netherlands received a boon in February 2000, when all remaining records (most in Dutch) of all railway companies in the Netherlands were housed in the Utrechts Archief, the state and municipal record office in Utrecht. Inventories, lists, and other aids make these records highly accessible.

LITERATURE

Little literature is available in languages other than Dutch. In this bibliographic essay, I have tried to bring together all pertinent works in English and the most important works in Dutch as well. For those who want to go deeper into the subject, the extensive bibliography of *De IJzeren Weg in een Land vol Water* is a useful Dutch source of secondary literature.

GENERAL HISTORY

For the history of the Dutch Republic the best recent work available is Jonathan I. Israel, *The Dutch Republic: Its Rise, Greatness, and Fall, 1477–1806* (Oxford: Oxford University Press, 1995). For the later period, E. H. Kossmann, *The Low Countries, 1780–1940* (Oxford: Oxford University Press, 1978), is an excellent survey and as a bonus includes Belgium.

ECONOMIC HISTORY

For the period of the Dutch Republic, the recent work of Jan de Vries and Ad van der Woude, *The First Modern Economy: Success, Failure, and Perseverance of the Dutch Economy, 1500–1815* (Cambridge: Cambridge University Press, 1997), is an invaluable survey, and the authors argue convincingly that the first—wind-powered—industrial revolution occurred in the Zaan region north of Amsterdam in the late sixteenth and early seventeenth centuries. What is commonly known as the industrial revolution in England was only the second, in their opinion. The important commercial connections between the Netherlands and the Prussian hinterland are described in Joachim F. E. Bläsing, *Das Goldene Delta und sein Eisernes Hinterland 1815–1851: Von Niederländisch–Preussischen zu Deutsch–Niederländischen Wirtschaftsbeziehungen* (The golden delta and its iron hinterland, 1815–1851: From Netherlands-Prussian to German-Netherlands economic relations) (Leiden: Stenfert Kroese, 1973). The development of Dutch industry during the first half of the nineteenth century is covered in Joel Mokyr, *Industrialization in the Low Countries, 1795–1850* (New Haven: Yale University Press, 1976), and R. T. Griffiths, *Industrial Retardation in the Netherlands 1830–1850* (The Hague: M. Nijhoff, 1979), although the latter work has been critized as being too negative. A more balanced attitude toward the industrialization of the Netherlands is to be found in H. W. Lintsen et al., eds., *Geschiedenis van de Techniek in Nederland: De wording van een moderne samenleving, 1800–1890* (History of technology in the Netherlands: The growth of a modern society), 6 vols. (Zutphen: Walburg Pers, 1992–1995). Lintsen and his authors argue that industrialization in the Netherlands in many respects proceeded differently from that in other European countries, but not necessarily later. J. A. de Jonge, in *De industrialisatie in Nederland tussen 1850 en 1914* (Industrialization in the Netherlands between 1850 and 1914) (Amsterdam: Scheltema and Holkema, 1968; reprint Nijmegen: Sun, 1976) argues much the same point. In his view the takeoff, as formulated by W. W. Rostow in *The Process of Economic Growth* (Oxford: Oxford University Press, 1960), took place between roughly 1870 and 1890, without singling out a really leading sector, although the textiles and machine and metal industries developed faster than others. For the twentieth century there is nothing comparable in English, but in Dutch an excellent survey is J. L. van Zanden and R. T. Griffiths, *Economische geschiedenis van Nederland in de 20e eeuw* (Economic history of the Netherlands in the 20th century) (Utrecht: Spectrum, 1989).

TRANSPORTATION HISTORY

Jan de Vries has covered the prerailway era of barges and boats in his fine *Barges and Capitalism: Passenger Transportation in the Dutch Economy (1632–1839)* (Utrecht: Hes, 1981). H.P.H. Nusteling examined the Rhine navigation in his *De Rijnvaart in het tijdperk van stoom en steenkool 1831–1914* (Rhine navigation in the era of steam and coal), (Amsterdam: Holland University Press, 1974). J. H. Schawacht, *Schiffart und Güterverkehr zwischen den Häfen des Deutschen Niederrhein und Rotterdam vom Ende des 18. bis zur Mitte des 19. Jahrhunderts* (Cologne: Rheinisch–Westfälischen Wirtschaftsarchiv, 1973), does the same from the German point of view. Both give a lot of figures and hard facts on this important navigation.

RAILWAY HISTORY

Old, but still a most useful and authoritative source for the political background of the history of railways is J. H. Jonckers Nieboer, *Geschiedenis der Nederlandsche Spoorwegen 1832–1938* (2d ed., Rotterdam: Nijgh and Van Ditmar, 1938). Nothing is said in this study about the actual working of the railways, the technology involved, or the staff. Early finance is covered in excellent detail by W. van den Broeke, *Financiën en financiers van de Nederlandse spoorwegen 1837–1890* (Zwolle: Waanders, 1985). His chief argument is that the Dutch capitalists were not averse to investing in the early home railways. Only when the financial results were disappointing did they turn to more profitable investments elsewhere. In my own *De IJzeren Weg in een Land vol Water,* I have tried to give a succinct survey of all aspects of railway history. The only recent contribution in English is my article "Railways in the Netherlands, 1830–1914," in the U.S. journal *Railroad History* 173 (autumn 1995), pp. 5–57. It does give a lot of literature to help readers along. For the dates of opening and closing of railway and tramway lines in the country, and for the dates of incorporation, mergers, and so on, of companies, one should consult the invaluable little book by J. W. Sluiter, *Beknopt overzicht van de Nederlandse spoor- en tramwegbedrijven* (2d ed., Leiden: Brill, 1967). A new edition is in preparation.

COMPANY HISTORIES AND MEMORIAL BOOKS

The Holland Railway was the first to mark its half century with an elaborate memorial book: *Hollandsche IJzeren Spoorweg–Maatschappij 1839–1889* (Amsterdam: HIJSM, 1889). The Rhenish Railway was no longer in existence when it would have passed the fifty-year mark, but the State Company produced a very nice photo album in 1913 to mark its anniversary: *Maatschappij tot Exploitatie van Staatsspoorwegen 1863–1913* (Utrecht: SS, 1913). The Central and North Brabant–German companies were too poor to do anything in this respect, but Netherlands Railways did bring out a beautiful illustrated volume to celebrate the centenary of railways in the country: *100 jaar spoorwegen in Nederland. Overzicht van het ontstaan en de ontwikkeling der spoorwegen in Nederland van 1839–1939* (Utrecht: NS, 1939). Serious company histories are rather scarce, but fortunately K. H. Beijen, formerly connected with the Rhenish Railway, chronicled his memories in his *Geschiedkundige herinneringen aan de Nederlandsche Rhijnspoorweg Maatschappij* (Haarlem: Tjeenk Willink, 1893), and D.A.E. Immink, secretary of the Central Company, did the same in his *De Nederlandsche Centraal Spoorweg Maatschappij van 1863–1913* (No place, no year [1913]). More superficial but interesting nevertheless are three books by N. J. van Wyck Jurriaanse, *De Hollandsche IJzeren Spoorwegmaatschappij* (2 vols., Rotterdam: Wyt, 1975–1977) and *De Nederlandsche Centraal Spoorwegmaatschappij* (Rotterdam: Wyt, 1973). Recently, to mark 150 years of railways in the Netherlands, J. A. Faber edited *Het Spoor. 150 jaar spoorwegen in Nederland* (Amsterdam: Meulenhoff, 1989), but the result is somewhat spotty—very good for the first fifty years, but much less so for the rest of the period. Quite recent is Michael Lehmann's history (in German) of the North Brabant–German, *Der blaue Brabant. Die Geschichte der Boxteler Bahn* (Uedem: Guntlisbergen Verlag, 1998), a serious story with a lot of local lore. The impact of war on the railways and its dramatic consequences for all concerned are covered by A.J.C. Rüter in his well-researched *Rijden en Staken. De Nederlandse Spoorwegen in oorlogstijd* (The Hague: M. Nijhoff, 1960). Rüter manages to give a careful, balanced, and overall fair judgment of the directors, and especially of Hupkes, president of Netherlands Railways, in their dealings with the German authorities.

Local and regional studies concerning railway history are much too numerous to list them all here. Interested readers are referred to the bibliography of my *De IJzeren Weg in een Land vol Water*, where at least the most important ones are given. An exception should be made here for J. W. van Borselen's *Sporen in Rotterdam. Stadsgeschiedenis rondom de trein* (Rotterdam: Stichting Historische Publicaties Roterodamum, 1993), and H. Kaas, *Amsterdam Goederen. De geschiedenis van de goederenstations in Amsterdam* ('s-Hertogenbosch: Stichting Rail Publications, 1996). The first gives an all-round history of railways in and around Rotterdam, while the second concentrates on freight yards and terminals but includes a lot of general railway history in Amsterdam as well. Comparable railway histories of other major cities are not available, not even of Utrecht, which was a major railway town.

Histories of regional and local tramways systems abound, too many to enumerate here. A useful and fairly complete survey in English is given by G. E. Baddesley, *The Continental Steam Tram* (London: Light Rail Transit Association, 1980), who lists all companies operating in the Netherlands, with their lines and rolling stock, on pp. 146–174. J. W. Sluiter, in his *Beknopt overzicht* (noted earlier), also lists all tramway companies, with their dates of incorporation and such.

Of the Dutch factories active in the railway field, Beijnes brought out a very nice company history by H. Asselberghs, *Een eeuw van arbeid* (Haarlem: Beijnes, 1938), while Werkspoor did the same later with *Werkspoor 1827–1952. Gedenkboek samengesteld ter gelegenheid van het honderd vijf en twintig jarig bestaan* (Amsterdam: Werkspoor, 1952). A short survey of all machine works, iron foundries, and related industries is to be found in W.H.P.M. van

Hooff, *De Nederlandse machinefabrieken 1825–1914* (Amsterdam: NEHA, 1990); the same author wrote a more in-depth study of the same subject with his *In het rijk van de Nederlandse Vulcanus. De Nederlandse machinenijverheid 1825–1914, een historische bedrijfstakverkenning* (Amsterdam: NEHA, 1990).

Railway bridges, very important in a country with so much water, are described in H.M.C.M. Maarschalkerwaart, J. Oosterhoff, and G. J. Arends, *Bruggen in Nederland 1800–1940* (3 vols., Utrecht: Matrijs, 1997–1998, 1999). Bridges in all construction materials, wood, iron, steel, and concrete, and all kinds of bridges, fixed or with opening spans of some kind, are covered in this exhaustive survey.

SURROUNDING COUNTRIES

The connections by steamboat with England are given in Cecil J. Allen, *The Great Eastern Railway* (London: Ian Allan, 1955), especially pp. 190–219, where the Harwich-Rotterdam services are described, and in Rixon Bucknall, *Boat Trains and Channel Packets: The English Short Sea Routes* (London: Vincent Stuart, 1957), for the Flushing-Queenborough service. Belgian railway history is covered by U. Lamalle, *Histoire des Chemins de Fer Belges* (Bruxelles: Office de Publicité, 1953), while W. Klee, *Preussische Eisenbahngeschichte* (Stuttgart: W. Kohlhammer, 1982), and H. J. Gaida, *Dampf zwischen Weser und Ems. Die Geschichte der Grossherzoglich Oldenburgischen Eisenbahn* (Stuttgart: Motorbuch Verlag, 1979), describe the other neighboring countries. The interesting first Prussian connection is treated in more detail by W. Steitz, *Die Entstehung der Köln–Mindener Eisenbahngesellschaft* (Cologne: Rheinisch–Westfälischen Wirtschaftsarchiv, 1974), and K. P. Ellerbrock and M. Schuster, *150 Jahre Köln–Mindener Eisenbahn* (Essen: Klartext, 1997).

ROLLING STOCK AND WORKSHOPS

The general history of steam locomotion is covered in detail by E. L. Ahrons, *The British Steam Railway Locomotive* (London: Ian Allan, 1963), and R. von Helmholtz and W. Staby, *Die Entwicklung der Lokomotive im Gebiete des Vereins Deutscher Eisenbahnverwaltungen* (vol. 1, 1835–1880, Munich–Berlin: R. Oldenbourg, 1930); a second volume by E. Metzeltin (1880–1920, Munich–Berlin: R. Oldenbourg, 1937) brings the story forward into the twentieth century. Ahrons pays some attention to British exports to Holland, while von Helmholtz gives a lot of particulars of the Borsig engines of the Holland Railway. The story of the Borsig Company itself is to be found in K. Pierson, *Borsig. Eine Name geht um die Welt. Die Geschichte des Hauses Borsig und seiner Lokomotiven* (Berlin: Rembrandt Verlag, 1973). R. L. Hills and D. Patrick, in their *Beyer, Peacock, Locomotive Builders to the World* (Glossop: Transport Publishing, 1982), do the same for that famous English firm and list all locomotives built for the Dutch State Railways.

The bible for Dutch steam locomotive aficionados still is H. Waldorp's longlasting work, *Onze Nederlandse stoomlocomotieven in woord en beeld* (8th ed., Alkmaar: De Alk, 1986), which describes and illustrates every class of steam engine that ever rode on Dutch rails. J. J. Karskens, *De locomotieven van de H.IJ.S.M.* (Haarlem-Antwerp: Stam, 1947), does the same in even more detail for the locomotives of the Holland Railway, while G. F. van Reeuwijk, *De breedspoorlokomotieven van de H.IJ.S.M.* (Alkmaar: De Alk, 1985), concentrates on the early broad-gauge period of that same company. C. Hamilton Ellis, in his *Some Classic Locomotives* (London: Allen and Unwin, 1948) and his *The Engines That Passed* (London: Allen and Unwin, 1968), describes some outstanding Dutch engines in a pleasant literary style.

The locomotives of the Belgian railway companies operating in the Netherlands are to be found in Phil Dambly, *Vapeur en Belgique* (2 vols., Brussels: G. Blanchart, 1989–1994).

Contemporary workshop practice is to be found in Friedrich Oberstadt's *Die Technologie der Eisenbahn-Werkstaetten. Lehrbuch für Maschine–Techniker* (Wiesbaden, 1881). Oberstadt was the first chief of the Tilburg works of the State Railways, so his book is mostly based on Tilburg practice. H. Waldorp and J.G.C. van de Meene, *Locomotiefloodsen en tractieterreinen in Nederland 1839–1958* (Haarlem: Schuyt, 1992), list and depict all engine sheds and related installations in the country.

A. D. de Pater, in one of the few publications in English, *The Locomotives Built by Machinefabriek 'Breda,' voorheen Backer and Rueb* (Leiden: Brill, 1970), gives particulars of all steam engines built by that firm. Although most of its products were tramway locomotives, Backer and Rueb also constructed small engines for the State Railways and for the Netherlands South African Railway as well. H. de Jong, *De locomotieven van Werkspoor* (Alkmaar: De Alk, 1986), does the same for the engines built by Werkspoor of Amsterdam, for foreign and domestic railways, including rare 2-12-2 narrow-gauge tanks and gigantic 2-8-8-0 Mallets for the Dutch East Indies.

The history of the first electrification in the country is to be found in J. F. Smit, *Rotterdam Hofplein–Den Haag–Scheveningen Kurhaus. Hoe het spoor elektrisch werd* (Rotterdam: Phoenix and Den Oudsten, 1989). The transition to electric and internal combustion is covered by I. Franco and P. Labrijn in their *Internal-Combustion Locomotives and Motorcoaches* (The Hague: M. Nijhoff, 1931), and N. J. van Wijck Jurriaanse, *Van stoom tot stroom. Het blokkendozenmaterieel van de N.S.* (Alkmaar: De Alk, 1980), the latter especially for the electrification of 1924. C. van Gestel and B. van Reems describe the electric locomotives in *Elektrische locomotieven in Nederland* (Alkmaar: De Alk, 1988), the multiple-unit trains in *Elektrische treinen in Nederland* (3 vols., Alkmaar: De Alk, 1992–1997), and the diesel-electric and diesel-hydraulic trains in *Dieseltreinen in Nederland* (Alkmaar: De Alk, 1989). About locomotive-hauled rolling stock, hardly anything is available apart from a few small books and scattered articles in the railway press.

RAILWAY ARCHITECTURE

Two well-illustrated books cover the whole history of railway architecture in the Netherlands. H. Romers, *De Spoorwegarchitectuur in Nederland 1841–1938* (Zutphen: Walburg Pers, 1981), covers the earlier period, while C. Douma, *Stationsarchitectuur in Nederland 1938–1998* (Zutphen: Walburg Pers, 1998), describes the postwar years.

SAFETY AND ACCIDENTS

Easily the best source for a history of railway accidents in the Netherlands is R. T. Jongerius, *Spoorwegongevallen in Nederland 1839–1993* (Haarlem: Schuyt, 1993). Jongerius carefully examines the causes of every major accident, based chiefly on original records and the (printed) annual reports of the Railway Supervisory Board, and describes their consequences and the measures taken to prevent recurrence. L.H.N. Dufour, chief of the signaling department of the State Railways, wrote a solid technical book about his achievements: *Het seinwezen op de Nederlandsche spoorwegen 1915* (Utrecht: Kemink and Zoon, 1916). H. G. Hesselink gave a more popular version of the story of signals in his *150 jaar seinen voor treinen* (150 years of signals for trains) (Rotterdam: Wyt, 1978).

STAFF AND ENGINEERS

H. W. Lintsen wrote a major study on the development of the engineering profession in the country in his *Ingenieurs in Nederland. Een streven naar erkenning en macht* (The Hague: M. Nijhoff, 1980). Individual engineers may be found in my own small contribution: "De kennisoverdracht op het gebied van spoorwegtechniek in Nederland 1830–1870" (Transfer of railway technology in the Netherlands), in *Jaarboek voor de Geschiedenis van Bedrijf en Techniek* 7 (1990), pp. 54–82. Gerrit Middelberg, one of the leading mechanical engineers, found his biography in my own "Gerrit Middelberg, een veelzijdig spoorwegingenieur uit de 19e eeuw", in the same *Jaarboek* 1 (1984), pp. 231–255. Other short biographies of railway directors and engineers are to be found scattered in biographical dictionaries such as the *Nieuw Nederlandsch Biografisch Woordenboek* (10 vols., Leiden: A. W. Sijthoff, 1911–1937) or the *Biografisch Woordenboek van Nederland* (4 vols., The Hague: M. Nijhoff–Institute of Netherlands History, 1979–1994, to be continued). Unfortunately, a handy survey such as J. A. Marshall's *A Biographical Dictionary of Railway Engineers* (Newton Abbot: David and Charles, 1978) is not available for the Netherlands.

The working conditions of the lower staff of the companies are amply covered by A.J.C. Rüter in his classic history of the strikes of 1903, *De spoorwegstakingen van 1903, een spiegel der arbeidersbeweging in Nederland* (Leiden: E. J. Brill, 1935). P.W.N.M. Dehing studied the strong tradition in a large number of families of working for the railways in his

"Eene soort van dynastie van spoorweg–beambten". Arbeidsmarkt en spoorwegen in Nederland, 1875–1914 (Hilversum: Verloren, 1989). A more general social history by I. J. Brugmans, *Stapvoets voorwaarts. Sociale geschiedenis van Nederland in de negentiende eeuw* (2d ed., Haarlem: Fibula–Van Dishoeck, 1978), is still useful for a succinct survey of working conditions, wages, and such, of the working class.

RAILWAYS AND LAW

E. van Citters and J.C.A. van Roosendaal published their first collection of laws pertaining to the railways in *Verzameling van wetten, besluiten enz. betreffende de spoorwegen in Nederland (1832–1943)* (The Hague: M. Nijhoff, 1879, with many later updates), a most useful and factual source. For the Berne Convention and its consequences for international freight traffic see C. D. Asser, Jr., *De Bernsche Spoorweg-conventie van 14 october 1893* (The Hague, Gebroeders Belinfante, 1893).

JOURNALS AND MAGAZINES

The Netherlands Royal Institute of Engineers (Koninklijk Instituut van Ingenieurs, KIvI), founded in 1848 by F. W. Conrad, among others, published its proceedings since 1848 as *Verhandelingen van het Koninklijk Instituut van Ingenieurs* until 1869, when it was superseded by its journal, *Tijdschrift van het Koninklijk Instituut van Ingenieurs,* which existed until 1916. A competing organization, the Vereeniging van Delftsche Ingenieurs, has published its journal *De Ingenieur* since 1886. From 1900 (volume 15), *De Ingenieur* was also the official journal of the Royal Institute, and as such it is being published to this day. Roughly until 1940 these journals contained a lot of rail-related material, but later only occasionally. During the years of the first competition from road traffic, S. A. Reitsma founded his weekly *Spoor– en Tramwegen* (1928–1965). It was continued as *Rail and Weg* in 1966 and 1967, and since then as *Openbaar Vervoer.* The Nederlandse Vereniging van Belangstellenden in het Spoor- en Tramwegwezen (Netherlands association of those interested in railway and tramway matters), founded in 1931, the foremost rail-fan organization in the country, has published its *Maandblad* since 1931; in 1947, this monthly was renamed *Op de Rails,* and it is still being published under that name.

Page numbers in *italics* refer to illustrations.

West India Company, 5

Westendorp, F., Dutch railway engineer, 117

Westerbork (Drente), German concentration camp, 170

Westervoort (Gelderland), railway bridge at, 15, *16*, 112

Westinghouse Brake Company, 57, 72

Westland Steam Tramway Company (WSM), 141

Weyers, A., Roman Catholic priest and trade union leader, 106

White and Company, American contractors, 120

Wijck, W. F. van der, Dutch railway director, 129

Wilhelm II, German emperor, 99, *129*

Wilhelmina, Queen of the Netherlands, 125, 126, 169

William I, King of the Netherlands, 2–4, 7, 8, 12, 125

William II, King of the Netherlands, 12, 125

William III, King of the Netherlands, 74, 125

Willink, J. J., Dutch railway promoter, 78

Winterswijk (Gelderland), 41

Wolfheze (Gelderland), 57

World Jamboree, *146*

World War, First, 91, 123, 127, 128

World War, Second, 126, 143, 164, 167–77; damages caused by, 167, 168, 174–77

Wright, Robert, English engineer, 122

Xanthippe, steam locomotive, 63

Zaandam (North Holland), 44

Zaltbommel (Gelderland), bridge at, 33, 76, 180, 181

Zandvoort (North Holland), 78, 99

Zeeland (province), 3, 94

Zeeland Flanders, 24, 69

Zeeland Packet Company, 43

Zeist (Utrecht), 95

Zeitung des Vereins Deutscher Eisenbahn-verwaltungen, 49, 77

Zevenaar (Gelderland), 57

Zoetermeer (South Holland), 206, 207

Zutphen (Gelderland), 41, 58; railway bridge at, 65, 76, 181

Zwolle (Overijssel), 3, 79, 93, 96, 111, 152, 181; railway station at, 24, *35*; railway works at, 38, 64, 168